DESPERATELY SEEKING SOMETHING

Photograph by Owen Franken

DESPERATELY SEEKING SOMETHING

A MEMOIR ABOUT MOVIES, MOTHERS, and MATERIAL GIRLS

SUSAN SEIDELMAN

ST. MARTIN'S
PRESS
NEW YORK

First published in the United States by St. Martin's Press,
an imprint of St. Martin's Publishing Group

www.stmartins.com

Designed by Steven Seighman

Library of Congress Cataloging-in-Publication Data

Names: Seidelman, Susan, author.
Title: Desperately seeking something : a memoir about movies, mothers,
   and material girls / Susan Seidelman.
Identifiers: LCCN 2024003567 | ISBN 9781250328212 (hardcover) |
   ISBN 9781250328229 (ebook)
Subjects: LCSH: Seidelman, Susan. | Women motion picture producers and
   directors—United States—Biography. | Women television producers and
   directors—United States—Biography.
Classification: LCC PN1998.3.S3944 A3 2024 | DDC 791.4302/33092
   [B]—dc23/eng/20240208
LC record available at https://lccn.loc.gov/2024003567

Our books may be purchased in bulk for promotional, educational, or business use. Please
contact your local bookseller or the Macmillan Corporate and Premium Sales Department at
1-800-221-7945, extension 5442, or by email at MacmillanSpecialMarkets@macmillan.com.

First Edition: 2024

10 9 8 7 6 5 4 3 2 1

For Ozzy, with love always

Contents

ACT ONE

ACT TWO

The reward for conformity is that everyone likes you but yourself.
—Rita Mae Brown

Call Me by Your Name

Out of the ground the Lord God formed every beast of the field and every bird of the sky, and brought them to the man to see what he would call them; and whatever the man called a living creature, that was its name.

—Genesis 2:19

My parents named me Susan.

It was a popular name in the 1940s through the 1960s. A name identifies you, gives you a sense of who you are and your place in the world. Mine is a Baby Boomer name, and while there are various shades of Susans, many are white.

It's an ordinary name, not exotic or posh like Cordelia or Ghisele. But not as plain as Jane.

It's a biblical name of Hebrew origin meaning "lily," associated with hope and the number eleven.

The name has several notable forbearers: the nineteenth-century suffragette Susan B. Anthony; the *Britain's Got Talent* singing phenomenon Susan Boyle; the essayist and critic Susan Sontag; the Academy Award–winning actress Susan Sarandon. Even Queen Elizabeth's first corgi, given to her on her eighteenth birthday, was named Susan.

But there was another Susan, a Hollywood actress famous for playing bold and shameless women in the 1940s and '50s whose name was Susan Hayward. My mother tells me I was named after her.

The name Seidelman also identifies me. Although there are German Sie-delmanns (spelled *ie* and double *n*), it's often a Jewish last name. The word *siedeln,* the etymology of Seidelman, means "to settle down; to create a new life in a before unknown place." And that's what I've spent a lifetime trying to do.

So, my name has four identifying features. I'm a Baby Boomer, white, Jewish, and have settled in a new place.

Last year I turned seventy, and after spending forty years on the less-glamorous side of the camera telling other people's stories, I've decided to tell my own. This is not a memoir about extraordinary ambition or enormous drive leading to success. Yes, I had ambition and drive, but really what I had was a vision about the kind of movies I wanted to make and the stamina to make them.

This is a story about persistence. About putting one foot in front of the other, heading down a path, and, after several wrong turns, eventually ending up where I wanted to go.

It's also a tale of transformation, one I've played out in real life as well as on film.

History likes to mythologize artists as struggling and tortured souls who rise above their circumstances. There's nothing dramatic about growing up *normal* and relatively happy in a middle-class suburb outside of Philadelphia. When I was young, I thought that having such a boring origin story disqualified me from being a *real* artist, so at times I created my own chaos just to shake things up.

But here's the question: Can you be *ordinary* and still have something extra-ordinary to say?

Jonathan, my partner of thirty-seven years (most of them good), tells me memoirs need to involve death, drugs, war, dysfunctional parents, sexual abuse, or mental illness. Is he right?

And then comes the self-doubt. Shit! That's the way it works. Dammit! He's planted that seed of uncertainty in my head and it begins to take root. I mean, what have I got to say that would be of interest to anyone other than my mother, who loves everything her kids (and grandkids) create, including those kindergarten popsicle-stick paintings and macaroni collages?

Will this embarrass my son?
Do I have any life lessons worth sharing?
(Long pause here to contemplate, then—)
Fuck, yeah!

ACT ONE

Season of the Witch

(Donovan)

When I look in my window. So many different people to be.

Like other people living in quarantine during the pandemic, I spent far too much time online googling people I knew, reading social media, and, admittedly (yes, embarrassingly), googling myself. Since my daily life had become so isolated, I hoped I was having more fun in cyberspace. Many of the online posts were connected to Madonna or *Sex and the City* and its reboot. I was featured in articles about women directors of the 1980s and blogs about the New York indie film scene. Revivals of my movies were still playing in repertory cinemas, and there were reviews of my films that were now streaming on cable.

It was therefore a surprise when in one of my bored and narcissistic check-ins I found the following question posted under my Wikipedia page: *Whatever happened to Susan Seidelman?*

Women don't age well in the film business, neither in front of nor behind the camera. Had I been invisible for too long? Had I been erased? My first film, *Smithereens,* was made forty years ago, and I haven't directed a new movie in a decade.

Girls of my generation were brought up to be humble. I have no delusions of grandeur, but no false modesty either. I've played my part in the earlier wave of trailblazers who paved the way for the women directors of today. I've broken barriers, too.

In the early 1980s, I directed the first American independent film to officially compete in the Cannes Film Festival. A few years later, I made one of the first Hollywood hits that was directed, produced, written by, and starred women. I cast Meryl Streep in her first movie comedy, then fast-forward a decade, and there I am directing the pilot for an HBO series about a group of thirty-something gal pals dealing with life and sex in the city—a show I had no idea would become iconic. And I've managed to maintain an aesthetic playfulness and outsider perspective for the past forty years out of sheer tenacity.

I've also had my share of flops and endured the slings and arrows of naysayers. Like others, my life is dotted with woulda, shoulda, couldas, several linked to my gender. Back then, women weren't supposed to make movies—certainly not movies that told stories about women's lives.

Thankfully times have changed and it's no longer strange to see a woman's name on the *directed by* credit of a movie or TV series. It's true, more change is needed, but there's no denying that the world is different now.

But in 1980, with a few rare exceptions, it was nearly impossible to become a professional film director if you were female, especially not in a studio system that was still run like an all-boys club.

There were others before me, pioneering women who wrote, directed, and produced movies in the Silent Era. Successful women who had been almost entirely written out of cinema history, like Alice Guy and Lois Weber. Because once movies started to talk in 1927, Wall Street realized that the film business could be Big Business, and women were systematically shut out.

Yet, there were still a few (very few) exceptions, such as Dorothy Arzner in the 1930s and '40s, Ida Lupino in the 1950s, and Joan Tewkesbury and Elaine May in the 1970s. There were also women making their mark in Europe. Agnès Varda and Chantal Akerman in France, Lina Wertmüller in Italy, and Margarethe von Trotta in Germany. And, of course, there were a few women who made one beautiful movie then quietly disappeared for reasons unknown.

But I wanted a career, one that would last for decades. Making movies was not a hobby or a vanity diversion. I had no fallback position. It was my passion, but it was also my job. Occupation: Film Director. This is what has paid the bills.

There's a kind of self-absorption that comes with getting older. A lot of navel-gazing at a time in your life when you do less and think about more. So, this is a collection of musings and memories about what it was like in the movie industry at a time when there were fewer than a handful of us women. Back when "girl boss" wasn't a term and social media wasn't a thing.

Trust me, I have no intention of trash-talking anyone. I love Hollywood. I love the indie film community in New York. I treasure the Land of Make Believe and the creative people who live there. Even the sharks and schemers have taken on a warm and fuzzy glow with the passage of time. I feel privileged to have been a part of this industry for many years.

This is a story about people whose lives intersected with mine. Family, friends, artists, colleagues, some famous, some not—a mix of what I remember as seen through the lens of how I've chosen to remember it. And if how one sees the world is a reflection of who they are (and I believe it is), then you can look at the world reflected in any of my films and see little pieces of me. Like Where's Waldo?, I'm hidden somewhere in each of them.

Memory plays tricks over time, but it doesn't totally gloss over the truth. Although it might put a soft filter on some of life's wrinkles.

Wake Up Little Susie
(Everly Brothers)

A part of me will always be a Philly Girl, even though I lived for forty-three years in New York City.

Philly Girls are tough. This story begins in Northeast Philadelphia in a working-class part of town called Oxford Circle. This was before my father made enough money to move us all to the suburbs.

I was born in a semidetached house on Kerper Street in a neighborhood where Jewish newlyweds bought their first homes in the early 1950s for about $5,000. The streets were filled with young mothers pushing baby strollers while their husbands worked as clerks at shoe stores, managers of small furniture shops, and (like my dad) salesmen in their fathers-in-law's hardware stores.

My mother got married at eighteen, shortly after high school. My father was twenty. My maternal grandmother liked my father because he was generous, ambitious, and dependable. She encouraged my mother to get married quickly before he got snatched up by someone else. Although she was shy and studious in high school, my mom blossomed once she got married. My dad adored her, which gave her confidence. She was fun-loving and always saw the bright side of everything.

My mother had no particular interest in housekeeping or cooking. Years later, after my father passed away at eighty-one, she confided to me they had a good sex life for their entire marriage.

A year and a half after my parents wed, I was born. They were probably too young to have kids, but people grew up faster back then. They would figure it out as they went along. They bought a small house in a neighborhood where there were several other little girls named Susan and Debbie and there were a shitload of Barbaras. Little boys wearing cowboy hats and shooting cap guns played in tiny backyards while their sisters fed baby bottles to Betsy Wetsy dolls and changed dolly diapers.

Let me start with some basics. I am *petite, diminutive*—the fact is, I'm short. I mention this because my size has defined me for much of my life. No, let me clarify—others have tried to define me by my size, since it's probably the first thing about me you notice. I'm four feet, eleven and one-half inches tall (but I round up to five feet on my driver's license).

I've seen the look of surprise on the faces of Hollywood executives when I first enter a room. *"She's* the film director!?" they say with a sideways glance. And they're right. I look nothing like you'd imagine a film director to look. But over the years I've learned to use my height to my advantage. Here's the rub: I've also had to work five times harder and be ten times as tenacious to be taken seriously in a world that believes "bigger is better."

I'm the only short member of my immediate family, although my grandparents on both sides were small. I inherited their short genes. There were times I tried to guilt my mother into believing my small stature resulted from being deprived of genuine food as a child. And that part is true. In the 1950s my thoroughly modern mother refused to be tied to the kitchen stove, so it wasn't until high school that I realized vegetables weren't cubed soggy things from a can.

At home we ate three-course meals covered in tinfoil and served in a Swanson's TV dinner tray. Pasta was Chef Boyardee. Fruit came in a can labeled Del Monte. Although, as times changed, my mother did experiment with a few homemade recipes; they all involved Campbell's soup.

Mish Mosh: Take one can of Campbell's minestrone soup. Add one pound of ground meat, and salt, pepper, and ketchup to taste. Heat, then serve over Uncle Ben's Instant Rice. This was my mom's signature dish.

* * *

When I was young, I was verbal, outgoing, and self-assured. My mother told me I was "cute." Of course, that was a decade before she called me a disobedient teenage tramp. (I was going to write "Ha-ha" but at the time it wasn't funny.)

Recently I came across a school photo of my kindergarten class taken in 1957. There I am, front and center, because on photo day the students were arranged in size order, starting first row, center. I'm dressed in a Little Red Riding Hood cape. (I'm not sure what my mother was thinking that morning.) My legs are carelessly spread apart; my feet—in little white socks and Mary Janes—barely touch the floor. My cape is full and draped across the lap of the timid little boy in a bowtie sitting next to me. I have long dark hair pulled back in a ponytail, a fringe of bangs cut straight above my eyebrows. My smile is filled with confidence.

There were several advantages to being petite. At age three I was selected to perform on *The Horn and Hardart Children's Hour*, a local televised kids' talent show, and scheduled to sing the teapot song: *"I'm a little teapot, short and stout. Here is my handle, here is my spout."* I practiced performing it with elaborately choreographed hand and body gestures, coached by my mother. Unfortunately, I came down with chicken pox the morning of my TV debut, so I never made it onto the show.

Being pint-sized was also fun. My older cousins and uncles picked me up and tossed me high into the air like a beach ball. It was only when I got older that I found out being small can be a liability in an industry where size matters. The size of your weekend box office, the size of your production deal, the size of your house, the size of your _____ (fill in the blank).

At age eight, I would play Thumbelina in a summer camp musical based on the Hans Christian Andersen fairytale. Although I had limited singing ability, I was the only camper who fit into the costume and could remember the lines. I got to twirl around onstage while everyone sang about precious little Thumbelina. But it didn't take long before I realized that I actually didn't like being center stage. I preferred staying behind the scenes, where I could organize, create, and boss other people around.

What I really wanted to do was direct.

Somewhere over the Rainbow

(Judy Garland)

Twenty-five years later I find myself standing on another stage. Actually, it's a stage on a movie set. There's fifty crew members, mostly men, busy at work all around me. Two actresses are there, as well, and a crowd of movie extras. Both actresses are pretty and blond, about the same age: twenty-seven, twenty-eight. And they look somewhat similar. Similar height, similar build. A harder and softer reflection of each other.

It's our seventh week of filming, and we're shooting a scene in a dilapidated building once known as the Audubon Ballroom on West 165th Street. It's where Malcolm X was assassinated in 1965 while giving a speech. We've turned the crumbling ballroom into a funky, punk-retro nightclub, with a showcase of oddball entertainers. There's a neon sign out front that blinks MAGIC CLUB. Inside, there's a magician wearing a cape and a turban, a ventriloquist and his dummy, a comedian in a shabby tuxedo who tells corny jokes, and a house band of geriatric musicians. Just the kind of club I like. Everyone looks like background extras who stepped out of Woody Allen's *Broadway Danny Rose.*

Today there's a new electrician working on set. It's his first day on the job and it's apparent he knows nothing about the film or its participants. He sees me standing off to the side, watching as the grips and gaffers adjust lighting and assemble dolly track. He walks over and asks me to bring him a bottle of water, assuming I'm a production assistant and it's my job to look after the crew. I look like I could be one, since it's 1984 and that's the job most of the women on set have.

I say nothing, but go over to the nearby craft service table and return with a bottle of water. I hand it to him. I don't remember if he thanks me. Maybe he did. I smile to myself, but can't wait to see the look on his face when he finds out that I'm the director and could easily have him fired. I look nothing like what he'd expect a director to look like. I'm young, girlish, and I don't wear a reverse baseball cap or have a scruffy beard.

Unfortunately, I won't get to see his reaction when my identity is revealed, because he's now disappeared into the shadows and I'm too busy rehearsing with the actors to look around for him.

Madonna enters the Magic Club wearing a sexy black-sequined jacket and the black mesh rhinestone boots that will one day be collectable. She takes a seat near the stage. She's playing a character named Susan who has come to watch the magic show. In real life, her music career is skyrocketing, but no one could imagine the superstar she will become, and remain, for the next four decades, turning feminism inside out along the way.

Rosanna Arquette is onstage, dressed in a pink tutu and a blond wig. She's playing a magician's assistant and is about to climb into a casket-like box and get sawed in half. She, too, plays a character who thinks her name is Susan.

I wish I could have told her then what I know now. That this would probably be the most memorable role of her film career.

But I didn't know that at the time.

The cinematographer, Ed, comes over and tells me the lights are set and we are ready for a take. The first assistant director, Joel, calls out, "Quiet on set!" The sound rolls, the camera rolls, the clapboard is clapped.

I shout "Action!"

But I'm jumping ahead of myself. So, before you get confused, let's rewind to 1959, where I'm still a seven-year-old, impatient to grow up.

You Don't Own Me

(Lesley Gore)

was a restless kid. I could concentrate when something grabbed my attention, but some part of my body was always in motion. My parents told me I had "ants in my pants." The "heebie-jeebies." My grandmother called it *shpilkes*. As a teenager I was nicknamed the Energizer Bunny and Road Runner. I was always doing three things at once. Today it's called multitasking, and it's a skill that comes in handy if you ever want to direct a movie.

My favorite retort as a child was to put my hands on my hips and say, "You're not the boss of me," which usually got me a spanking or my mouth washed out with soap. Corporal punishment was not yet frowned upon in the late 1950s, and although my parents were loving and affectionate, my father was not averse to taking off his belt and chasing my younger sister and me around the dining room table. Girls were not supposed to be assertive or bossy. (But that, too, comes in handy as a director—just add a smile.)

Back in the 1950s and '60s, children were more independent than they are today. By the age of seven, I was walking eight blocks to school, alone—crossing double lanes of traffic, my ponytail swinging. My mother never thought it was dangerous to let her little girl walk alone down city streets. She knew there were bad people in the world, but not in *our world*. She had always felt safe. So did I. Plus, I was now a big sister, which made me feel self-sufficient and grown-up. My younger sister, Denise (called Zeesie), was born two and a half years after me, followed by Richie (the Bird Baby), in 1957.

For my father, having a baby boy was like winning the lottery, and my parents sent out birth announcements: *The King Has Arrived*. It was decided from birth that the Bird Baby was going to be a doctor, and that is exactly what he became.

The Bird Baby, big sister Sue, and Zeesie

* * *

I discovered my vagina one day while watching the *Mickey Mouse Club*. I was lying on the carpet, staring at the small, black-and-white console television in our living room. I was probably five or six at the time and fascinated by perky Annette Funicello and Tommy, the cute boy Mouseketeer. Distractedly, my hand wandered down to my private parts and I discovered something pleasurable there. My mother walked into the room, saw whatever it was I was doing, and scolded: *"Susan, don't touch your tussy!"[1]* I quickly moved my hand away. I didn't know what I'd done wrong—I just knew it felt good—but now I knew it was forbidden.

I was learning that some things that bring you pleasure are best kept secret.

* * *

I had two grandmothers, Nana H and Nanny S. One cooked, the other didn't.

Nana H was my mother's mother, a pretty but nervous woman who stood about four feet, eleven inches. She was always proud of her good posture and would push back my shoulders and tell me to stand up straight. Her short gene skipped my mother and was passed down to me. At night, she kept her false teeth in a glass of water on her bedside table. She was probably only fifty at the time, but people aged differently back then. Everyone looked old by forty.

Nana H pretended to enjoy cooking, but she really thought of it as a chore, like sex, that a wife was obligated to perform for her husband. Over the years she perfected the art of boiling the flavor out of everything. This was a skill that would be passed down from mother to daughter for the next three generations.

Nanny S, my father's mother, was an excellent cook. She made a fantastic lemon custard poppyseed cake that still makes my mouth water. She wore a

---

1. The word "tussy" may be derived from the Yiddish word "tuchus" in combination with the English word "pussy."

poufy blond wig she kept on a wig stand on her dressing table. Actually, she had two wigs: her daytime wig and her "special occasion" wig—the one she saved for weddings and bar mitzvahs.

My father's side of the family were colorful storytellers, especially if the stories involved growing up during the Depression in West Philadelphia in a noisy house filled with unmarried aunts and unemployed uncles. All my relatives were supported by my sweet-natured grandfather, Harry. My father shared a bed with Uncle Ockie, sleeping head to toe.

There were also my great-aunts, Uttie and Tootie. Uttie was the family beauty. She had been engaged many times but never married, and never gave back any of her engagement rings. Years later, when my father's sister, Aunt Phyllis, began to suffer from dementia, she told me that Uttie was a prostitute, but I'll never know if that was true. I was probably only six the last time I saw Tootie, and mostly what I remember was that she was a heavyset woman who would always say, "I could eat you all up." And I believed she could. Tootie had whiskers. Not obvious ones you could see, but you could feel little stubbly pricks on your cheek when she gave you a big, wet kiss.

There's a strong, stubborn streak that runs through all the Seidelman women on my father's side. A tell-it-like-it-is outspokenness that can sometimes seem blunt, but is never intentionally mean-spirited. This would be passed on to me.

My mother's side were more concerned with manners and appearances, but under the surface they were tightly wound, and a few suffered from depression. Except for my mom, who is genuinely the most enthusiastic person I know. She can turn picking up the dry cleaning into an exciting adventure. My mother hit the jackpot when they handed out the happy gene.

We Are Family
(Sister Sledge)

When I was ten, my family moved to a new middle-class, suburban development just outside of Philadelphia, in a town called Huntingdon Valley. It was 1962 and my father's business, a family-owned hardware company, was booming due to the growing market for affordable housing and the popularity of aluminum siding. More Americans were becoming homeowners and needed reasonably priced hardware, so my dad and my uncle Arnold built a small factory in an industrial park outside of Center City, Philadelphia. They now had well over a hundred employees. All my father's childhood dreams had come true. He had a loving wife, three healthy kids, a custom-built colonial house, and a Cadillac parked out front.

The first night in our new house, the entire family piled into the big walk-in shower together. My father had the letter *S* for Seidelman etched in fancy script on the glass shower door. All five of us, in bathing suits, stood inside, shampooing our hair at the same time. It was a big change from the small bathtub with the plastic shower curtain we had before. A clear sign that we had moved up a rung on the social ladder. It felt like we were rich.

Our suburban development had the mellifluous name June Meadows and was a storybook version of the American dream—an instant neighborhood that had popped up almost overnight, built on what was once farmland. Nearby was a new shopping center: a large parking lot surrounding a row of single-story shops with a roof to protect shoppers from inclement

weather and a built-in sound system that played Muzak. A supermarket an-
chored one end, and a bowling alley the other. It was our suburban version
of Main Street, U.S.A.

There were basically three styles of houses to choose from: the Ranch,
the Split-Level, and the Colonial. My father bought an oversized two-acre
lot at the end of a cul-de-sac. Here he built our custom colonial with white
pillars and a circular drive. In the center of the lawn were two large metal
lawn sculptures, each about six feet tall. A king and a queen that looked like
enormous chess pieces. Potted flowers grew from the crowns on top of their
heads. This house would be our castle, so I guess that made my sister and
me the princesses, my brother the prince.

My parents could have afforded one of the older Tudor-style homes in a
nearby fancy area called Rydal. These were elegant stone and stucco houses
built in the 1920s, with creeping ivy, sweeping drives, and stone terraces.
This is where the doctors and lawyers lived. But my dad always liked being
a big fish in a small pond, so we had the biggest house in the less-upscale,
but spanking-new, development of June Meadows.

The suburbs were not just a place, they were a state of mind. Living there
whittled the complexities of life down to a manageable size. It was like living
in a protective bubble. Looked at from the outside, it had many advantages.
It was safe, clean, and well organized. But it had disadvantages, too. It was a
homogeneous world inhabited mostly by people who wanted to live among
"people like us."

It provided a safety net that could also feel like a noose.

* * *

In fourth grade I transferred to a suburban elementary school where I was
now the new kid. Although I was bright and outgoing, my fourth-grade
teacher, Mrs. Kirschbaum, didn't like me. This was upsetting because I'd
been popular with teachers in the past, but Mrs. Kirschbaum didn't like the
way I would slip off my Capezios and twirl them around with my toes under
my desk. By the end of class one shoe had landed under the desk three rows
in front of me. The other, three rows behind. Mrs. Kirschbaum thought I
was twirling my shoes for attention. I knew it was nervous tension about

being the new kid, combined with boredom. As punishment, Mrs. K made me stand out in the hallway by my locker. Mostly you'd find boys standing in the hallway, but every once in a while there would be a girl. Me.

Back then, test papers were handwritten by teachers onto a stencil, then copies were run off using a manual mimeograph machine located in the school's supply room. I would readily volunteer to help crank out the copies and bring them back to class, hot off the press. Mrs. Kirschbaum saw this as an activity to keep me busy, wear me out. I saw it as a treat. I loved inhaling the dizzying smell of the deep-purple ink on my fingers as I walked the fresh copies back to the classroom. Every once in a while, I still catch a whiff of that scent and it instantly takes me back to my childhood. Xerox photocopy machines would soon replace the mimeograph machine and kill all the fun.

Despite my love for books and stories, Mrs. K put me in the Low reading group with the dumb kids. There were three reading groups, tactlessly named the High, the Medium, and the Low. You'd think an elementary school teacher could come up with more creative names to make the ranking less obvious. Maybe something cute, like the Sparrows, the Robins, and the Hummingbirds. But Mrs. Kirschbaum was a nasty and sadistic bitch who enjoyed traumatizing her students. She would be my bête noire my entire life, even after I'd achieved some level of success.

The Low group was told to bring their chairs up to the front of the room, where we formed a circle and took turns reading aloud. All the other kids would stare at us, the dummies, which added to my anxiety. When it was my turn to read, my voice would stammer, and I developed a fear of public speaking that would continue well into adulthood. Years later, when my film career took off and I was invited to speak at film festivals or do radio and television interviews, I would flash back to Mrs. Kirschbaum. I hoped she was still alive and saw me on TV. I desperately wanted to prove I was no dummy.

As a kid I thought my mother was like Lucille Ball. Not the real Lucille Ball, but the character she played on TV. And like Ricky Ricardo (the TV version), my father worshipped her. They argued. At times, animatedly. But there was never any ugliness in their squabbles. Usually, it was about some silly household repair or interior decoration. It was a loud house, filled with commotion, filled with life. But at times the noise could get overwhelming, and I would retreat to my bedroom to escape and go somewhere else in my head.

My dad had flashy taste. He had grown up poor during the Depression and as a young boy went to school wearing his sister's girly hand-me-down coats. He quit high school in eleventh grade, too impatient to graduate and eager to get out into the world and make his mark. So when he started to make money, he enjoyed showing off the things he'd been denied as a child. My dad was a hard worker and a straight shooter who never forgot where he came from. To outsiders, he might have appeared gruff. My friends were afraid of him. But inside, he was a teddy bear and a fiercely loyal family man.

On Sunday afternoons we would go out for long family drives in my dad's big-finned Caddy. Now, take a moment to imagine what the car must have smelled like. My dad would be puffing on a Kool menthol with the windows rolled up (he didn't like his Brylcreemed hair blowing in the wind) and the air-conditioning on high. His face was splashed with Old Spice aftershave. My mom smelled like a mix of Aqua Net and Fabergé Tigress. Now, add in the scent of new leather car seats. This was the smell of my childhood. And here's the soundtrack: the car radio blasting pop songs from Chubby Checker, Dion, Ray Charles, and my own personal favorite, "The Loco-Motion" by Little Eva. Three kids squabbling in the back seat. No seat-belts. We went flying whenever my father hit the brakes, then all laughed. It was the summer of 1962, a time of prosperity and peace. President Kennedy was in the White House, and the world was perfect.

My dad also had a borscht belt sense of humor. He loved jokes about shitting, farting, and belching. I confess, I'm still a sucker for a good fart joke.

Question: Why is love like a fart?
Answer: If you have to force it, it's probably crap.

My father would laugh so hard that tears would stream down his cheeks. He was also very affectionate. A big, noisy kisser. When he gave you a kiss, he would suck in your whole cheek. Once, my dad gave my sister, Denise, a kiss on her neck that resulted in a purple hickey. It involved nothing inappropriate and we all thought it was funny at the time. But my sister went to school the next day with that big, purple hickey, and my mother had to call the principal to explain. Innocent Denise, the middle child, who would grow up to become a successful attorney—the most stubborn and argumentative of us all.

For a short period of time Denise and I took piano lessons from a teacher who went by the name of Professor Marquez. Whether he was an actual professor or not was never questioned. He would come to our house once a week in the evening, and we would sit next to him on the piano bench, often in our pajamas and bathrobes, and do keyboard exercises. Sometimes, he put our small hands on top of his to follow along with whatever he was playing. But at one point he got a little touchy-feely with eight-year-old Denise, resting his hand on her thigh. My sister (not fully aware of what was going on, but sensing it was creepy) casually mentioned this to our mother and the professor was abruptly fired. But it was 1963 and people kept quiet, so his inappropriate behavior was never reported to the police. However, that was the end of our formal music education. Although I never learned to read sheet music, my fingers had been trained by rote to play the opening few bars of Rachmaninov's Prelude in C-Sharp Minor and Beethoven's "Für Elise," which I continued to play on autopilot for the next twenty years.

Glory Days
(Bruce Springsteen)

had the random good fortune to be born into a cheerful family. A lucky roll of the genetic dice. My mother had married an adoring man who protected her and gave her a comfortable lifestyle: family Christmas trips to the Caribbean, summers at the Jersey Shore, department store credit cards, and the resources to redecorate the house every few years—which she did, just to keep busy and express herself artistically.

The living room in our home was spacious, with velvet flock wallpaper and a never-used white marble fireplace. In fact, the entire room was unused and pristine (thankfully without the plastic slipcovers that covered Nana H's good furniture). We only walked into the living room once or twice a year and never for long. When my parents' friends came over, they would head down to the den, where my dad had built a long wood-paneled bar with mirrored shelves and six barstools. My father wasn't a drinker, so all the alcohol on the shelves were the sweet liqueurs you could pour over vanilla ice cream and turn into dessert. Kahlúa, amaretto, crème de menthe, and, later, Baileys Irish Cream. It made me feel grown-up to sit at the bar, eating my Swanson's TV dinner—Salisbury steak, mashed potatoes, and apple cobbler. To this day, I still like eating at bars.

The den was where my parents entertained their friends before they headed out for their date nights. My parents would dress up every Saturday evening and go to a restaurant in Center City or a popular nightclub in

Cherry Hill, New Jersey, called the Latin Casino (which wasn't Latin, nor was it a casino). It was a large, Vegas-style dinner theater that brought in top acts like Johnny Mathis, Brenda Lee, Tony Bennett, and Frankie Valli and the Four Seasons. Women wore cocktail dresses and men wore dinner jackets to attend the shows, but unlike Vegas, it was family-friendly, so you could bring along Granny and the kids to the early shows.

Mom dressed up for "date night" in little white gloves and beehive hairdo

Around this time, my parents became friendly with a couple named Bunny and Norman. Norman was a business associate of my father's, and Bunny looked like a movie star. She wore her blond hair up in a French twist, like Tippi Hedren. Bunny and Norman didn't have children, which was pretty unusual for a married couple at that time. All my parents' other friends had two or three. Instead, Bunny and Norman had dogs. Poodles. On the few occasions Bunny stopped by in the afternoon to visit, I remember her wearing capri pants and bringing along a young male companion. He was her hairdresser. I thought he dressed in a dapper European style, very different from my father and our suburban neighbors.

This was my first glimpse of people living lives distinctly different from our own. It wasn't that Bunny was an important figure in my life—I hardly knew her. But she made an impression. She was glamorous and unique, and that's probably why after all these years I remember her, her poodles, her capri pants, her French twist, and her hairdresser.

Bunny died mysteriously a few years later from a gunshot wound to the head. It was rumored that there had been foul play and Norman was involved. But I'll never know the truth. Norman disappeared from our lives shortly thereafter.

My final reminder of Bunny was our family dog, bought from a breeder she had recommended. It was a champagne-colored poodle named Chi Chi. Unfortunately, Chi Chi had a high-strung, miserable disposition and would often hide under the bed, growling. She did not like being tormented by three boisterous children. She would have much preferred strolling down the Champs-Élysées in Paris to roaming the asphalt cul-de-sac of June Meadows.

One day Chi Chi ran out of the house and was hit by a delivery truck. Chi Chi, like Bunny, was suddenly gone. The next week we got a golden cocker spaniel named Corky, who had a much sweeter temperament and more tolerance toward both suburban life and kids.

* * *

For a while we had a mother's helper who slept over at the house on Saturday nights when my parents went on their date nights. Her name was Margie. She was a Black teenager of about fifteen. She lived in North Philadelphia, the rough part of town. Her aunt was a housekeeper for someone in our neighborhood.

Margie was the first person who talked to me about sex. We would sit up for hours after my sister and brother had gone to bed, and she would tell me fascinating stories about her escapades with her boyfriend. They were sexy and romantic. She taught me the words "jizz" and "blowjob." I had never heard of fellatio before and found the concept strange and exciting at the same time. But I was confused about why anyone would put their mouth on the thing a boy peed out of.

Of course, I had to tell my girlfriends all about our conversations the following Monday. This would be a PG-13 version of a scene I would direct thirty-five years later in *Sex and the City,* but instead of gathering at a chic restaurant in Tribeca and drinking cosmos, we were sitting at a Formica table in the lunchroom of Rydal Elementary School, drinking cartons of milk through paper straws and snorting with laughter until the milk spewed out of our noses.

Adolescence was a confusing time. I got my first stretch bra and faked my first period, wanting to be ahead of the curve. (Then, a few months later when I really did bleed, I had to act blasé since I'd already told some friends I'd had it.) My girlfriends were the center of my life, and I had several different best friends. They alternated every few months because adolescent girls can be fickle. But at age twelve, losing a bestie can be dramatic (hurt, anger, rejection), almost like a divorce.

Did I mention I became superstitious in an attempt to make sense out of the hormonal chaos? I invented a series of magic rituals I performed every night before going to bed. I would open my sliding closet doors exactly one fist wide. This way I would know if any ghosts or evil spirits had entered my closet while I was asleep. I would re-measure the opening in the morning to make sure the gap was still exactly the same size. I'd walk around my room pairing objects and stuffed animals into groups of two. Everything needed a partner to talk to, in case they came alive in the middle of the night. I believed in magical thinking. I believed that if you thought of something hard enough and visualized it in your mind, you could make it happen.

I was obsessed with the number eleven and, for years, every time I glanced at my bedside radio alarm clock, the number had just flipped to 11:11. This necessitated getting out of bed (no matter how tired), going on my knees, and reciting a prayer of my own invention. I sprinkled in a few Hebrew words I'd picked up at synagogue without knowing their actual meaning, but they sounded holy. Needless to say, going to bed was a long and arduous process.[2]

* * *

2. An interesting fact about the number 11: Armistice Day, also known as Veterans Day in the United States, commemorates the armistice signed between the Allies of World War I and Germany for the cessation of fighting on the Western Front, on the 11th day of the 11th month (November) at 11:00 a.m. 11-11-11!

At school, I became friendly with some of the cool Italian kids who had left Catholic school after sixth grade. I was fascinated by Catholicism because it had sacraments, symbols, and fantastical objects. It appealed to my sense of mystery and high drama. The clear-eyed logic of Reform Judaism seemed bland by comparison.

Although we weren't religious, we celebrated the major Jewish holidays, like Hanukkah, where I got practical gifts like underwear with the days of the week printed across the backside, pajamas, or a Jean Naté bath set. Most of our family rituals centered around food. Bagels and lox on Sunday mornings. Chinese food on Christmas Eve (all the other local restaurants were closed). And we did a Yom Kippur break-fast with whitefish salad and kugel. For Passover we had a big family seder, read the Haggadah, and asked the Four Questions (*"Why is this night different . . ."*). We put out a symbolic glass of wine for the Prophet Elijah, but when we opened the front door to welcome the Prophet inside, my father would shout, "Enough already, you're letting out the air-conditioning!"

I had heard that Italian and French families regularly drank wine with dinner, but the only wine I'd ever tasted was Manischewitz, which, in the 1960s, tasted like cough syrup, sweet and thick. I couldn't imagine why Europeans would want to drink this sickly stuff every night.

Doctor My Eyes
(Jackson Browne)

There was an amusement park not far from our house, in Willow Grove Park. It had roller coasters, a fun house, a tunnel of love, and a big Ferris wheel. My mother would take my sister and me to go on the rides, eat cotton candy, and visit the sideshow. Why my mother took her young daughters to a sideshow is puzzling, but we were all fascinated by life's quirks and peculiarities.

The first celebrity autograph I ever got was from Percilla the Monkey Girl, a bearded lady dressed in a Victorian gown, sitting on a makeshift wooden stage. Everything about her—her voice, her gestures, her facial features—was feminine. Except for her long beard, mustache, and unibrow. This was the first time I noticed that the line between what was considered masculine and feminine could be ambiguous. I also got an autographed photo from Hank, the armless man, who signed it with his feet. There were a fat lady, a reptile man, a sword swallower, a giant, and a contortionist. I felt immediate empathy with the performers onstage. I'm not sure why, but their "otherness" made them special to me. I'm sure being a performer in a traveling carnival was a harsh life, but in my mind I had romanticized their itinerant lifestyle. Even at that age, I was itchy to move around.

The sideshow existed in Willow Grove until the mid 1960s. In the 1970s, the park was shut down, and by the early '80s, the grounds were turned into a generic shopping mall. Where the sideshow tent once stood there is now a TGI Fridays.

My sister, mother, and I also enjoyed thumbing through art history books with paintings of martyred saints and pictures of the cruel punishments meted out by capricious Greek and Roman gods. When we went to the Philadelphia Art Museum, we headed straight for the Rubens painting *Prometheus Bound*. It depicted an eagle pecking out the liver of Prometheus, who was bound to a rock. We sat for half an hour, mesmerized, discussing all the horrific things the ancient gods did to mortals. We loved Medusa, with her headful of snakes. We were riveted by Cronus, who ate his children. We hunted down the painting of Saint Sebastian tied to a tree; we needed to see his bloody body pierced with arrows.

But despite her fascination with the macabre, my mother had an upbeat, optimistic disposition that she passed on to her daughters. She was the mom all my friends wanted as their own. She willingly drove the carpool, schlepping us to movies and dance classes. She could be relied upon to throw on a bathrobe in the middle of the night to pick everyone up from a party when the designated driver didn't show. So, I'm not sure why, at fourteen, I felt the need to rebel, or exactly what I was rebelling against. But at some point, I knew that if I wanted the adventurous life I'd fantasized about, I'd have to create it myself. But the pathway there was fuzzy.

So was my eyesight. My vision had begun to blur.

* * *

I'd always suspected I saw the world through a slightly different lens than my friends and family. Now I knew it was true. I was diagnosed with uveitis, an inflammatory condition inside my eye that can be caused by infection, injury, or, in my case, an autoimmune condition of unknown origin. It can cause pain, redness, and blurry vision. And in extreme cases, blindness.

I'd been experiencing blurry vision and "floaters" for a few months and was sent to see several ophthalmologists who confirmed the condition, but had no idea what was causing it. I spent a week at Wills Eye Hospital, where I was poked and probed and punctured. I had a spinal tap and nightly IV drips. The veins in my arms were so bruised I had to get the drips in my feet. The doctors said the problem was systemic, although they couldn't pinpoint an exact diagnosis—except that my body was attacking itself from within.

I don't know how seriously I contemplated the possibility of going blind, but it was obviously on my mind. I'm sure I was terrified, but I've edited most of this chapter out of my memory.

Eventually, I was sent home and prescribed weekly shots of cortisone to reduce further inflammation. I remember closing my eyes at night and feeling my way around my bedroom, practicing how I could navigate as a blind girl, like Audrey Hepburn in *Wait Until Dark*. Over the next few years, my vision gradually improved, although the floaters have stayed with me to this day. But I was determined not to give them the attention they were demanding. I looked at myself in the mirror, put my hands on my hips, and muttered to the uveitis, "I'll show you . . . You're not the boss of me."

Runaround Sue
(Dion)[3]

Being the oldest of three, and only twenty years younger than my mother, I was the one she tested her nascent parenting skills on. Raising an adolescent with a rebellious streak was uncharted territory. A lot of trial and error.

Here's one of our eighth-grade mother-daughter conversations:

ME: Mom, can I shave my legs?
HER: No.
ME: My legs look like a gorilla. Kids are going to make fun of me.
HER: I said no. No means no.
ME: Well, can I at least shave under my arms?
HER: No. Once you start shaving, you can never stop. It's a vicious cycle.

So I would go over to my friend Barbara's house after school (she had one of the few professional working moms, so the house was empty in the afternoon) and I'd shave my legs, put on a pair of tights, then walk home. I didn't like being deceitful or sneaky, but in my mind my mother had forced me into this untenable position. It was her fault if I was rebellious. Having hairy legs is a burden no eighth-grade girl should have to bear.

---

3. Fun fact: The second most popular name in a song title is Susan, along with its derivatives Sue, Susie, and Susanna. This was particularly true for country songs of the 1970s. The most popular sung girl's name is Mary.

Once I committed to being a sneaky person, I was able to expand that skill to other areas of my life. Like slipping my parents' tiny airplane-sized bottles of alcohol into my handbag to take to parties. Or sneaking boys into the house when my parents were away.

By the time my younger sister turned twelve, my mother was feeling more confident about her parenting skills and loosened her grip. Denise had much more freedom and didn't have to skulk around. As a result, she became the most straightforward person I know. And by the time my little brother, Richie, hit puberty in the early seventies, my mother had started college as a full-time student and was busy reinventing herself. Consequently, she didn't notice the marijuana plants growing on Richie's bedroom windowsills. Or maybe she did, but didn't care, since the boundaries of her own world had opened up. Richie told her they were tomato plants, and she encouraged his new interest in horticulture.

*   *   *

In high school I started to call myself Sue. It sounded more casual. More laid back, like a real teenage name. I also tried out Suzi with a ♥ above the *i*, but Sue sounded cooler.

There's a cardboard box I recently found on the top of my closet. Inside were a bunch of old diaries. The kind of adolescent diaries with daisies and red polka dots on the cover that you close with a little lock and key. They were written when I was between the ages of twelve and fourteen.

I used little symbols as code for different secret activities—sort of like primitive emojis. The code was easy to break, since I'd written a code guide on the back page of the diary in case I forgot what the symbols meant.

★ meant I kissed a boy. ★★ meant with tongues. As I got older, the variety of symbols grew more complicated. ●● meant second base. ⬇ meant third. I never had a home run. That would wait until my fourth week of college.

For some reason I named my diary Harriet, perhaps in memory of my grandfather Harry, who had recently passed away. I was also very meticulous about writing down the exact time I finished each entry and signing my full name to the bottom of each page as if it was an official document.

Some of the entries were about boys I liked and girls I didn't. They described petty grievances, small injustices, flashes of jealousy, and moments of adolescent insecurity.

March 3, 1964
Dear Harriet,
Today I went to Charm and Poise Club after school. I'm going on a diet because I weigh 91 and I want to get down to 85. I talked out in science class so now I have to write an essay on why I shouldn't interrupt people. Gary S was talking too, but he didn't get caught. Unfair.
—Sue Seidelman, 10:31pm

October 4, 1964
Dear Harriet,
Wendy had a sleepover Saturday night and I wasn't invited. Wendy's such a bitch. I caught her picking her nose during math. I'm sure that's why she didn't invite me. I thought Ivy was my best friend, but she told Brenda she was <u>her</u> best friend. They better not be talking behind my back.
—Sue Seidelman, 9:05pm

May 17, 1965
Dear Harriet,
Went to school and wore a sleeveless shell (which I was kind of embarrassed to wear because of my hairy arms). After school, went to Barbara's house, then to Strawbridge's to buy bell bottoms. Had a fight with mom again. Bobby C. came by with his brother and some older kids in a car. ★ ★ ● ●
—Sue Seidelman, 10:56pm

November 12, 1965
Dear Harriet,
This morning I broke a mirror and I've been having good luck all day. Barbara, Ellen, and I went to Cedarbrook Mall and got silver friendship rings. We were all going to get our ears pierced, but Ellen chickened out. Bobby called twice.
—Sue Seidelman, 8:42pm

I was surprised to see how often my diaries mentioned movies. Who starred in them, what the actors wore, their hairstyles, the decoration of the rooms. I never thought about the film's director or even knew what a director actually did. I went to whatever movie was playing at the local movie theater without discernment. I just liked escaping into other people's more exciting lives projected up on a big screen. At the time there was still a large, four hundred–seat theater where you could smoke in the balcony. That was before it got divided into a multiplex in the late 1970s and lost its magic.

I also wrote entries about movies I'd watched on late night TV. My sister, brother, and I huddled together in bed, watching black-and-white B movies starring Vincent Price and Christopher Lee, and getting high on our childhood farts. We were night owls and loved staying awake until the *Late Late Show* ended and the national anthem played, followed by the Indian-head test pattern signaling the end of the broadcasting day.

* * *

Around this time, I developed a fascination with bad boys. Actually, they weren't really bad, but they put on a tough rebel attitude, passed down from their older brothers, probably inspired by James Dean and the young Marlon Brando. Most came from the other side of town, the blue-collar neighborhood near Willow Grove Park where the houses were smaller and closer together. I also developed an interest in kissing. My hormones were raging and making out with boys (we called it "macking") was a cheap and readily available weekend entertainment. It was also a form of rebellion. Plus, it gave your mouth something fun to do.

Every Friday night there was a make-out party in someone's basement while their parents were out. That's when we invited the bad boys over. Sometimes they arrived drunk. Sometimes they were high from huffing glue, which, at the time, was a cheap buzz. All you needed was a paper bag and a tube of model airplane glue easily bought from HobbyLand. Back then, marijuana was still only smoked by New York City beatniks and jazz musicians, and the methamphetamine and opioid plague wouldn't hit the suburbs until a few decades later.

My mother warned me: "We didn't move to Huntingdon Valley so you could run around with hoodlums. You're going to get a reputation!" And she was right. By ninth grade, I had one.

There was one boy I liked in particular, Bobby C. He dressed like a "smoothie." Smoothies wore cuffed khaki pants, tucked-in Banlon shirts, and desert boots. They were generally bad students, but good dancers and sharp dressers.

One night, I invited Bobby C over to my house knowing my parents would be out for the evening. He arrived with a group of friends. (They traveled in packs.) While Bobby and I were making out in the den, his friends were robbing the house and rifling through my mother's handbag. I wasn't aware of this until my parents returned home that night and my mother found the contents of her bag scattered around the room. The next day she called Bobby's mother, whom she had never met, and told her about the incident. That evening Bobby's mother drove him to our house and made him apologize in person to my parents. Mortified, I hid upstairs in my bedroom.

Bobby and I broke up right after that. More specifically, he broke up with me, but I was never quite sure about the sequence of events. We just stopped talking. That's the way it was with eighth-grade romance. We turned our heads in opposite directions when we passed in the hallway and ignored each other totally. But I was upset and remember locking myself in the bathroom at home, turning on the water full force so my mother wouldn't hear me crying. Melodramatically, I vowed that I would never allow myself to feel this kind of rejection again. I felt used and tossed away like an old tissue. ("Used and tossed away" dialogue borrowed from an old 1950s movie.)

"I'll show him," I sniffled to my reflection in the mirror above the bathroom sink. "One day, I'll show you all!"

Theatrical at 12. (Yes, that is a "bubble" haircut!)

There's a quote by Graham Greene in his book *The Power and the Glory*. He writes: "There's always one moment in childhood when the door opens and lets the future in." I didn't have that one big moment. Instead, I had several small moments that merged together to form a big one.

My reaction to the breakup with Bobby was one of those moments.

Disappointment would fuel my fire. Success would be my revenge.

* * *

Fifty years later, at a high school reunion, I bumped into my old friend Gary, who had kept in touch with Bobby C over the years. Gary had wanted to be an actor, moved to NYC, but after a few early successes, got cold feet and returned to Philly to become a county judge. He was curious to know how I, a mediocre high school student and the recipient of many "Does not live up to her potential" report cards, ended up becoming a film director. After a few glasses of wine, I told him jokingly about how after being dumped by Bobby C in eighth grade, I vowed to use my hurt and rejection to prove something to myself and the world.

Gary thought the story was funny and asked if he could tell Bobby, who had moved to San Francisco many years earlier and was working as a photographer. I was happy to hear that he had left the neighborhood and was doing something creative, but doubted I would even recognize him if we passed on the street.

A week later Gary called me. He had spoken with Bobby, who said he thought I was the one who had dumped him in eighth grade. I dumped Bobby?! How could I have gotten that so wrong? This had been a defining moment in my childhood. My *I'll show you!* moment. All I could think about was how glad I was not to know this at the time, or I might never have made that vow and my entire life's journey could have been totally different.

Dazed and Confused
(Led Zeppelin)

Here's an example of why I lost my parents' trust in high school.

I had been caught shoplifting trinkets from Woolworth's with a group of girlfriends. (I confess, I was the group's ringleader.) I knew it was wrong and I could have easily bought the cheap items I pinched: a tube of pale pink CoverGirl lipstick and a bottle of peacock blue ink for my fountain pen. But I looked at it as a challenge, an adventure, with just enough real-life danger to make it exciting. I had been inspired by a scene in *Breakfast at Tiffany's* (every teenage girl's favorite movie), where Audrey Hepburn and George Peppard wander through a five and dime store looking for some small thing to pilfer, then run out laughing wearing stolen Halloween masks. They didn't get caught. But I did. My mother made me return the items to Woolworth's and apologize for my criminal behavior to the pimply teenage girl snapping gum behind the cash register.

And, of course, the stolen car incident was a total misunderstanding.

What happened was, we were on summer vacation and staying at a motel in Margate City, a seaside town outside of Atlantic City. My mother allowed me to bring along my friend Debbie. It was the Fourth of July weekend and we heard about a late-night fireworks party on the beach by the Ambassador Hotel.

After my parents fell asleep, Debbie and I snuck out of the motel and took a jitney over to the Ambassador. By the time we arrived, the party was over. It was now 2:00 a.m. and the jitneys were no longer running, so we decided to hitch a ride back to the motel, which was only two miles away.

How could we have known that the boys who picked us up were fifteen and the car was stolen? We weren't mind readers! When we were stopped by the police and put into the back of a paddy wagon, I tried to explain the situation, but the officers wouldn't listen.

It was about 4:00 a.m. when the Margate police called my father at the motel. They said they had arrested his daughter for car theft and he should come down to the precinct. He said this must be a mistake, his daughter was sound asleep in the other room.

It soon became clear that Debbie and I had never met the boys before, but naturally my father was furious. I was grounded, Debbie was sent home. My parents had had enough of my bad behavior. My father said I was a juvenile delinquent destined for a life of depravity. (Sorry. I just lied. What he actually called me was a "slut." And that hurt.) Something inside me was broken and needed to be fixed. Why was I desperate for excitement? This and the shop-lifting incident were enough to drive my mother to seek professional help. I was her problem child.

*   *   *

The waiting room to Dr. Greenberg's office had kiddie magazines like *Highlights for Children* and *Jack and Jill,* scattered on colorful little plastic tables (the kind of tiny tables you'd find in kindergarten rooms) along with toys, stuffed animals, and puzzles. Back then, few kids went to psychiatrists—certainly none that I knew of. And I hated the psychiatrist for no other reason than I was forced to sit opposite him for fifty minutes whether I wanted to talk or not. I had no choice but to look at his ridicu-lously happy family photos (weddings, graduations, bar mitzvahs) in gold frames on his desk and lining his walls. Coincidentally, he was the father of a girl I vaguely knew from the Sunday school classes I was now forced to attend. I thought she was boring. After long periods of silence, when finally cajoled into speaking, I spent the remainder of the session talking about why I didn't like his daughter and the "matchy-matchy" clothes she wore. My behavior was obnoxious, but I felt like I was suffocating. Still, that's no excuse. The only trouble I had in my life was the trouble I was creating for myself.

After seven or eight sessions, it was decided that either I was cured, or never would be, and my therapy came to an abrupt end. But I was now a pariah. I was the girl my friends' parents didn't want their nice daughters to associate with. They said I was a bad influence. I pretended I didn't care, but secretly I did.

Back then, girls were put into categories. You were either a good girl or a bad girl. There was no in-between. And when you're told something enough times, you begin to believe it. So, I would take on a new identity. I would embrace my badness.

"I'll show you all!" I said (in my mind) to my friends' parents. Also to my own.

You Should Be Dancing

(Bee Gees)

My mother thought I needed moral guidance and had enrolled me in Sunday school classes at the local synagogue, Keneseth Israel. I knew I was walking on eggshells, so I went to avoid an argument. It also gave me the opportunity to skip out of class early and catch the bus up Cheltenham Avenue to Wagner's Ballroom with my friend Madeleine.

Madeleine came from the only bohemian family in June Meadows and her mother didn't make her go to Sunday school. Madeleine's mother wore her black hair pulled back in a ponytail with a headband. Madeleine's older sister was a beatnik who wore smoky eye makeup and went to art college in New York. Madeleine's mother wasn't judgmental. She was one of the few mothers who hadn't banned me from their house.

Wagner's Ballroom was where the badass Catholic school kids went to dance. Madeleine loved to dance and so did I. It's a Philly thing. Hometown to Dick Clark's *American Bandstand,* the first teenage dance show to be televised nationally in 1957. Madeleine took dancing more seriously than I did and was probably the better dancer, but we were the only two white girls in the Abington High School Dance Club. We knew the latest line dances along with all the choreography. We were obsessed with Motown. The other white kids at Abington did a lame version of the Hully Gully or the Frug, which we considered *queer.* (The word had a different meaning back then.)

In an act of half-assed self-reinvention, I called myself Sue Sidel when I went to Wagner's, as if that somehow blurred my ethnicity and suburban-ness. I thought it sounded tough. The dance was hosted by a legendary DJ, Jerry Blavat, aka "The Geator with the Heater," aka "The Big Boss with the Hot Sauce." He was a wiry little guy, half Jewish, half Italian, with a supercharged personality, a smile that took up half his face, and possible connections to the Philadelphia mob. This was back in the good ol' days of payola, when the mob and the record business were like husband and wife. Blavat had a radio show and played Black music at a time when few white radio DJs did. He was a precursor to the superstar club mixers of the '80s and '90s, one song seamlessly morphing into the next. He knew exactly how to rev up a room filled with horny teenagers. We would dance for three hours straight, our clothes drenched with sweat. Boys carried their mothers' dish towels hanging from their back pockets to mop their faces in between songs.

I also went to *Super Lou's TV Dance Party* after school with my friend Ivy. This was a televised dance show, broadcast live at 4:00 p.m. from the basement of an apartment building in Jenkintown, not far from our high school (and down the street from where actor Bradley Cooper would grow up eight years later).

The show, hosted by Super Lou, aired on Channel 29. It was 1967, before the advent of cable TV, so there were only seven TV stations. The big three: ABC, CBS, and NBC, plus three local UHF channels: 17, 29, and 48, but you needed a separate television dial to access those. There was also PBS, watched only by grandparents, geeks, and our World Civilization teacher, Miss Ripowski.

Channel 29 must have been desperate for cheap local programming since most of the shows were community news reports, religious talk shows, and a low-budget kiddie program that involved hand puppets (a copycat version of Shari Lewis and Lambchop).

I don't know why Little Richard would agree to be a guest on *Super Lou's Dance Party*. It must have been a very low point in his career, because the show had a tiny viewership—mostly the friends and family of the teenage dancers. But Little Richard lip-synced his way through "Tutti Frutti," while a bunch of white fifteen-year-olds tried their best to keep up.

I remember his appearance because it was the first time I'd ever seen a man wearing a black wig and pancake makeup with plucked, arched eyebrows. It was unusual. So, naturally, I was fascinated.

Born to Be Wild
(Steppenwolf)

In the 1960s there were minimal expectations placed on young women, other than to look pretty and be smart enough to catch a husband. And it was never too early to start planning for the future. Maybe you'd go to college, get a job for a few years, teach kindergarten (a job that had a practical application for motherhood), then give it all up when you got your MRS degree. In fact, if you were too intelligent, you didn't want to show it. Being smart wasn't attractive. But I was secretly competitive and determined and those were not considered positive traits in a girl, so throughout high school I hid that as best I could. Ambitious men were strong and enterprising. Ambitious women were bitches.

I was an artsy kid who wanted to color outside the lines. I liked designing things and became my family's official hairstylist—although my sister still blames me for cutting her long locks into that asymmetrical Vidal Sassoon haircut made popular by Barbra Streisand in 1967. You know the one—rounded on top, short on one side (to show an ear), longer on the other. It was the night before Denise's bat mitzvah, so that hairstyle will forever be memorialized in my parents' laminated photo albums, along with my Marlo Thomas–inspired *That Girl* flip.

At some point, I decided to channel my creativity into fashion. I became obsessed with Swinging London. That was the groovy, free-spirited lifestyle I fantasized about. I loved the miniskirts, Mary Quant tights, patent leather boots, pale Yardley lipstick. The music of the British Invasion: the Spencer Davis Group, the Kinks, the Rolling Stones. The style of Julie Christie. I wanted to be tall, leggy, and stick-thin like Twiggy, Penelope Tree, and Veruschka. Flat-chested women with androgynous bodies who looked great in A-line dresses. Women physically my opposite. They were a counterpoint to the big-breasted, wasp-waisted women of the '50s. Curvy women, like my mother, who wore longline bras and tight elastic girdles to squeeze their stomachs and cinch their waists.

I experimented with a variety of creative but misguided, beauty tips. Twiggy-inspired painted-on bottom eyelashes that looked like spiders' legs crawling out from under my eyes. Black cat's-eye liner (post–Ronnie Spector, pre–Amy Winehouse), with a thin white line painted above it like a skunk. I even shaded a dimple on my chin, like Diana Ross. At some point I decided to shave off my eyebrows and re-create them in a more dramatic arch with a kohl pencil. I bleached two stripes down the sides of my hair like Cruella de Vil. I was trying on various identities to see if any would stick.

For my senior year class trip, I went to London, the mod capital of the world. I had little interest in seeing Big Ben, Buckingham Palace, or the Changing of the Guard, but couldn't wait to get to Carnaby Street and the Biba department store. It was a few years after Carnaby Street's heyday, so it had gone from being a trendy shopping area to a tourist attraction, but still it was eye-opening for a seventeen-year-old aspiring fashionista. I bought my brother, Richie, an ice-blue satin shirt with a ruffle down the front and billowy sleeves—the New Victorian style worn by the band members of the Dave Clark Five. Richie thought the shirt was cool and wore it to school for his fifth-grade photo day. Unfortunately, he almost got beat up by a neighborhood bully named Chipper on his way home. I felt terrible. My little brother was a fashion victim and it was all my fault.

In 1967, a new girl arrived at Abington High who looked like Twiggy, but smaller. Her name was Gail and she was my first girl crush. In fact, I think everyone had a crush on Gail. Boys and girls. Probably teachers, too. She had huge blue Kewpie doll eyes and a short pixie haircut like Mia Farrow's in *Rosemary's Baby*. She looked like an exotic creature who had just temporarily landed in suburbia, but would not be staying for long. She was also slightly dangerous, which was part of her allure.

Rona Gail (she actually had a stage name!) had been a child actress, star of the original New York production of *The Miracle Worker*—a role that would eventually be played by Patty Duke on Broadway. Her photograph had been in newspapers, and she'd traveled around the world, performing. I hoped some of her worldliness would rub off on me. I was excited when we became friends and both got a job go-go dancing wearing minidresses, white go-go boots, and fishnets in the window of a hip British clothing boutique called Paraphernalia in Center City. She was an exhibitionist and I was her exhibitionist-in-training.

At sixteen, Gail quit school and left the suburbs to move to Manhattan and restart her acting career, but what she was really chasing was adventure. The suburbs of Philadelphia were too small for her. Although Huntingdon Valley was only ninety miles away, NYC was another planet.

Gail's parents allowed her to move into the Barbizon Hotel for Women on East 63rd Street, thinking that living in a women's residential hotel might protect her. They still had women's hotels back then, where no men were allowed above the first floor. It was intended as a safe refuge for young women who had come to the big city seeking fame or fortune as journalists, actresses, dancers, or executive secretaries. Some of the Barbizon's famous guests included Lauren Bacall, Grace Kelly, and Joan Didion.

But nothing could protect Gail from herself. We lost touch for a few years. While I was living the life of a college student in Philadelphia, she was trying out the life of Holly Golightly, but in reality, it was far less glamorous than in the movie. I bumped into Gail when I moved to NYC in the midseventies and was sad to see that the sparkle in her eyes had dulled. She looked emaciated and pale, like the blood had been drained out of her. The person I'd known was no longer there. I don't know how she was earning money, but it wasn't from acting. A few years later she was found dead from an overdose on the bathroom floor of a restaurant in midtown Manhattan. She was twenty-eight.

Another adventuress who left Huntingdon Valley for the Bright Lights, Big City was Nancy Spungen. Like Gail, she met an early end, in 1978 inside the Chelsea Hotel, presumably stabbed to death by her punk musician boyfriend, Sid Vicious of the Sex Pistols. Their turbulent, heroin-fueled relationship would later be turned into the cult movie *Sid and Nancy*.[4]

I didn't know Nancy Spungen personally, she was a few years younger, but I knew where she came from and what she was running to. I've heard she was self-destructive and emotionally unstable, and I have no doubt that was true. She was only twenty at the time of her death, and when I later saw a photo of her mother—a pretty dark-haired woman—I realized she could have easily been a friend of my mom's. I could imagine them sitting around our suburban kitchen table chatting and drinking Sanka.

Gail and Nancy were both buried outside of Philadelphia on October fifteenth, exactly one year apart.

Their life stories would influence a fictional character I named Wren, the protagonist of my first film, *Smithereens*. But that's a decade and a daydream away, because right now, I'm still in high school trying to figure out who I want to be when I grow up.

---

4. Actor Gary Oldman would play Sid—but more about him twenty-five years from now.

Dream a Little Dream of Me
(The Mamas & the Papas)

In the beginning of senior year, students were given an aptitude test by the school's guidance counselor. The test was a series of multiple-choice questions to help you focus on a future career path and figure out what college options best suited your interests.

My test result said I should be a librarian. A WHAT?! At first I was horrified. A librarian? BORING! Wasn't a super-exciting job, like being the fashion editor of *Glamour* magazine, obviously a much better fit? Librarians were old maids who wore glasses on chains around their neck and smelled musty.

What I didn't realize was that the aptitude test got it right. A librarian loves stories—so did I. I had become an avid reader. (My personal fuck-you to Mrs. K, my fourth-grade teacher.) I would go to the Wanamaker's Department Store in downtown Philadelphia and search through the book department, often buying paperbacks based on their striking graphic cover designs. These were books I couldn't find in our school library—slim volumes of poetry written by poets like Gregory Corso, Lawrence Ferlinghetti, Leroi Jones, and Allen Ginsberg. Novels by French writers like Albert Camus and Jean-Paul Sartre. Although I'm not sure I fully understood all of what I was reading, I liked the flow of the words. I knew they were pushing boundaries, and that made them exciting. They also held the promise of taking me somewhere I might want to live one day. London, Paris, New York. Maybe San Francisco, home to hippies and beatniks.

My sister and I kept our books stashed privately in our bedrooms. The only books I remember in our den (the suburban word for family room) were volumes of old leather-bound books with gold trim that my mother's interior decorator, Mr. Alice Andrino (a man with a girl's name—fascinating!), had placed on the shelves of our built-in bookcase as set dressing. The book covers were color-coordinated to match our couch and shag rug.

*   *   *

Being a film director wasn't a career option on a high school aptitude test in 1969. But filmmaking is about storytelling, so I guess I ended up in the right place. My mother suggested I consider becoming a lawyer. Law school involved books and a lot of reading. All Jewish parents want their kids to become doctors or lawyers. In the case of a daughter, if not become one, marry one.

I think my mother was living out her own fantasies through her children. She was a savvy operator and often succeeded in convincing you that her ideas were your own. But being her firstborn, I was strong-willed and figured she still had two more shots with my siblings. I was not interested in studying law, nor had I been very good at abiding by it. There was a creative world out there I wanted to be a part of and hoped art might be my entrance ticket, so I applied to the fashion design program at Drexel University (then called by its less fancy name, Drexel Institute of Technology) and was accepted. A few years later my mom was successful at convincing my younger sister to go to law school. But Denise always loved a good argument and was a natural debater. And as for my pot-growing baby brother, who fantasized about being a rock 'n' roll drummer, well, he would become the doctor, a pulmonologist, as determined at birth.

*   *   *

I've always had an interest in people who were different. That's what led to my friendship with Billy B.

Billy was gay at a time when no one was out of the closet, especially not in high school. Especially not in Huntingdon Valley. I knew he was gay, but it was something we never spoke about. I was waiting for him to bring it up, but he never did—until the year after he graduated high school. This was decades before gay and lesbian couples could even dream of marrying, having kids, and becoming just as boring as their suburban heterosexual neighbors.

What made things more difficult for Billy was that his father was a well-known college football coach back when the words "gay" and "football" were not mentioned in the same sentence. In fact, homosexuality officially didn't exist in our suburb, although everyone knew that the hairdressers at the shopping center beauty parlor were *effeminate*.

Billy had a larger-than-life personality and lots of platonic girlfriends. He had a loud, excitable laugh and a camera usually dangling from his neck to document his friends' daily lives. He enjoyed sitting around a kitchen table late at night, gossiping. My mother was also a big talker, and I remember several times, after a long night out, Billy would come back to my house, I would be tired and go to bed, leaving my mother and Billy laughing and drinking coffee until 3:00 a.m.

Billy was my date for senior prom. He could always be counted on to fill in in an emergency. Somewhere, I have a prom photo of the two of us, arm in arm. I'm wearing black satin bell-bottoms, a turquoise blue cummerbund, and a black magician's cape with turquoise lining. It's unclear what fashion statement I was going for at the time (Merlin, perhaps?), but it was definitely a misfire. Billy is dressed in a classic black tux with red paisley trim.

He went to college for a few years at Penn State, then escaped to NYC to become a photographer. I caught up with him when I moved to the city. He was the only person I knew in Manhattan, and by that time he was out and living a *fabulous* life with a group of young, up-and-coming fashion designers, one of whom had a promising career that would be cut short by a mysterious gay cancer no one had ever heard of before.

In the fall of 1973, Billy would get me my first paying job as a dresser for an afternoon fashion show at the Continental Baths, a gay bathhouse in the basement of the Ansonia Hotel. It was the first time I'd ever been to such a theatrical and decadent place. I loved it. It was a hint of all the secret worlds that existed in NYC, hidden away in surprising places at unexpected times of the day.

All the models walked down a makeshift runway in just bath towels. (I'm not sure what they were actually modeling. Towels?) It was my job to make sure they were wrapped and pinned in such a way so as to keep their towel on. Although walking the runway naked was also an option. The entertainment for the event was a young Bette Midler (nicknamed Bathhouse Betty), with Barry Manilow on piano and Melissa Manchester singing backup, but I was so mesmerized by the weirdness of the experience, I paid little attention to the performances of these soon-to-be very famous entertainers.

Billy and I continued to hang out occasionally, but he was now living a fast life, clubbing downtown, partying on Fire Island, and I was an exhausted film student. A few years later, he would move to LA and start a lucrative greeting card company featuring drag queens like Divine on the cover. Inside were messages like: *Turning 30 is a drag.*

But, oh no! I've done it again! I've let my story jump ahead. . . . New York City is still ninety miles away and the gay cancer wouldn't make its terrifying appearance for another decade.

Who Are You
(The Who)

When I left for college, I wanted to start fresh. I no longer felt like a "Sue" and wanted to distance myself from that rebellious, confused teenager. I was still searching for a new identity and for a moment thought about changing my name to Suzanne, Susanna, Suki, or Olivia—my middle name. Someone named Olivia sounded sophisticated and intellectual. But, in the end, I went back to just plain Susan.

I moved into Drexel's women's dorm, Van Rensselaer Hall, in the fall of 1969. It was an ugly white stone building on Powelton Avenue and 33rd Street, in a deteriorating part of West Philadelphia. House rules were strict. You had to sign in and out at the front desk every time you came and went. There was an 11:00 p.m. curfew on weeknights and a 1:00 a.m. curfew on weekends. Boys were not allowed above the lobby floor. Powelton Avenue would make national headlines a few years later when a large, crumbling house occupied by the members of MOVE, a controversial Black Power group, had a shoot-out with the police that left one officer dead and nine MOVE members in jail. Protests to free the MOVE members would lead to police firebombings in 1985 that would destroy two city blocks and leave six more dead.

I shared a dorm room with a friendly heavyset girl named Michelle. Her mother had packed her off to college with a supply of diet pills. This was back when family doctors thought nothing of handing out amphetamines as casually as jelly beans. Michelle became very popular with the other girls in the dorm, especially around finals time.

Design classes were taught by instructors who took the train in from Manhattan twice a week. There was a sophistication about them that the Philadelphia faculty members didn't have, as if inhaling New York City air automatically made you chic.

At Drexel, the male-female student ratio was five to one. Many of the men were slightly geeky engineering, computer science, and business majors. (Who knew they would become the rock stars of the 1990s! In the '70s they were still just nerds.) The female students fell into two categories: library science and home economics majors (conservative girls from Western Pennsylvania and Central New Jersey), and design majors, artsy girls who wore Native headbands with long, poker-straight hair parted down the center, bell-bottoms, leather fringe vests, and clogs.

The disproportionate number of male students would have been advantageous for a girl who was husband shopping. I wasn't. Although within a month of my arrival, I had a boyfriend named Michael and quickly went about the business of losing my virginity. I wanted to get it over and done with so I could stop thinking about it and move on. I remember waking up the next morning and looking in the mirror surprised to see that nothing had changed. Would other people notice a difference? I don't know what I was expecting, but I was still me.

Fashion tip: For hair this straight, sleep all night with tresses wrapped around a large orange juice can, then wrap entire head with a tight scarf.

Michael and I were boyfriend and girlfriend for the entire freshman year. We went to movies, to concerts, listened to scratchy Jefferson Airplane albums on his record player, and smoked lots of pot—the harsh kind, full of seeds. I drew naked charcoal sketches of him for my life drawing class, feeling very creative and grown-up.

In November of my freshman year, I was chosen as Drexel's homecoming queen. There was nothing about me that was typically homecoming queen-ish. Personally, I identified more as a *hippie* than a *rah-rah,* but my (pre-feminist) ego was stroked. I also had little interest in football (or most sports, for that matter). I didn't understand the rules and why there were so many stops and starts. Seated on a cold metal bleacher in a plaid miniskirt and crocheted vest on a blustery afternoon, what I remember most was wishing someone would offer me a flask to keep warm. Still, I was flattered to be part of an American tradition that in the rapidly changing world of 1970 suddenly seemed anachronistic.

Queen for a day!

* * *

Hippie culture was taking hold on college campuses across America. This was a time when students smoked weed with their professors. It would be the year of Kent State. I remember walking into the quad, Drexel's student gathering hall, on December 1, 1970, the day the draft lottery system started. Your birthdate would now dictate the order you were called up for military service. A bunch of college students quit school the following week after they found out their lottery number was high and would now be last in line to be drafted for Vietnam.

Everyone read books by Kurt Vonnegut, *Catch-22* by Joseph Heller, *Siddhartha* by Hermann Hesse, and *Future Shock* by Alvin Toffler. I ate my first kiwi and tasted my first avocado. I tried Indian curries and went to macrobiotic restaurants—a radical change from the TV dinners and all-you-can-eat Chinese buffets I'd grown up with. I listened to James Taylor, Joni Mitchell, and played Carole King's first album over and over and over. I joined an encounter group. I chanted *nam-myoho-renge-kyo* at a makeshift Buddhist temple in the basement of a coffeehouse near Rittenhouse Square. I dropped acid and watched my fingers melt into multicolored waves of light, feeling at one with the universe.

I also received news from my friend Debbie that her high school boyfriend had been killed in Vietnam after being there for only a month. I remember exactly where I was standing at the time: talking to her from a pay phone in the hallway of my dorm. I was stunned. I'd never known anyone who was killed in a war before.

During my last year of high school, I'd become friendly with a German exchange student named Toni. We'd kept in touch, and she invited me to stay at her family's apartment in Frankfurt the summer after my freshman year of college.

I took a cheap Pan Am flight to Frankfurt with a copy of Arthur Frommer's *Europe on 5 Dollars a Day* and two hundred dollars' worth of American Express travelers checks tucked inside my embroidered Indian shoulder bag. I also had a student Eurail pass that was good for unlimited train travel for a month. I'd never traveled south of Miami, north of Montreal, or west of Scranton, Pennsylvania.

My world was about to expand.

Magical Mystery Tour

(The Beatles)

I arrived in Germany and loved everything about its foreignness. I loved that the buildings were old, the streets were cobbled, the people spoke a language I couldn't understand and ate foods I'd never tasted.

I stayed for a week with Toni and her parents in their apartment above the restaurant they owned in Frankfurt. I remember the first time her mother brewed chamomile tea. I had never tasted chamomile before and liked its floral aroma. It was very different than the Lipton's powdered tea mix we drank at home. As her mother poured tea, I noticed the faint blue numbers tattooed on her forearm. Her father had them, too. I knew what the numbers signified—a horror I couldn't possibly imagine. Still, I wondered why after the Holocaust Toni's parents would return to Germany, a place that had caused them so much suffering. Toni told me they had been unable to enter the United States because of restrictive immigration policies, so they went to Palestine instead. But Palestine was a harsh desert land, and they were city people, Europeans, and felt like strangers in that dry Middle Eastern place. Despite all the unspeakable things they'd lived through, they returned to the country where they had once been part of a community, hoping they could pick up some of the pieces and start again. And they did. They now owned several restaurants in Frankfurt and had prospered. The irony was that Toni had met a Sabra (Israeli-born) boy when she was visiting relatives in Tel Aviv and had fallen in love. She planned to return to Israel to see if, unlike her parents, she could start a new life there.

After a week in Germany, Toni and I drove her Mustang from Frankfurt to Venice, where it was put on a ship to be ferried to Tel Aviv. I left Toni in Venice and decided to bum around Europe for a few weeks. I had a Eurail pass, so I could move around easily, sometimes sleeping overnight in the train compartment rather than paying for a room. Once I woke up to find a sad-looking young German soldier fondling my bare feet.

At the time, the US dollar was strong and Europe was cheap. There were plenty of youth hostels, and you could actually bump into people you knew from back home while checking out the message board at the American Express office in any major city.

For a while, Amsterdam was the place to be. It was crowded with American and European hippies hanging out at Dam Square, camping in sleeping bags, so at night you'd have to step over sleeping bodies to get across the plaza. Marijuana was legal, cheap, and readily available. Youth hostels had co-ed dorms, some with bunk beds, that cost only seventy-five cents a night.

What was originally intended as a twenty-one-day trip stretched to four months. Needless to say, my parents were not pleased and were unwilling to support my extended stay. I decided to join Toni in Israel because if you worked on a kibbutz, you could get free room and board. I found a kibbutz near the Golan Heights, where I spent two months sleeping on a military cot in a corrugated metal hut with four other women. We picked grapefruit each morning. Our afternoons were free for sightseeing or swimming because it was too hot to work in the fields.

I befriended a girl from Boston named Rona, and we took a cheap flight to Istanbul, another hippie destination at that time. With the help of Arthur Frommer, we found an inexpensive *pensione* near the majestic Blue Mosque. We spent our afternoons hanging out at a nearby café called the Pudding Shop, eating baklava and kunefe and drinking thick Turkish coffee.

The Pudding Shop was also a boarding point on the Hippie Trail. This is where a battered, psychedelically painted bus loaded up with passengers before heading overland through Iran, Afghanistan, Pakistan, and India, eventually ending up in Nepal. The goal was to get to Nepal as cheaply as possible. There were ramshackle hotels at stopping points along the way.

Back then, Nepal was a popular destination for nonconformist travelers because it was the birthplace of Buddha. (Not to mention the cheap cannabis and opium that could be bought along the way.)

Every afternoon, the military police would raid the Pudding Shop, ostensibly looking for drugs, but mostly as an excuse to pat down (feel up) the American hippie chicks hanging out there. The Hippie Trail would come to an abrupt end by 1979 due to the military dictatorship in Pakistan, the Iranian Revolution, and the Soviet invasion of Afghanistan, which closed off tourism to Westerners. I never hopped on the bus, but it was wonderful to know that for a brief period of time, this magical mystery tour had actually existed back when the world was a very different place.

I'm Every Woman

(Chaka Khan)

I returned home a different person. It's like a switch had been turned on in my head. In many ways I'd been a typical suburban teenager, until one day I wasn't. I'd walked through souks in Turkey and had sex on a beach by the Red Sea. I'd eaten fresh figs in Rome and lamb shawarma in Jerusalem. I'd gotten a taste of a bigger, more colorful world that I now wanted to be part of. I couldn't go back to Beefaroni.

My sophomore year at Drexel had been in session for two months when I returned to Philadelphia. I tried to get back into the swing of college life, but the idea of living in a women's dorm on Powelton Avenue was depressing, so I moved into an apartment on 44th and Spruce with three other roommates.

The courses in the fashion design program had become more technical: sewing, tailoring, patternmaking. I knew that if I wanted to be a professional fashion designer, I'd need to have those skills, but I was nineteen and too impatient to sit behind a sewing machine. Besides, it reminded me of my tenth-grade home economics class, where girls were taught how to sew aprons and make cinnamon toast, while boys took shop and made wooden birdhouses.

There were now other things I wanted to learn, so I transferred out of the fashion program and into the humanities department. This was the dumping ground for all the disenfranchised engineering and design students who wanted to change their major but didn't want to lose academic credits by transferring to another university. I enrolled in a German language class, nineteenth-century Russian literature, and a course called Film Appreciation 101. It was a Mickey Mouse class where I could earn an easy four credits just by watching movies and writing about them.

The world is seemingly random and irrational, yet the paths we take often make sense, if only in retrospect. Here's an example: instead of Film Appreciation 101, I could have chosen Music Appreciation 101, or Introduction to Psychology. All had the same number of credits and were of equal interest at the time. But Film Appreciation 101 was taught in a time slot that better fit my schedule, so I enrolled. I had no idea this would change my life.

* * *

I didn't come from a highly educated family. My mother had natural intelligence, but having married straight out of high school, she'd never gone to college. I think that bothered her. So with one daughter already out of the house and another soon to graduate, she decided to go back to school. My mother and I would both be college students at the same time, although, thankfully, not at the same school. And here's what I recognize now, something I didn't realize back then. From the outside, my mother's life looked happy and content, but I think she was seeking something, too. She wanted to be someone different from whom she'd been brought up to be. Maybe someone more worldly, more knowledgeable, more creative. And that aspirational desire to push boundaries would be passed on to her kids. It wasn't an actual goal, it was an attitude. The confidence to move beyond your comfort zone without fear of failure.

I remember coming home one weekend to see my mother with her new college friends, women my own age, sitting around our kitchen table, laughing and drinking coffee, and I couldn't help but wonder if my mom was having a better college experience than I was. But I was happy that at forty she was getting the education she'd always wanted. And my father, the self-made, self-confident, successful businessman who had dropped out of high school, was never threatened by anything my mother wanted to do, always supportive of her new goals.

* * *

During my junior year at Drexel, I had a teacher that I'll call Phil. I had just turned twenty. He was twenty-seven and a freelance movie critic for a local Philadelphia newspaper. He showed classic American and foreign films in his Film Appreciation 102 class. I'd never seen *Citizen Kane* or Ingmar Bergman's *The Seventh Seal*. I'd never heard of directors named Truffaut, Fellini, or Antonioni. It was like having cataracts removed from my eyes only to realize there was an entirely different world of filmmaking I knew nothing about.

I'd originally taken the class merely to get an easy four credits toward graduation. Unexpectedly, I had my mind blown. I was suddenly paying attention to things I hadn't noticed before: How a shot was framed, how a character was introduced into a scene, how a screenplay was structured. I realized that you can tell a compelling story and give it an ambiguous ending, as Truffaut did in *The 400 Blows,* or Fellini in *Nights of Cabiria*. You could capture psychological truths and inner emotions using camera framing, as in Bergman's *Persona*. You could disrupt the traditional flow of the narrative— even break the fourth wall and look directly into the camera—like Jean-Luc Godard did in almost all of his films. There were so many different ways to tell stories I hadn't thought about before.

Phil became my mentor. He took me to morning film screenings, the kind that only critics get invited to. He also became my *lover* (that sounds romantic, doesn't it?). Basically, we just started having sex midweek after class. Our pedagogic relationship had turned personal, not uncommon in the heated college campus atmosphere of the early seventies, a time when workplace ethics ranged from ambiguous to nonexistent. When I view this now through a twenty-first-century lens, I can't help but feel some mixed emotions. He was my teacher, I was his student. There was definitely an imbalance of power, but at the time I didn't see it that way.

Phil was funny, acerbic, and loved talking about movies. And I loved listening. Actually, he loved holding forth about many things, but neglected to mention that he was in a long-term relationship with another woman he saw on weekends (hence our midweek sex). I would find this out, eventually.

Her name was Marion. She was ten years my senior, had a beautiful three-year-old daughter, Jillian, from a previous marriage, and was working on her PhD in psychology. Marion knew about me and was very clever. Instead of feeling threatened or angry, she invited me to Phil's birthday party at her home, where we spent the entire evening holed up in her bedroom, sitting on a big pile of coats, talking. Surprisingly, we liked each other almost immediately, and she asked me to join her women's group.

It was 1972. *Ms.* magazine, the first American feminist monthly magazine, was now available at newsstands, and women's consciousness-raising groups were all the rage. I was the youngest member of my group, but figured I could learn something from the others. These were not women sitting in a circle examining their vaginas with hand mirrors. These were intelligent women talking about sexual politics, female empowerment, equal rights. Several had married straight out of college and were now divorced or in the process of becoming so. They felt they had been sold a false bill of goods back when being married was a sign of a woman's worth.

I ran out and bought books by Betty Friedan, Kate Millett, and Germaine Greer.[5] I read *Our Bodies, Ourselves* and privately studied my own vagina with a mirror. I bought poetry and novels by Sylvia Plath, Virginia Woolf, and Anne Sexton and wondered why talented women committed suicide. Was that the fate of a smart, creative woman? Sticking your head in the oven? Walking into the sea with a pocketful of stones?

Before then, I had never thought much about feminism. I had been focused on escape. But now that I understood what the term meant, I realized that this was what I was—a feminist. I wanted to be independent and empowered. I wanted the opportunity to be whoever the hell I wanted to be (as soon as I figured out what that was). And I got the message that if a male-dominated society was going to stand in my way, I'd have to create these opportunities for myself.

---

5. Germaine Greer—the author of *The Female Eunuch,* a 1970 feminist treatise about female sexuality—famously said that a woman isn't truly emancipated until she has tasted her own menstrual blood. This was a gastronomic treat that would never make it onto my menu. Years later, when I was about to give birth to my son, someone gave me a recipe for placenta soup. Another dish I never tried, although I've heard that eating placenta has now become popular. Apparently, celebrity moms trade recipes online for how to make the best placenta smoothie.

Long story short, sisterhood won out. I became friends with Marion and ended my fling with Phil, although we would remain friendly for the next few years. Eventually we lost touch, but I'll forever be grateful to him for opening my eyes to the possibilities of cinema. And for introducing me to Marion. Marion and I would remain friends for life.

By my final year of college, I'd taken Film Appreciation 101, 102, 103, and 104. There were no hands-on production courses at Drexel, so I never got to actually make a short film.

Graduation was rapidly approaching and I still didn't know what I wanted to be, but I now had a general direction. Although I loved watching movies, I'd never thought seriously about making one. Were there even any female movie directors? Was that a realistic goal?

On a whim, I applied to three graduate film school programs. Two in Philadelphia. One in New York City. I had nothing to show as a film sample and was rejected by the two in Philly.

Those would be the best two rejections of my life.

Blinded by the Light
(Manfred Mann's Earth Band)

Maybe I would have made it to New York City anyway, but this gave me the push I needed to get there.

Film schools were not very popular in 1973 when I took the train into Manhattan for an interview at New York University's Graduate Film School. The idea that you could teach film in an academic setting wouldn't become widespread until the '90s, when suddenly every major university had a film department, and independent film academies were popping up like weeds all across the country. Filmmaking programs were sexy academic money-makers. Every kid suddenly wanted to direct.

I had a meeting with the admissions committee, a group of four men and one woman. I was sure the other applicants had been making movies with their parents' Super 8 cameras since they were ten and was worried about my lack of hands-on experience. I had nothing to show except my early fashion design portfolio, but hoped my enthusiasm for cinema would come through. It did. I was accepted.

* * *

Unlike warm, sunny West Coast cities, Manhattan is not a place where young people go just to hang out. The pulse of the city is not *chill*. Rents are high. Apartments are small. And the weather is bad in winter when bus fumes turn the snow into gray slush and the sidewalks are covered with frozen piles of dog poop. But New York City is electric. A magical place where you could meet fascinating people who did interesting things.

There were no artists in my family. No one thought being creative was a realistic career goal. I came from business people with no connection to the entertainment industry. My dad, my uncle, and my grandfather manufactured hardware—practical items that people used in their daily lives. A door lock for security. A screen door to keep out flies. Aluminum siding! Art was a hobby, not a job.

I don't know if my mother thought I'd ever actually become a movie director, but at least I was getting a master's degree, and she believed in higher education. Maybe film was something I could teach. In her mind, the fallback position was that eventually I'd marry a guy who would take care of me—same as she had. And as for my dad—well, he went along with everything my mother said when it came to the children.

Moving to Manhattan was something I'd fantasized about ever since I was a young girl, but as the reality approached, I felt a wave of insecurity. In the suburbs, being different made you stand out. In New York City, no one cared where you came from; everyone was on the go. It was a tough, competitive town, and I knew only one person there.

I found a tiny furnished studio apartment in a 1950s brick building (with an elevator!) on East 9th Street. It was a furnished sublet and the rent was $135 a month. (Not cheap at the time.) The apartment had a single window that looked onto an alleyway between two buildings. The man who sublet it to me, a guy in his forties, had moved in with a woman on the top floor. She had a larger, two-bedroom apartment, but smoked like a chimney, so he would have to live in a cloud of cigarette fumes. It was a trade-off. He would sublet his tiny studio to me and live rent-free with her. Love and real estate go hand in hand in Manhattan.

I arrived with two suitcases, a carton of books, a typewriter, toiletries, bed sheets, a pillow, and a few personal knickknacks. The existing furniture consisted of a twin-sized cot, a brown plaid couch, a functional wooden coffee table, and two folding chairs. In the teeny kitchen nook there was an under-the-counter mini-fridge, a two-burner stove, and some basic pots and pans. But following in the Seidelman family tradition, I wasn't much of a cook anyway.

I came across some books and old photos stacked in his small closet. Looking through them, I discovered that the man had been a child actor— one of the gang in an early TV series called *The Little Rascals,* later renamed *Spanky and Our Gang.* He must have been four or five at the time. I'm not sure what he did once he grew up, but his apartment was spartan and sad, and it made me realize that Manhattan was filled with all sorts of aspiring people. Some on their way up, others on their way down.

Living in New York City changes your sense of privacy, so there's a certain reluctance to become too friendly with your neighbors. You can hear conversations through the wall. You get to know your neighbor's bathroom habits. Toilet flushes sound as loud as PA announcements at an airport. I'd seen the tenants across the alleyway walking around naked. I'd listened to my upstairs neighbor having noisy sex. I was hoping that one day he might hear the same sounds coming from my apartment, but since I hadn't yet made any friends, my romantic life was on hold. I was lonely that first month in the city.

* * *

My first friend in the building was a slightly stooped elderly man in his mid-seventies who lived in a larger apartment down the hall. I would sometimes see him waiting for the elevator and we would exchange smiles and say hello. His name was Mr. Schlanger and he reminded me of my grandfather. He told me he had once owned a small hot dog manufacturing company in Brooklyn and made the best frankfurters in town. I'd always enjoyed the stories older people told about growing up during the Depression or their experiences in World War II, so Mr. Schlanger and I would exchange a few words when we bumped into each other in the hallway. I sensed he was lonely, too.

One Sunday afternoon, Mr. Schlanger invited me into his apartment for a cup of coffee. We sat on the couch chatting, his radio tuned to a classical music station. He put out a tray of Ritz crackers and little cubes of orange cheese with individual fancy toothpicks. I thought it was sweet, something my grandmother might do. His apartment was furnished with an assortment of French Provincial furniture that came from his former living room in Queens. It was the kind of furniture his wife must have picked out in 1950, still pristine as if it had been covered in plastic for the past twenty years. Mr. Schlanger told me stories about the sausage business. How he sold his hot dogs to some of the small kiosks in Coney Island. I asked him about his wife, his children. He was a retired widower and his kids no longer visited him very often. Then he leaned over and tried to kiss me on the lips. The old-fashioned music playing in my head came to a screeching halt. I pushed Mr. Schlanger away and tried to stand up. He tried to hold me down, but there was no force in his action. I easily managed to get off the couch and hurried out of his apartment. I felt more shocked than violated. My faith in the sweetness of little old men instantly turned sour.

From then on, I would peek out of my apartment door to make sure the coast was clear before heading to the elevator. Once classes started, my schedule changed. I was busy and no longer home in the afternoons. I avoided bumping into Mr. Schlanger for several months, sometimes dawdling on the sidewalk if I saw him entering the building to avoid an awkward elevator encounter.

Around Christmastime there was a knock on my door. I peeked through the viewing hole and saw Mr. Schlanger standing in the hallway, but I pretended I wasn't home. He slid an envelope under my door. It was a holiday card along with one of those old-timey promotional wall calendars, the pinup kind you see hanging on the walls of gas stations and auto body shops. His company's name was printed boldly across the top, and each month featured a photo of a different sausage that was manufactured by Schlanger and Sons.

That was my introduction to dating in NYC.

With a Little Help from My Friends
(The Beatles)

NYU's Graduate Film School was located on 7th Street near Second Avenue, in the heart of the East Village. The famous, now-defunct rock venue, the Fillmore East, was located in the same building. Jim Morrison and Janis Joplin had played there only a few years earlier. Ratner's restaurant was nearby. This is where I'd eat scrambled eggs, lox, and onions for dinner several times a week, served by cranky old Jewish waiters. Other days I'd buy a one-dollar hot dog and orange mystery drink from Gray's Papaya on Eighth, or dine on cheap Japanese comfort food at Dojo on St. Marks Place, famous for their delicious carrot-ginger salad dressing (the original recipe is still a secret).

When I arrived in the East Village in the fall of 1973, the '60s counterculture was already beginning to fade. The neighborhood's burnt-out hippies and junkies, the Hare Krishnas dressed in fraying orange robes, and the peaceniks with beat-up guitars were slowly being overtaken by younger kids, louder and more aggressive, dressed in tight black jeans, leather jackets, and metal-studded collars. Blue spiked hair was replacing graying ponytails. The drugs were changing, too. Pot, hash, and psychedelics were swapped for coke, crack, and heroin. Maybe it was a cynical reaction to the dark turn the counterculture had taken after the maniacal delusions of Charles Manson. The flowers in everyone's hair had wilted.

* * *

At the time, NYU film school felt detached from the mainstream film industry. Few of my teachers had connections to the LA studio system. There were
thirty-five students in the class: thirty men and five women. Our aspirations
were about self-expression and creativity. Our heroes were the French New
Wave film directors: rebels like Jean-Luc Godard, François Truffaut, Alain Resnais. This was a time before artistic value was linked to commercial success.

We didn't read trade papers like *The Hollywood Reporter* or *Variety*. We
didn't know who the LA power agents were, nor did we care. We were naïve
about the workings of Hollywood. For me, this had a major upside. Had I
known how few women would ever get a shot at directing a movie, I might
have been demoralized and given up. Ignorance was bliss.

* * *

New York still had several large repertory cinemas that showed a vast array
of foreign films, cult films, and old movie classics. I was hungry for knowledge and had a lot of catching up to do. I'd take the subway up to the Carne-
gie Hall Cinema on 57th Street and watch three movies in a row, starting at
noon. For $3.50 you could stay all day. I became a *cinemaniac.* I scheduled my
weekly activities around the screening times of the films I wanted to see. I
set my alarm clock for 2:00 a.m. to watch Preston Sturges's *Sullivan's Travels,*
or Mervyn LeRoy's *I Am a Fugitive from a Chain Gang* on the *Late Late Show.*
Since there was no video yet, your only chance to catch an old movie on TV
was to wake up at whatever time it happened to be airing.

I took classes on American cinema, looking for role models. Several of
the directors we studied were macho men who resembled cowboys or military
generals: John Ford, John Huston, and Cecil B. DeMille (who actually wore
knee-high riding boots and jodhpurs on set). Some were cigar-smoking,
larger-than-life guys in suits (Hitchcock, Orson Welles).

There was also a new breed of directors: hipper, younger men who had
graduated from the burgeoning film schools on the East and West Coasts.
Coppola, Lucas, Scorsese, DePalma, Milius, and Spielberg. (Okay, Spielberg
had applied to USC's film school and been rejected a few times.) These were

guys with long hair and scruffy beards who smoked weed and wore baseball caps. Although I respected their talent and rebellious spirit, they seemed as macho in a countercultural way as their predecessors. They were telling stories about machismo and power and viewed the world with a male gaze.

I was looking for a woman who might help guide me through uncharted territory. Someone whose work I knew and respected. But I could count the number of American women who had directed a film I'd actually seen in a commercial movie theater on one finger. Elaine May, 1972. *The Heartbreak Kid.*

Then along came Lina Wertmüller.

Wertmüller was Italian and had been a protégé of Federico Fellini. She branded herself with large, attention-grabbing glasses. She was brazen. Fearless. And small (five feet tall)! But her films were big. She was rebellious, and you could sense her naughty mind at work in all her movies.

Wertmüller directed several films in the early to mid-1970s (*Swept Away, Seven Beauties, The Seduction of Mimi,* her three most popular) using dark comedy to make social and political observations. Everything about her films was slightly exaggerated, but still grounded in real human emotion. And although the star of her movies was a man, Giancarlo Giannini, you could feel Wertmüller's touch. Her female characters had strength. Her male characters had vulnerability. And she was developing a large body of internationally acclaimed work. Something few women had done before her. Something I wanted to do.[6]

Let me tell you the best thing about film school. You had access to a student crew who would work for free, usually without complaint. (Okay, maybe a little complaint, especially if you didn't feed them well.) You also got to use the school's camera equipment and editing machines. Plus, you could screw up, and no one made fun of you. Then you could fuck up again the second year, and the third, hopefully learning from your mistakes.

---

6. Wertmüller would become the first woman director nominated for an Academy Award in 1975 and was awarded an honorary Oscar in 2019. She died in 2021 at the age of ninety-three.

1975. Making an NYU short film. Student crew and free camera equipment!

Cinema is a language that I needed to learn. I wanted to understand when to use a close-up, a wide master shot, a two-shot, an over-the-shoulder. When to use an objective or subjective camera. How to film a scene by choreographing the actor's movement to the movement of the camera. I needed to learn the rules of screen direction so a dialogue scene between two characters looked like they were actually talking to one another when edited together (not facing in opposite directions, as happened in my first disastrous film exercise). It was like learning a foreign language. There would be lots of trial and error before I understood the basic rules. Rules I wanted to learn so I'd have the confidence to break them one day.

I realized that each individual choice made by the director had a cumulative effect on the storytelling. These were the elements that gave a film its personality, its point of view.

"We see new things through the lens of what we have already seen," said poet laureate Natasha Trethewey. So, for my first student short film, I decided to explore my suburban past with all my complicated feelings toward it. I would make a movie about a female character I intuitively understood. Someone I could have been. The short film, *And You Act Like One Too,* would be a story about a frustrated housewife who stumbles into an extramarital affair on the day of her thirtieth birthday. She would be a woman who feels restless, unappreciated, and is desperately seeking something—a reoccurring theme in the films I would go on to make (although I didn't know that at the time).

Jillian Frank and Karen Butler

By 1975, you could feel it in the air—women reevaluating their traditional role as homemakers in pursuit of power over their own lives. "The Personal Is Political" was a motto increasingly embraced by feminists over the next few decades.

I now had a mission. I wanted to be: 1) a professional woman film director, 2) who told tales about women's lives, 3) as seen through a female lens. Stories that needed to be shared.

At NYU we formed crews of six people and rotated positions. We were loaned a 16mm camera and a sound and lighting package and given some rolls of black-and-white 16mm film. Each student would write, produce, direct, and edit their own short movie. When it was my turn, I took my crew to Huntingdon Valley, to my parents' house. I would film in my parents' bedroom, kitchen, bathroom (the one with the big *S* etched on the shower door). I would shoot at the shopping center where I hung out as a teenager, smoking cigarettes behind the bowling alley. I would try to capture the texture of the world I'd grown up in—the place I'd left behind.

I filmed my script in a straightforward dramatic style, but with enough flexibility to allow for spontaneous discovery on set and give the actors some room to improvise. The film had a traditional narrative structure, but an ending with an emotional punch.

When the film was finished, I made three 16mm prints. Every few weeks I'd lug a print in its heavy metal carrying case over to the post office and wait in line to ship it to a film festival, or a library, or a museum somewhere across America in the hopes of setting up a screening. It was a time-consuming job that involved a lot of schlepping. (Today filmmakers just email a Vimeo link.)

It takes a certain amount of arrogance and self-delusion to think that anyone other than your family or best friend might be interested in your creative endeavors. So, I was genuinely surprised when I got news that my film had been nominated for a 1976 Student Academy Award and the Academy of Motion Picture Arts and Sciences was going to fly me to Los Angeles, along with eleven others, selected from across the country. They would put us all up in a hotel for three nights and there would be an awards ceremony and a cash prize. I'd never been to California before, so this was a fairytale way to visit Hollywood for the first time. But more importantly, it gave me the confidence to think that I could actually direct a film that others might enjoy watching. Maybe filmmaking was something I might be good at.

Hotel California
(The Eagles)

At the Beverly Hilton Hotel I shared a room with another film student, named Karen, the first woman I'd ever met who was an aspiring cinematographer. I lost track of her a few years later so I don't know if she succeeded in her chosen field, but she had probably picked the one film career even harder for a woman to break into than directing. Being a professional director of photography was basically a closed shop for women wanting to join the camera union in those days.

*   *   *

My film didn't win the Student Academy Award, but I was still reeling from the fact that I'd been nominated and got to meet Jack Nicholson at a cocktail party given by the Academy in our honor. He had just won the Oscar for Best Actor for *One Flew over the Cuckoo's Nest* the year before. I'd never seen a real movie star up close. They actually glow. I have a photo of the two of us. Me with a ridiculously starstruck grin on my face. Him, looking down with a quizzical expression. Smack in the center of the photo is a stranger caught in an awkward gesture, his hand reaching up to his nose like he's about to pick a booger.

Looking gaga meeting Jack Nicholson

Rather than return straight home to New York, I decided to extend my stay by a few days. Who knew what other celebrities I might meet in this star-studded city? So I got a cheap motel room somewhere off Sunset Boulevard. I wanted to walk around and get a feel for the city. (Not a realistic plan, I'd soon find out.) I don't remember who recommended the motel, or exactly where it was located (I've never had a handle on the street system in LA), but it was clearly in a sketchy part of town, and the excitement and glamour I'd initially felt quickly started to fade. I walked around deserted streets for about an hour, then returned to the motel mildly depressed. Because I didn't have a car, it was impossible to get around other than by taxi. Coming from New York, I was used to walking and public transportation. But without a credit card, a rental car wasn't an option.

New York City may be brash and noisy. But LA suddenly felt lonely. Or maybe it was just me feeling lost in this sprawling city that had no center. I spent the night alone, eating take-out in the motel, God knows where.

* * *

Before leaving for Los Angeles, I'd been given the phone number of a friend of a friend who had recently moved out west from New Jersey. The next day

I called him up, and he offered to take me to a barbecue at his girlfriend, Rhea Perlman's, house. He mentioned there would be a lot of people there from the East Coast.

A little while later, a beat-up jalopy pulled up in front of the crappy motel and a cheerful guy stepped out. I was surprised to see that he was even shorter than I was, and I'm often the shortest one in the room. It turned out he was an aspiring actor named Danny DeVito and he drove me to a backyard barbecue at the home of his girlfriend, Rhea Perlman. I didn't know anyone at the party, but everyone was friendly and very optimistic about their future. And I realized that was the key to survival in LA. You needed unwavering hope and an unquestioning belief in yourself. I stayed for a while, trying to muster up my own unbridled enthusiasm, then took a taxi back to the motel.

After realizing I was stuck in a creepy part of town, with no way to get around and no idea where to go, I called an old high school friend named Linda, who was living in Brentwood. She kindly invited me to stay a few nights with her.

The street where Linda lived had a cluster of two- and three-story mid-century U-shaped apartment buildings with small swimming pools in the center. She had a cute one-bedroom with a queen-sized waterbed (one of the worst fads of the '70s, along with the Dorothy Hamill bowl haircut). I was grateful she offered to put me up. I spent a few nights in her bed trying not to squirm because the waterbed's undulations made me a little nauseous and I didn't want to wake up my sleeping friend.

Linda was working for a TV production company and had a hunky non-working actor boyfriend who had once played a comic book hero in a short-lived series. He got to wear a red-and-blue spandex costume. And tights. This was long before wearing tights and a cape made you extremely rich and famous. He had one of those Hollywood actor names, like Garrett, although I think his real name was Walter. He had blue eyes, sandy blond hair, and a slightly round face that is cute at twenty-eight, but might not age well.

For the next two days Linda, Garrett, and I lounged around Linda's palm tree–lined swimming pool along with a bunch of other aspiring twenty-somethings.

Now, I admit, there were a few things about Los Angeles that made me anxious. The sky was too blue, the bougainvillea too pink, and the palm trees looked like set dressing. There was a distinct California style. LA was a city filled with tall, tanned blondes with hair like Farrah Fawcett's. Even Brooklyn Italian, Jewish, and Puerto Rican girls looked Californian after moving there. Whereas Manhattan was a town for sharp-edged brunettes like Dorothy Parker, Nora Ephron, and Fran Lebowitz. I was a brunette, not just in hair color but also in temperament.

The insightful (and underappreciated) LA writer Eve Babitz once said something like this: The reason people in LA are so good-looking is that LA always attracted the body-beautiful people and New York attracted the smart ones. After a few decades of beautiful people mating with other beautiful people, you end up with a town filled with a lot of beautiful-looking offspring.

Even the homeless people in LA looked sort of attractive. At least they were tanned.

Without a doubt, the town and many of its inhabitants were lovely on the surface, but underneath I could feel a hint of desperation, as if everyone knew there was a ticking clock and within a few years they would be substituted by another group of pretty young people already waiting in line to take their place.

Maybe I also feared that living in such postcard surroundings would take away my edge or make me insecure. Without the daily hassles of NYC life, I could easily fall into distraction. Or become a recreational drug enthusiast. And living in a town where inside every coffee shop there was an aspiring writer-director-actor-producer pitching a project to another aspiring writer-director-actor-producer would be demoralizing.

I'd enjoyed my visit to the City of Angels but was looking forward to returning to the rough-and-tumble streets of downtown New York. I realized that was where I felt most at home. A few days later, I boarded a plane and flew back to JFK with an Academy Award Nomination Certificate in my suitcase. It was embossed with a little gold Oscar statuette on the letterhead and signed by the (then) Academy's president, Walter Mirisch. I also took home a runner-up check for $250.

When I got back home, it hit me that film school was over, and I wasn't sure what to do next. I had left my NYU nest, but didn't know if I was ready to fly.

New York State of Mind

(Billy Joel)

In the mid-1970s, NYC was a mess and on the verge of bankruptcy, but it was a great time to be young, creative, and reckless.

In response to the city's financial crisis, Mayor Abe Beame had laid off thousands of municipal workers and cut back on services such as sanitation pickup and other social programs. Businesses were closing, there was massive unemployment, and many of the city's middle-class residents were moving to the suburbs for work and safer surroundings. They called it white flight.

Crime was rampant. Drugs, vandalism, and theft became the norm. Budget cutbacks meant that there were few police on the streets of Manhattan, now nicknamed "Fear City." Garbage piled up on the sidewalks. The subways were filthy and broke down frequently.

Maybe coming from the protected bubble of the suburbs, I didn't fully comprehend how dangerous the city was. I had little fear taking the subway home alone at 3:00 a.m. from midtown to Astor Place. Or walking down deserted streets at dawn. I was oblivious to danger, even though the newspapers reported daily stories about subway muggings and chain snatchers. But I wore no jewelry and blended in easily. It wasn't until David Berkowitz, "the Son of Sam," began his killing spree in July 1976 that I became more cautious, since he targeted mostly white women with long dark hair and I fit that description.

And out of this mess came a movement that would change New York culture. Because no one was paying attention, the Lower East Side morphed from a run-down slum into a creative incubator for aspiring artists. In chaos lies opportunity. Subway cars became huge canvases for graffiti artists. Crumbling walls and storefronts became bulletin boards covered with fly posters advertising the latest clubs and emerging bands. Some walls, like the one on St. Marks Place, were so overlaid with xeroxed flyers that you could pull off chunks half an inch thick.

Abandoned tenement buildings became pop-up galleries and performance spaces where electricity was shared through a Rube Goldberg-esque tangle of wires and cables reaching into adjoining buildings. A shithole country and western bar on the Bowery became the landmark punk club CBGB. Even Ratner's kosher dairy restaurant became became a hip hangout.

And suddenly everyone had a band. It didn't matter whether you could actually play an instrument. Musicianship was not the point. The music was intentionally confrontational; so was the performance style. The angrier and more offensive, the better. Rock 'n' roll had gotten too slick, overproduced, and there was a growing rebellion against its manufactured sound. Punk also became the antidote to the growing popularity of disco, which had taken hold all across America after the release of *Saturday Night Fever*.

I didn't go to Studio 54 when it opened in 1977 and soon became the epicenter of Manhattan's chic uptown nightlife. Although I wish I had, just to say that I did. I liked pulsating dance music and the glamorous, decadent lifestyle on display. Maybe I was afraid I wouldn't make it past the velvet rope, lorded over by a nineteen-year-old dictator-doorman. The downtown punk clubs were grungier, more egalitarian, and easier to get into.

Okay, some punk music sucked. But there were legendary performances by Talking Heads, the Patti Smith Group, Blondie, Television, the Police, and the Ramones. I went to CBGB, Max's Kansas City, and the Mudd Club mostly to people watch. I was a natural voyeur, fascinated by the subversive subculture surrounding the punk scene. But whether you were a fan of the music, a fan of the attitude, a fan of the anarchy, or just a fan of the widely available cocaine, it was clear that something raw and rebellious was happening. I watched as it began to spread, taking field notes like a cultural anthropologist.

There are some people who have a clear goal and a focused plan about how to achieve it. I had a general direction, but lacked a road map. My parents were helping with my rent, but I knew that wouldn't last for long. I had pushed their generosity to the limit and hated myself for it. I was no longer a student.

I needed to find work.

9 to 5

(Dolly Parton)[7]

B ack in the late seventies, there wasn't much film work in NYC. I helped
out on a few low-budget movies, but indie film jobs barely paid (if at all),
so I enrolled with a Gal Friday temp agency and got some part-time office
gigs. I did fine if they put me behind the reception desk or had me filing
papers, but if the job required typing, I was a disaster. This was a time before word processing—when everyone used manual typewriters, Wite-Out,
and carbon paper—so every time I made a mistake, I'd have to start from
scratch. I'd crumple the messed-up letter into a ball and hide it in my handbag. By the time I left work, my bag was bulging.

I got a job as a production assistant on a commercial that featured a
famous basketball star, but I don't remember who it was. I had minimal
interest in basketball or its players. (This would come back to haunt me in
2012 when I found myself directing a women's basketball comedy. But more
about that later.)

The job mostly involved sweeping the set in between takes and bringing
people coffee. But I got to listen in as a group of advertising execs sat around
a bank of video monitors critiquing the shot being filmed over and over and

---

7. Dolly Parton was a role model not just because of her enormous talent—having written one of
the most beautiful love songs of all time, "I Will Always Love You"—but because of her big personality and diminutive size. She was five feet tall, or maybe only four feet, eleven and a half inches
and rounded up.

over. It was a close-up of the basketball player's feet stepping out of a limo wearing Converse All Stars. The execs drove the director nuts with their notes. One said the shoelaces should hang more to the right. Another said more to the left. A third said the laces should be tucked inside the shoe. Too many cooks, too many opinions. It seemed like a very frustrating job that put me off ever wanting to direct a TV commercial.

Missing the camaraderie of being around film students, I took a screen-writing class at the New School and wrote a film treatment with a classmate named Peter. It was based on the true story of a Vietnam vet who had committed a robbery and would be one of the first veterans officially diagnosed with PTSD, which was then used in his legal defense. My sister had recently started work as a public defender in Manhattan and was involved in the case. (Taking our mother's advice, Denise had become a lawyer and moved to NYC.) She put me in touch with the Vietnam vet. Peter and I optioned our treatment to a TV producer, so I made my second trip to LA and stayed at the Chateau Marmont. Back then, the Chateau was shabby chic and relatively inexpensive. The only room service available was a turkey or cheese sandwich. And beer. Our project never went beyond the treatment stage, and I realized that many projects get optioned, few get made.

Over the next year, I made several more trips to LA, taking advantage of the generosity of my friend Linda and learning to like the undulations of her waterbed. I sat around her apartment complex swimming pool listening to other young hopefuls pitching projects as they sunbathed. I met with a few junior executives at production companies, but despite their casual friendliness, I felt like I was running in circles. I could knock on doors until my fists were bloody, but chances were slim to none I'd get a shot at directing a movie. Maybe if I was lucky, I'd find work as a gofer, or an assistant to one of the D-girls[8] at a studio.

The industry was filled with intelligent young women, former English majors from Ivy League universities, who were now reading scripts and writing coverage reports. But I was determined to be a director. I'd had a promising start. My short student films had won awards. I'd received prestigious

---

8. Development girls, or D-girls as they were called back then, were often attractive young female executives with no power. Thankfully that pejorative term is no longer in use. These days studios develop very few in-house scripts.

filmmaking grants from the New York State Council on the Arts and the American Film Institute. I didn't want to be read scripts—I wanted to direct movies. The male directors who were getting attention (Spielberg, Coppola, Scorsese, De Palma) had started out directing low-budget films and B-movie horror flicks for renegade producers like Roger Corman. I respected that kind of independent spirit. That was the path I wanted to take, and if no one was going to hire me, I'd just have to hire myself.

So, I returned to New York determined to make a low-budget indie feature film that I would write, direct, produce, edit, and cater, just as I'd done at NYU. Somehow, I'd pull all the pieces together. Then something unexpected happened that caught me off guard.

I fell in love. Just the thing to distract me from my goal.

What's Love Got to Do with It
(Tina Turner)

Yan was a professor at NYU. (Do you see a pattern here? Clearly, I had a thing for pedagogues.) He taught economics and was a friend of a friend from film school. They had both emigrated from Poland to New York in the late 1960s.

I met Yan at a New Year's Eve party held somewhere in New Jersey. We had arrived with other people. All I remember is that at midnight, after quite a few glasses of champagne and *Wiśniówka* (sour cherries soaked in vodka), we found ourselves in the corner of the room, kissing. It turned out that Yan lived on 9th Street, not far from me.

By now, I had moved into a new apartment, another tiny L-shaped studio in the same building. It was no bigger than the first, but at least my own name was on the lease and I could list my name and address in the Manhattan phone directory. That made me feel like an official New Yorker.

I bought a cheap pullout sofa bed and furnished the studio with leftover stuff from my teenage bedroom, U-Hauled up to New York. When the pullout was open, there was no space to walk between the bed and the desk, so I had to crawl across the bed to reach the kitchen nook. But what made me feel most like a real New Yorker was that I hired a telephone answering service. The cassette message machine had not yet been invented, so anyone who wanted to receive phone messages hired a service where a live human actually answered your number. Then you'd call in to the service to retrieve your messages. Most of the services hired out-of-work actors, which was pretty cool since they added in a touch of method acting as they recited your messages. ("Susan, your mother *r-e-a-l-l-y* wants you to call her back! She'll be up until midnight and needs to know if you received the book of two-for-one restaurant coupons she sent last week.")

Yan called the following day and asked me out for a drink (via phone message). I told him I was busy (via phone message). I wasn't, but remembered my mother's old-school advice to always play a little hard to get. It must have worked because he asked me out for the next night. And the night after that. And then we saw each other almost every night for the next three years.

Yan was cute, super smart, and just a little bit arrogant, which was part of his charm. He also had a voracious curiosity about all things cultural, academic, idiosyncratic, and a little bit naughty—along with a mischievous, dark sense of humor that came from growing up in a Communist bloc country. I'd always had a thing for foreigners. I liked their otherness. And for an Eastern European, he had surprisingly good teeth.

* * *

During the 1970s, sex was everywhere. The Sexual Revolution was in full swing. Birth control was readily available and sex was presumed to be safe, fun, and guilt-free. Even healthy. No one had a clue what dangers were lurking around the corner.

In LA, it was the height of the porn industry. Hundreds and hundreds of porn films were being shot in the San Fernando Valley, which gave employment to many young filmmakers eager for any kind of work behind the camera. Francis Ford Coppola said he got his industry start on the set of a porn film. Others included Barry Sonnenfeld (*Men in Black*), then working as an up-and-coming cameraman, Abel Ferrara (*Bad Lieutenant*), and Wes Craven (*A Nightmare on Elm Street, Scream*). Craven's debut feature film had the provocative title: *9 Lives of a Wet Pussy*. Soft-core porn was also a way for some now very famous actors, like Sylvester Stallone, to get their on-screen start. The porn wars of the 1980s would erupt a few years later with the anti-porn feminists on one side of the battlefield and sex-positive feminists on the other. Some say this polarizing division marked the end of second wave feminism, ushering in the third wave, the riot grrrl punk subculture feminism of the early '90s.

We had read a *New York Magazine* article about a new club called Plato's Retreat. It was a swingers' club that had opened in the Ansonia Hotel, in the space where the Continental Baths had once been. We were not swingers, but decided it was a cultural experience worth investigating. You could only enter Plato's Retreat as a straight couple, or a single woman. Single women got a discounted rate, but groups of men alone were not allowed in. You were encouraged to leave your clothes in a changing area and handed a towel. Or, you could choose to stay dressed and be a voyeur. I draped myself in a towel and remained wrapped the entire evening, as much out of vanity as modesty.

The club was an exhibitionist's playground, with some guests parading brickhouse bodies, others with saggy boobs and flabby bellies. There was a long buffet table that served crackers, fruit, carrot and celery sticks, juice, and soft drinks. Alcohol was not available, but I'm sure many couples brought along a personal stash of quaaludes. There was a dance floor where they played disco songs like "The Hustle" and a large room filled with thin mattresses where you could watch people having sex. Or join in, if you could find a non-sticky spot on the mat. (That alone was a turnoff.)

The clubgoers were a mixed bag. A few curious celebrity types, some uptown Manhattanites looking for adventure, some polyester-clad bridge and tunnel swingers. These were reckless Dionysian times. Post-Vietnam, pre-AIDS. Yan and I flitted around like flies on a wall, me in my towel and platform shoes, him in his Top-Siders, taking it all in.

* * *

Many nights we would stay up late watching shows on Manhattan Cable TV (which later became HBO). It was the very early days of cable, and there were public access programs that ranged from televangelists to Glenn O'Brien's *TV Party,* where Mr. O'Brien interviewed downtown celebs about all things cool and trendy. There was even a Wiccan chat show. But most popular were the naked talk shows.

A chubby, bearded fellow named Daniel J hosted a program where he interviewed adult entertainment stars along with an assortment of naked guests who sat cross-legged, yoga style, on the floor around him. Then there was the queen of public access, Robin Byrd, a former porn star who hosted her own talk show in a crocheted bikini and ended each episode by dancing with her guests to a theme song she'd written called "Baby Let Me Bang Your Box." And how can anyone forget *The Ugly George Hour of Truth*? Ugly George wore a silver lamé singlet and carried a bulky 1970s video rig on his shoulder. He would follow women down deserted NYC streets and film his attempts to get them to undress in public. He had a fifty-fifty success rate. I guess everyone wanted their fifteen minutes of fame, even if that meant flashing their titties on a public access TV show, watched only by insomniacs.

* * *

Yan was erudite. He introduced me to *The New York Review of Books* and authors like Milan Kundera, Italo Calvino, and Renata Adler. He bought me the diaries of Anaïs Nin and we read them aloud in bed, smoking pot. We went to see experimental theater at La Mama. He introduced me to Dean & DeLuca when it was just a small specialty food shop on Prince Street. Joel Dean and Giorgio DeLuca were behind the cash register and Soho was still a funky neighborhood filled with cheap artists' lofts and small factories making notions: buttons, snaps, fashion accessories, and underwear, bras, and panties.

It's hard to imagine, but back in the early 1970s Soho was scary at night. It didn't have an acronym until 1974. In the late nineteenth century, it was called Hell's Hundred Acres. In the early twentieth, it was simply called the area south of Houston Street.

Once the sun went down, the streets were dark and deserted. There were a few blocks of four-story tenement apartments on the west side, bordering Greenwich Village, where the Italian families lived. But much of Soho was made up of small factory buildings and workshops with cast-iron façades. Many were empty after the dry goods manufacturers moved out. These open workshops, with large windows and rickety wooden floors, were slowly being transformed into artists' lofts. But in the midseventies they housed an assortment of squatters, artists, and drifters who had managed to get to New York with nothing more than a backpack and the scribbled address of a place to crash passed on by a friend.

I remember one gigantic loft sectioned off into a warren of tiny bedrooms, divided by opaque plastic shower curtains hanging from poles on the ceiling. Getting up to the third or fourth floor involved knowing how to work a manual freight elevator that ran on a system of pullies and chains. Or you could climb the treacherous, incredibly steep stairs that induced vertigo if you dared to look down.

When I moved to Soho in 1983, the neighborhood had just started to gentrify. But that's still four years away, because right now it's 1979 and I'm about to move in with Yan.

Don't Do Me Like That

(Tom Petty and the Heartbreakers)

I'd been seeing Yan for three years when we decided to live together. He had just gotten tenure at NYU, so he was eligible for faculty housing in a modern high-rise building designed by I. M. Pei, near Houston Street. It was a subsidized three-bedroom apartment for only $350 a month. There was a reproduction Picasso sculpture in the front courtyard, a dishwasher in the kitchen, and a underground garage down below. I gave up my tiny studio apartment, donated my childhood furniture to the Salvation Army, packed my books and clothes, and moved into the appropriately named Silver Towers.

Little by little I found myself immersed in Yan's academic lifestyle. Looking back on it now, I think it was a distraction from my own film career, which seemed to be on hold. It was like I was trying on another new identity to see if one day it might fit. At the time, I thought I was happy, but maybe you can be unhappy and not know it.

And there was another thing. As modern as my mom was, in some ways she was still a traditional Jewish mother, although far from stereotypical. But she was truly happy being married. After marriage she had come out of her shell, grown more confident and more adventurous. So she wanted everyone she loved to be married, too, seeing it as a launching pad for future happiness. And in Huntingdon Valley, if you weren't married by twenty-seven, your shelf life was beginning to expire. Even my twenty-five-year-old *younger* sister had recently gotten married. I was about to turn twenty-eight, so somehow the thought that since Yan and I were living together and his career was going well, maybe we should get married bubbled to the surface.

But was marriage something you did with the best available person who sauntered into your life before your desirability expiration date? Unlike some of my high school friends, being married had not been my priority. I'd been focused on a career. Making movies. But once the idea of marriage was out of the box, it lodged itself in my brain.

* * *

I don't remember the exact sequence of events. There had been no wedding proposal, no ring, no declarations of eternal love, not even printed invitations! But the next thing I knew, my mother had planned an engagement party. At her house. With her friends. My mother loved organizing things. Even the smallest event was reason for celebration. I was reluctant to ask any of my NYU friends to travel to the Philadelphia suburbs. Maybe I was secretly embarrassed that I was turning into the person I had tried to escape.

The engagement party was just me, Yan, my relatives, and a lot of my mother's friends. I'm sure we both felt disconnected from what was going on around us. Yan looked like a fish out of water. I opened our presents, oohed and aahed, and passed them to Yan. He smiled, numbly.

My aunts had pooled together to buy us sterling silverware—eight six-piece place settings from Christofle. We were given crystal wine glasses, decanters, casserole dishes, and Danish modern plates. All the lovely things newlyweds might want to start a life together. But the atmosphere of the party was surreal. On the ride home from Philadelphia, I could tell Yan was edgy. I decided to ignore it, hoping it was just premarriage jitters.

I should have seen it coming.

As it happened, the following week we were invited to a cocktail event at the Afghan Consulate in New York. One of Yan's colleagues, a professor from a prestigious family in Kabul, had organized the party to raise awareness about the recent Soviet invasion of Afghanistan that had taken place on December twenty-fourth. Several of Yan's NYU coworkers were there, as well as a pretty young woman who worked part-time as an assistant in the economics department. Someone I'd never met before. She'd come to the event alone, but was hanging around the group of NYU professors. She was hanging around Yan.

After the party, a bunch of us decided to go to Hurrah, a dance club on West 62nd Street. The club was crowded, the music was thumping, and the dance floor was packed. I went to the bar to get a drink and when I returned, Yan was gone. I looked around the room, but couldn't find him. I made my way to the dance floor and scanned the crowd. There he was, in the middle of the room, dancing like a fool with the economics department assistant. And Yan never danced.

As a filmmaker, I'm often in the position of being an observer—an outsider watching the action from behind the camera, through a lens. So, at first, I watched them smiling and dancing as if they were actors in a film. That was how I could separate myself from the shock. It would be a coping mechanism I'd use throughout my life.

I replayed the dance floor scene in slow motion. I broke it into master shots and close-ups and over-the-shoulder shots. I tried to edit out the parts that were the most disturbing. I played the scene in fast-forward. In reverse. In black-and-white. But it was always the same scene, and the close-up of Yan's face revealed he was in love. (Or was it just lust? No . . . it looked like love.)

I left Hurrah and took a taxi back to our (his) apartment in Silver Towers. It was now about 1:00 a.m. I sat at our (his) dining table, in our (his) darkened living room, feeling dazed. Yan returned home about an hour later. I'm sure we had an argument that night, but I've edited that scene out of my memory. Maybe I was expecting him to come up with an excuse that would soften the blow. Even a fake, corny excuse would've sufficed. "I'm sorry—I was drunk, I was stoned, I just wanted some exercise." But he offered no explanation.

A few days later, Yan moved out and into the economics department assistant's apartment uptown, near Columbia, where she was finishing her PhD in psychology. Oh fuck! She was pretty and *smart*!

I don't know if I was heartbroken because I'd lost Yan, or because I'd lost myself. I suddenly felt like I'd wandered down a wrong path and disappeared. I'd come to New York to be a somebody, not a somebody's wife. I was twenty-eight. Without a purpose. Without a partner. Without self-esteem. I'd given up my apartment to move into a (faux) Silver Tower with a (licensed faux) Picasso sculpture out front. Being a tenured professor, Yan was entitled to live there. I was not. I would have to move out within a few months.

* * *

I spent the month of January crying in the shower. At night, boo-hoo-hoo tears trickled down my cheeks as I lay alone in bed. I think part of me enjoyed playing the role of a jilted woman, like the ones I'd watched in those 1950s melodramas I loved—the parts played by my namesake, Susan Hayward. But I hid my feelings when Yan returned to the apartment on occasion to pick up some of his personal belongings: his books, his under-wear . . . even his fucking wok!

At times my hurt turned to anger. Yan had replaced me with someone he thought more worthy of his affection, someone he thought was smarter, or prettier, or who would have a more esteemed future. I needed to prove him wrong. So, after I had cried myself dry, I turned my anger into resolve. I would muster up the same "I'll show you" attitude I felt when Bobby C broke my heart in eighth grade. When Mrs. Kirschbaum put me in the dumb kids' reading group. When my high school friends' parents said I was a bad influence on their daughters.

I'll show you all!

I believed that art had the power to heal. (I still do.) So I decided to pour all my hurt into my work instead. Maybe fate had intervened to shove me back on track. Life is funny like that.

But first . . . What to do about all those engagement gifts? Some were still arriving in the mail. I imagined writing thank-you notes to my rela-tives: *Thank you for the lovely cast-iron cheese fondue set, but I will be returning it shortly as I will not be making cheese fondue for my husband or children any time in the near future. Instead, I will be making a major motion picture!*

I never did return the Christofle silver service for eight. I was going to, but my aunts had taken pity on their spinster niece and told me to "hold on to it for next time" (although dubious there would be a next time, given my age). I also didn't return the casserole bowl, which proved to be a very pragmatic gift that I still use to this day. I look upon it as a souvenir of an alternate reality that might have been mine.

Yan and I had goodbye sex when he came by to take his suits out of the closet. Goodbye sex is always good because it has hurt and guilt mixed in it, and we both knew this would be the last time we'd ever be physical together. I was not trying to win him back. He was not pretending he loved me. He had moved on to the woman who would become his wife. They would get married and have two children. She would become a psychotherapist and write some books. Within a few years, they would break up and she would change her ordinary first name to the more uncommon name of a western state. (I guess she, too, wanted to reinvent herself.) They would go through an acrimonious divorce and his kids would not speak to him for several decades.

* * *

It's funny how life is full of synchronicities. Around the time Yan and I split up, my grandmother, Nanny S, passed away. In her will she left me money intended for my upcoming wedding. Since there was not going to be a wedding, I suddenly found myself with $12,000. Perhaps not a fortune, but in 1979 it was enough to jump-start the indie film I had put off making.

I'd lost a fiancé and a three-bedroom apartment with a dishwasher and an underground parking spot, but I was now determined to make a movie. I had no excuse to delay. I just needed to figure out what I wanted to say, and how I wanted to say it.

Walk on the Wild Side
(Lou Reed)

Being alone, with no romantic attachment and only temp work, I had a lot of time to wander the city. I wanted to keep busy. And as my gloom began to lift, a sense of freedom crept in. I'm sure the feeling was forced at first, but gradually, it took hold for real. I was trying to get back in touch with the creative force that had drawn me to the city in the first place.

* * *

In 1980, NYC was still struggling with rising crime and decreased social services, but in the East Village, No Wave (cheap, guerrilla-style) film-making was flourishing, as the worlds of punk, rap, poetry, and graffiti art cross-pollinated. Inspired in part by the French Nouvelle Vague cinema of the 1960s—specifically the work of Jean-Luc Godard (every New York indie filmmaker's hero)—filmmakers like Jim Jarmusch, Amos Poe, Eric Mitchell, Michael Oblowitz, and later Scott B, Beth B, Sara Driver, Tom DiCillo, Bette Gordon, and Lizzie Borden were making personal, disruptive, and raw movies without money, without permits, without professional actors, without formal scripts (and in some cases, without any script at all).

Early '80s. Filmmaker Scott B, actors Amanda Plummer and James Russo, musician/author Adele Bertei, and me. (I never mastered the art of looking blasé.) *(Photo by John Clifford)*

I started going out more often to clubs and performance spaces. New spots, like the Pyramid Club on Avenue A, were popping up, with drag performances that brought together punk, queer, and straight clubgoers. Traditional boundaries were being blurred. There was a reckless energy you could feel in the air. A sense that anything was possible. If you could think it, you could be it. And the more I explored, the more my antenna went up as I searched out (or stumbled upon) unexpected facets of life in the city.

For years I'd taken notes about people I'd encountered who possessed some distinctive quality, some personal quirk that grabbed my attention. I was curious about human nature and carried a little notebook to write down observations—ideas for movie scenes, fragments of dialogue overheard in a bar or on the subway. I made sketches of what people were wearing. I doodled on napkins, matchbook covers, wrote words on my arms—whatever surface was available. Then I stashed my scribblings in a desk drawer, waiting for the right time to make sense of it all.

I'd heard about a mysterious place called the Hellfire Club, in the basement of a funky building in the Meatpacking district. (Thirty years later the club would become an expensive Mexican restaurant and tourist brunch spot.) It was a cavernous space with black walls, a long bar, and an edgy vibe. It seemed like a dark place I should steer clear of, which is probably why I was curious to go. I was hungry for new experiences and felt the urge to walk a little closer to the edge, but without falling off.

The club had a decadent BDSM following—a subterranean world of misfits and curiosity seekers. It was how I'd imagined a club in 1920s Berlin might be. The Velvet Underground's music played over the sound system. It smelled dank, like a gym locker. I didn't go there looking for romance, or even temporary companionship. I was looking for a story.

There were several small rooms off of the main room. In one you could watch a guy lying in a cast-iron bathtub being urinated on by whoever walked by and wanted to take a piss. There were men in studded black leather strappy things tied up and being spanked by dominatrices in black leather corsets. I walked past people in harnesses and chains, trying not to gawk. It was like an X-rated interactive museum exhibit with an assortment of deviant sexual activity on display. But after a while, I started to feel uncomfortable, so I went to the bar to get a drink before heading home. Standing there was a guy wearing Buddy Holly glasses who looked like a middle-aged accountant. While I was trying to get the bartender's attention, we struck up a conversation. The music was loud, so to be heard, he needed to stand very close and talk directly into my ear. What made this strange was that the man was totally naked except for a pair of black socks and tasseled loafers. I wasn't sure where to look, so we chatted for a few minutes while I finished my drink, then left.

I later thought about how comfortable, how at ease, this naked man in black socks seemed in this very strange place, casually sipping his drink. I wondered what it must be like to be him. And I realized that everyone is seeking a place where they can feel at home.

This scene wouldn't make it into the screenplay that was now percolating in my head. But I knew my film would be about someone searching for a place to fit in. I was inching closer to the story I wanted to tell.

Bad Girls
(Donna Summer)

I started to notice a certain type of girl hanging around the downtown club scene. I won't call her a groupie, but she had elements of that. She was someone looking for excitement. Driven by a need to feel special, eager for recognition despite no discernible talent . . . and inclined to sleep with anyone in a band. Like me, she came from a place she wanted to escape. Bit by bit, I began to draw a mental picture of this girl and realized she would be the protagonist of my movie.

I sorted through the pile of notes I'd written over the years to see where they would lead. I wanted the film to deal with the complications of love and romantic disappointment. Attraction and manipulation. And I wanted the plot to be a little bit messy, because life was messy. My protagonist would be a narcissistic young woman caught between two men. One, sweet and malleable. The other, a sexy manipulator.

I decided to name her Wren because she would be a birdlike creature who flies fast and keeps moving until she finds a place to land. Wrens build nests in old tree stumps, crevices of buildings, parked cars, flowerpots, drainpipes, even shoes. They are scrappy survivors.

I remember my father saying to me when I was a smart-aleck kid: "So, tell me something new." That phrase stuck in my head. I wanted to create a female protagonist that movie audiences hadn't seen a gazillion times before. I wasn't concerned about whether Wren was likable or sympathetic. I wanted her to be compelling, even infuriating. My favorite male movie characters always had a combination of good and bad qualities: Ratso Rizzo in *Midnight Cowboy*. Benjamin Braddock in *The Graduate*. Travis Bickle in *Taxi Driver*. There needed to be more guy roles for women.

I was also inspired by the multifaceted female characters I'd seen in European films. Roles for actresses in Hollywood movies of the '50s, '60s, and early '70s fell into two basic categories: the good wife/devoted girlfriend, or the slut/whore. This was infuriating after the heyday of great female roles in the melodramas and screwball comedies of the '30s and '40s. Post–World War II American cinema had created heroic male characters, but put women back in the kitchen, or the bedroom.

I watched the films of Jean-Luc Godard starring his wife and muse, Anna Karina. I wanted to be her! I watched the films of Claude Chabrol, mesmerized by his wife/muse, Stéphane Audran. I fell in love with the early movies of Federico Fellini because of the performances of his wife, Giulietta Masina. In *Nights of Cabiria,* Masina played a waifish prostitute, living in a hovel and roaming the streets of Rome looking for love, but finding only disappointment. The film would win an Oscar for Best Foreign Film in 1957.

The grittiness of Fellini's bombed-out postwar Italian neorealist settings reminded me of the dilapidated buildings and rubble-strewn lots of the Lower East Side in the 1970s. And although the film's subject matter was dark, the story sparkled with touches of genuine humor and hope. I loved that mix—dark and light. That was the tone I was looking for. But what I liked most was the pluckiness of Cabiria, the character that Giulietta Masina played. Her attitude, determination, even her wardrobe would inspire the character of Wren.

Wren   Cabiria

(Photo montage courtesy of Marya E. Gates)

Here are a few things I knew about Wren: She would have the gutsi-ness of Cabiria, the near-delusional ambition of Holly Golightly, and the self-destructive spark of the archetypal punk groupie, Nancy Spungen. She would be hungry for fame, but her best creation would be herself. She would use her day job working at a xerox copy shop to make photocopies of her face (*selfies,* before they had that name) with the caption: *Who is this?* She would plaster them all over the walls of the East Village. It would be her way of saying, "I exist. Pay attention to me!" She would be a precursor to a gener-ation of famous-for-being-famous social media influencers twenty-five years later. A legend in her own mind.

I wanted to create Wren without judging her.

* * *

There have always been girls like Wren (boys, too)—young people coming to the big city with the dream of reinventing themselves. Nobodies who want to be somebodies. And I admired Wren's resilience. When she got knocked down, she picked herself back up. Wren was no crybaby.

Because I didn't have much money, I decided to turn my financial limitations into an aesthetic. I was not looking for technical slickness or perfection (nor could I have achieved it). I was looking for the right edge, the right tone. The film's cheapness would become its style. The gritty streets, the crumbling buildings, the garbage-strewn sidewalks, and the graffiti-covered walls would be an important part of the production design.

1981. East 12th Street, near Ave A

Even though I'd been out of NYU for three years, I'd stayed in touch with some of my former classmates. I told them I was going to make a low-budget film. Since we'd had a good working relationship on my student films, they came onboard. Little by little the pieces came together. The notes scribbled on scraps of paper turned into a hundred-page screenplay and I set out to make a movie. All I needed was to find Wren.

I began the casting process following a traditional route. I placed an ad in *Backstage,* the weekly newspaper read by New York actors looking for work. This is how many student films were cast at the time—aspiring directors seeking aspiring actors to work on their films for free. I received hundreds of headshots. New York had no shortage of young hopefuls looking for a break. I sorted the photos into piles, then held auditions in a borrowed theater space in Times Square. There were a couple of potentially good candidates, but none had the edge, or the scrappiness I was looking for. They seemed to be acting the part, but lacked the authenticity.

An NYU friend of mine named Yossi happened to go to an off-off-off Broadway performance by an experimental theater group that was held in an abandoned downtown loft. Apparently, there were more actors onstage than people watching in the audience. The show was forgettable, but he spotted an actress he thought was unique. He gave me her phone number, and I called. We agreed to meet the following week.

The moment she entered the room I sensed she had the gamine quality I was looking for. I also knew it was fate that her name was Susan. Susan Berman. I had a thing about names. I had a thing about Susans.

In the end, *Smithereens* would take over two years to make, with several starts and stops and many complications along the way. Some of the problems were beyond my control. Some were financial setbacks I knew I'd eventually encounter (like running out of money). Sometimes I felt like a punch-drunk boxer waiting for the next blow. But each time it looked like the project would collapse, it made me more determined to get it made.

I'll show you.

One Way or Another
(Blondie)

On our fifth day of filming, Susan Berman fell off a rickety fourth-floor fire escape during a rehearsal. She dropped fifteen feet and could have easily been killed. Fortunately, she only broke her ankle, but it was a bad break that required her to be in a plaster cast for four months, and the film came to a screeching halt. I felt terrible for Susan (thankfully, she would be fine). I also felt sorry for myself. I'd already spent a third of my production money and there would be nothing to show for it. I feared the cast and crew would all go their separate ways and the whole endeavor would have been a total waste of time. What I didn't realize was that Susan's accident actually saved the movie. It gave me a chance to assess what I'd filmed—to see what was working and what wasn't—then adjust the script moving forward.

The scenes with Wren alone on-screen were powerful. We had created a unique character and Berman brought her to life. But the scenes with Wren and the French actor I'd originally cast as the male lead had no spark. It was no one's fault, there just wasn't chemistry between them. If Susan hadn't broken her ankle and I'd stuck with the original version of the script, I'm sure the film would not have been very good. It would have come and gone, and with it, my future directing career. But during the four-month hiatus, while Berman was recuperating, I decided to rewrite the script, with the help of an aspiring screenwriter named Ron Nyswaner, whom I'd recruited by cold-calling Columbia University's screenwriting department and asking the kid who happened to answer the phone if he had any suggestions. I lucked out finding Ron. I then recast the male lead, taking that character in a totally different direction. That's how bad luck can turn good.

* * *

Richard Lester Myers, aka Richard Hell, the lead singer of the Voidoids, was a Lower East Side celebrity. But despite his downtown fame, he was usually broke and hustling for money. He had a louche reputation that he fully lived up to. Richard had been in several influential bands—Television (with former friend Tom Verlaine) and the Heartbreakers—that played regularly at CBGB and combined poetry with posturing. He had written the punk anthem "Blank Generation" and, according to downtown mythology, was credited with having created the punk ethos before the Sex Pistols, Malcolm McLaren, and other British bands appropriated it. It's claimed he was the originator of the proto-punk fashion of ripped-up T-shirts held together by safety pins.

Somehow, we met through a friend of a friend of a friend. Richard had heard I was looking to recast my film and he was probably hoping there would be some money in it. We chatted on the phone, then he dropped by my (Yan's) apartment.

The first thing that struck me was his cinematic look. He was tall, thin, and handsome, with spiky hair and shabby glamour. We talked about filmmaking, and I was surprised to find out he was a serious cineaste. He had worked at Cinemabilia, the best film bookstore in town, and had an extensive knowledge of movie history. He had come from an academic family. His mother was a professor and he'd been a prep school dropout. He said he needed rent money and asked if the job paid. I told him no one else in the cast was getting paid (true) then offered him $200 a week for three weeks of part-time filming.

He was a smoker, so I threw in a professional teeth cleaning.

Richard would play "Eric," a diabolically seductive version of himself, and I wanted to capture his sexy bad boy allure on film.

Once Susan Berman got out of her plaster cast, I was able to pull the crew back together and we continued filming in one-week spurts due to weather and financial considerations. I would pepper the film with interesting people I'd met along the way—actress and writer Cookie Mueller, indie filmmaker Amos Poe, the singer and punk Brigitte Bardot, Kitty Summerall. When I ran out of money, I would stop to find more. But shooting in stops and starts also had its advantages. It enabled me to edit and make story adjustments as I went along. The tricky part was trying to hold the cast and crew together over the stretch of a year. Thankfully I'd inherited my mother's relentless optimism and didn't give up easily.

Yan's three-bedroom apartment in Silver Towers (where I was now living alone) became a combination production office and crash pad. There was a steady stream of colorful characters and oddballs coming and going. The script supervisor, my cousin Ira, slept on the couch in the living room. One of the assistant directors slept on a pullout sofa in the back room, and Richard Hell occupied the middle bedroom on the nights when he was filming the following day. It was a way to ensure that he would show up on set in the morning, clean, sober, and on time. (But as it turned out, my concerns were unwarranted. Richard was very professional when he wanted to be.)

*　*　*

My naïveté about filming in New York City turned out to be an asset. I didn't know you needed film permits to shoot on NYC streets, so we had none. We just ran around the city like outlaws, stealing locations, filming wherever we needed to, letting nothing get in our way. We shot the opening title sequence on the subway starting at 2:00 a.m. with our camera hidden inside a travel bag. There were six of us and we rode the trains all night until we got all the footage we needed, jumping on and off the train whenever we spotted a transit cop.

One night we were filming a scene in Times Square, which was still pretty squalid at the time. Most of the light on 42nd Street came from the neon-lit marquees of the XXX-rated movie theaters along the street. (This was still two decades before the area would be pedestrianized and turned into a Disneyesque theme park.) It was a scene where Wren and Eric, desperate for money, rob a tourist at gunpoint inside a taxicab. It was hard to rehearse the scene in advance and we didn't have a taxi at our disposal. So the actors and a small crew of four (cameraman, sound recordist, camera assistant, me) hailed a random cab on 42nd Street. I offered the driver fifty bucks and asked him to drive in circles around Times Square while we all squeezed into the taxi to film.

During a break in the shooting, while Chirine, the cameraman, was reloading his camera in the doorway of a peep show, I handed the prop gun to Ira, our script supervisor, for safekeeping. A pedestrian must have seen him standing there, holding a gun, and called the police. The next thing Ira knew, he was surrounded by cops with their weapons drawn. Luckily, he managed to talk his way out of being handcuffed and thrown in the back of a paddy wagon on a weapons charge. The cops then left, and we continued filming.

Our key location was an abandoned rubble-strewn lot around 47th Street, near the West Side Highway. This was a deserted stretch of highway well known as a cruising spot for hookers—and there were plenty hanging around, as well as the sketchy characters who watched over them. This is where the character of Paul (a drifter from Montana, played by actor Brad Rijn) lived in his graffiti-covered van, parked in an empty lot. During pre-production, I had met a young Puerto Rican kid—a subway graffiti artist named Lee

Quinones—and asked him to paint Paul's van in his signature style. I bought the spray paint and paid him $100. A few years later, after graffiti art became popular, Quinones's work would be in major museum collections around the world and auctioned for big bucks at Sotheby's. Regrettably, the old van he spray-painted for *Smithereens* had been junked as scrap metal. When I was unable to find cheap long-term parking in Manhattan, I'd asked my father if I could keep it temporarily parked in his driveway in Huntingdon Valley. But when the neighbors complained it was an eyesore, he had it shredded.

One of my favorite scenes featured an actress named Katherine Riley playing a zonked-out prostitute who propositions nice-guy Paul when she finds him sitting alone, at night, in his van. The dialogue (thank you, Ron Nyswaner) went like this:

> HOOKER
>
> Hi. You recognize me? I'm always hangin' around the corner when you walk by. Me and my friends always wave at you. . . . Listen, you want me to keep you company for a while? . . . Twenty bucks.

> PAUL (SHY)
>
> Uh . . . I don't think so.

> HOOKER
>
> You want me to go down on you? I'll do that for fifteen. With my hand, it's only ten.

> PAUL
>
> Uh . . . thanks anyway, but I don't think so.

> HOOKER
>
> Well, can I just sit here for a while? It's cold outside. . . .
> (She makes herself comfortable in the front seat)
>
> Crazy weather, huh? One day it's hot. Next day it's freezin'.

PAUL

I guess you gotta be outside a lot?

HOOKER

Yeah, well . . . it's the nature of my biz-ness. . . . You hungry? (She pulls a brown paper bag from her handbag, takes out a sandwich.)

PAUL

Nah, I don't want to eat your dinner.

HOOKER

You're lettin' me sit in your truck. Go ahead. I got an egg in here, too. It's chicken salad with may-o-nnaise. My mother made it.

(Reluctantly, Paul takes a bite. They eat in silence for a moment.)

HOOKER

I visited my mother the other day. Boy, was that a trip. She's sweet, but I think she's getting a little senile. . . . How's the sandwich?

PAUL

Uh . . . good.

HOOKER

So, what do you do?

PAUL

P-portraits. I draw portraits. I'm not an artist or anything. I just do it for the money.

HOOKER

Yeah, well, don't we all.

(They chat for a while, then, the hooker gets ready to leave.)

HOOKER

. . . Look, you sure you don't want to get it on with me? I got a scar. I'll show it to you for five dollars.

PAUL

A scar?

HOOKER

It's in a really interestin' place.

PAUL

Uh . . . thanks, but I don't think so.

This was the type of scene that didn't really advance the plot, but spoke volumes about the characters and mood, which was why I liked it. And Katherine Riley's deadpan performance as a sentimental hooker was brilliant. Both funny and sad. Unfortunately, this would be her last film role. She died four months before *Smithereens* was released and never got to read the rave reviews her performance received.

Occasionally, a few of the real-life prostitutes would stop by to chat, curious to check out what we were doing. And I realized that there was an alternate world of night crawlers who only came out after midnight— hookers and rent boys, night-shift taxi drivers, road maintenance crews, and the clubgoers who frequented the mysterious after-hours spots that didn't open until 4:00 a.m. We had temporarily become part of that secret universe. Someone with a gun could have easily shot us and stolen our expensive rented camera equipment. We were filming in no-man's-land, late at night, without protection or security. We were young and reckless and naïve. Creativity was the invisibility cloak that protected us.

I Will Survive

(Gloria Gaynor)

Around this time, I had to leave Silver Towers. I had overstayed my welcome and Yan wanted to move back into the (his) apartment with his new girlfriend and, besides, I had no legal right to be there. So I moved farther south to a converted office building on Maiden Lane, near Wall Street. Since artists had been moving steadily south from Greenwich Village to Soho, then farther south to Tribeca, I thought the Wall Street area would soon become the next artsy hot spot. I was wrong.

During the day, Wall Street was crowded with stockbrokers, lawyers, secretaries, and office workers. By 6:00 p.m., like clockwork, everyone went home and the streets were deserted. The coffee shops and fast food joints that fed the office workers closed early. There were few grocery stores and no supermarkets since this was not a residential area. If I ran out of milk, I went to the local Bun N' Burger on Broadway and pocketed a handful of those free mini plastic containers of half and half, then watered them down to use with my cereal. My refrigerator was empty except for individual-sized packets of mustard, ketchup, pickle relish, and duck sauce.

My apartment was pretty much devoid of furniture, since I'd given most of my old stuff away. I did have the big gray velvet sectional sofa that Yan and I had bought together that now looked lonely in my empty living room. The apartment had a tiny Juliet balcony, big enough for a folding chair and the plastic cube I used as a coffee table, and had a spectacular view of the Twin Towers only one block away. I would sit outside at night with a glass of wine and gaze at the magical cityscape, shimmering glass and chrome. Lights twinkled in thousands of empty offices where immigrant cleaning crews worked all night. That's the powerful and humbling thing about living in NYC. You are one speck of light in a gigantic grid. There were millions of stories out there, each as unique as your own. Looking out at the towering World Trade Center, I could never have imagined what would happen there twenty years later and that I would witness it firsthand.

I rented a Steenbeck editing table and put it in my living room. It was nearly the size of a professional xerox copy machine, with a monitor on top. I would thread the reels of celluloid film and magnetic sound through lots of gizmos, then physically splice and tape together the pieces I wanted to use. Plastic bins of outtakes (dangling bits of celluloid) were scattered about the room. My schedule was erratic, but I liked working best at night when the neighborhood was eerily quiet. I turned into a zombie. Anyone who has worked on a passion project knows the feeling of waking up at 3:00 a.m. with a sudden idea and leaping out of bed to jot it down before the thought vanishes. (In my case, running over to the editing machine to try it out.)

I spent months in my pajamas.

I had run out of money and still had lab bills, editing bills, and sound mixing bills to pay. I borrowed more money from my father and persuaded my Uncle Arnold to lend me $5,000, promising both they would be repaid shortly. I had no idea how, but I had no choice but to believe in myself. If I didn't, who would?

It was around this time that Ron Nyswaner met a director named Jonathan Demme, who had just made the movie *Melvin and Howard*. It received great reviews and won two Oscars. Ron put me in touch with Jonathan, who offered to take a look at a rough cut of *Smithereens*. He had a reputation for being supportive of young filmmakers and his generosity and enthusiasm were well known within the indie film community.

There's a funny thing about feedback. I was eager to hear what Jonathan had to say. He was far more experienced than I, but as we watched the rough cut together, I was also paying attention to how I felt sitting next to him. I was watching the film through his eyes, and there were times I got fidgety because a scene was paced too slowly. Times when my shoulders tensed, or my face involuntarily cringed, because a sequence was awkwardly edited. I could feel when Jonathan was engaged and when he was drifting. I was listening to what my gut was telling me.

We talked about music, a subject he loved, and the impact the right soundtrack could have on the movie. I'd listened to Lou Reed, the Clash, the Stooges, and David Bowie on heavy rotation as I was editing the film. It put me in the right zone. So when Jonathan mentioned that he knew a musician who might be interested in working on the film score, then said it was John Cale of the Velvet Underground, I was elated. Jonathan arranged for us to meet.

Unfortunately, our first meeting was . . . weird. Cale showed up at my apartment several hours late, high, and rambling in his Welsh accent. I was surprised to find out he had been a classically trained musician. Maybe he was going through a rough patch, but I'd put so much time, energy, and borrowed money into the project, I couldn't risk blowing it now. It was clear this would not be a productive working relationship as I watched him lay out lines of coke next to the editing machine and we got straight to work on them.

In all fairness, I would bump into Cale a few years later. I had no idea if he remembered me or our awkward meeting, but I was happy to see that he had pulled himself together, had a child, and had returned to producing new music.

Then Jonathan told me about a band called the Feelies. They had recently recorded their first album, *Crazy Rhythms,* for Sire Records. When I listened to their music, it sounded like it had been written specifically for *Smithereens.* The jittery guitar and restless melody line completely captured the energy of Wren. If she were music, this is what she would sound like. The Feelies' album, as already written and recorded, fit the film perfectly.

* * *

For the past two years, I had put all my passion into making *Smithereens* and had little left over for a social life. Frankly, I wasn't interested. But I was about to turn thirty, and that was a milestone. I was no longer a kid. I was happy I'd made a movie, but uncertain about its future. I was anxious and feeling a little melancholy.

To celebrate my birthday, I went uptown to Café des Artistes for a drink with my high school friend Madeleine. She, too, had left Huntingdon Valley for a reimagined life in NYC, and lived in a small walk-up on Thompson Street.

Manhattan is a cluster of small neighborhoods, each with its own distinct flavor. Downtown was my turf and I rarely ventured above 14th Street, so going to the Upper West Side was like visiting another country. In the late 1970s, the Upper West Side was not yet gentrified, and still home to many elderly Eastern European Jews. You saw them shopping for bagels and lox and lobster salad (which, it turned out, wasn't really made of lobster) at Zabar's, or smoked fish at Barney Greengrass. There were still old-fashioned dairy restaurants on 72nd Street where you could buy authentic blintzes and kugel.

The little triangle near the 72nd Street subway station was referred to as Needle Park because of the junkies and homeless people who hung out there. In 1980, the neighborhood had few baby strollers pushed by nannies, or women wearing expensive yoga attire. That would come a decade later.

Café des Artistes was on West 67th Street, across from Central Park. The closer you got to the park, the nicer the real estate. The restaurant, owned by a famous Hungarian chef-restaurateur, George Lang, was popular with the media crowd—journalists and TV stars like Barbara Walters, Diane Sawyer, and Peter Jennings. It had an elegant European ambience, soft lighting, and beautiful erotic murals of sea nymphs on the walls, painted by the artist and famous illustrator Howard Chandler Christy.

Madeleine and I could only afford one glass of wine each, which we sipped slowly so we could munch on the free quail eggs they kept in a bowl on the bar.

Afterward, we headed back downtown, stopping off for a much cheaper drink at a new place, the Red Bar, that had recently opened on Avenue A. Unlike most East Village hangouts of that time (dark dives with sticky wood paneling and a mix of young punks and old Ukrainian men from the neighborhood), the Red Bar was brightly lit, with big picture windows so everyone passing by could look in. I struck up a conversation with the guy seated on the barstool next to me. He was wearing a black leather jacket and a black beret. He told me his name was John, but somehow, I started calling him Turk. I don't remember how that nickname came about. Maybe the punchline to a joke I've long since forgotten.

In some ways, Turk was a kindred spirit. He had moved to Manhattan from Queens to pursue his passion for photography, but you could still hear Queens in his voice (as you could hear Philly in mine). He made a living as an assistant to a German fashion photographer named Chris von Wangenheim, whose images mixed sex and violence with edgy humor.

Turk had grown up in a split-level house, not unlike the houses in my own suburban neighborhood, but more modest. If the residents of June Meadows were Jewish accountants, insurance agents, and middle-management types, Turk's neighborhood was filled with Irish Catholic cops, firefighters, and union factory workers. Like me, he came from a place he wanted to escape.

He was Black Irish, a term I'd never heard before that referred to the Irish descendants of the sailors who had washed ashore after the sinking of the Spanish Armada. He had green eyes and dark hair—although it was hard to tell exactly what was happening on top of his head because he was wearing that beret. He must have noticed me staring and asked, "You're wondering if I'm bald?" Then he took off his hat and underneath was a thick mass of black curls.

For a while, Turk became my constant companion—a cross between my buddy and my boyfriend. I guess you could say we were cuddle-buddies. I learned he was a thirty-year-old widower. He had been married to a Sicilian woman everyone called Anna Big Eyes because she had strikingly large, soulful eyes, like a character in a Margaret Keane painting. She had died in her midtwenties from sickle cell anemia.

Turk was a vegetarian who occasionally ate fish, but mostly peanut butter sandwiches. He was eager to make a name for himself with his own work, so I asked him to take the subway photo that would become the poster for *Smithereens*.

(Photo by John Clifford)

Years later, he would be the on-set photographer for Woody Allen, Brian de Palma, Terry Gilliam, and others. You'd recognize his photographs that were turned into movie posters. The haunting young DiCaprio in *The Basketball Diaries,* the strung-out Robert Downey Jr. in *Less Than Zero.*

* * *

A few months ago, Turk called me to let me know he was in the hospital and dying. I was no longer living in the city, so I took the train in to see him at Memorial Sloan Kettering. He had suffered from a variety of ailments over the previous decade, always seemingly on death's door, but he always pulled through. I assumed (hoped) it would be the same this time around.

When I walked into his room, I was surprised to see how good he looked, with his stylish round tortoiseshell glasses and white hipster goatee. Even with a drainage tube up his nose, he didn't look like a dying man. He said he felt okay, he was on a relatively low-dose painkiller, and his mind was still sharp. That's what was so weird about the whole thing. He was so alive. But he had stopped eating over a week ago and his body was no longer absorbing any of the nutrition from a feeding tube. The tumor that surrounded his internal organs had made digestion impossible.

He asked his doctors to be straight with him, and they told him that he would probably die within a week from organ failure brought on by starvation. There was nothing more they could do other than make him comfortable and take away the pain. Turk seemed accepting of that, although still held out hope for a miracle.

He asked what I was doing, and I told him I was writing a memoir and he was in it. I asked if he wanted to read the part about himself, and he did. I guess I wanted his approval.

As he was reading the paragraphs above, I realized that his hair, now white, was still thick, but his curls had gone straight. I asked if he remembered why I called him Turk and why the name had stuck for all these years. Neither of us could remember how the nickname originated.

He liked what I'd written and asked for one change, which I made. I asked if he was afraid. He said a little, because the unknown is scary. He had been brought up Catholic, but was no longer religious. We joked that when he made it to the other side, he would send me a signal. It was a sad joke, but he said he would try.

As the doctors predicted, Turk died six days later. He was back in his apartment on 16th Street with his lovely Brazilian wife, Graca, by his side and just slipped away. It was the day before Easter Sunday. The strange thing was that the week after he died, almost every time I glanced at the clock, it was 11:11. It didn't matter, day or night—always 11:11. Turk was one of the few people who knew about my obsession with that magical number.

You often remember the people who were there for you in the beginning, when your grown-up life is just starting and the world is full of possibilities. Those are the people who stick in your head forty years later, even after they've gone. But back in 1981, Turk was a photographer's assistant, and I was an aspiring director with a lot of uncertainty about the future.

Walking on Sunshine
(Katrina and the Waves)

S mithereens was finished and I needed to figure out what steps to take next. I knew little about film distribution or the world of international film festivals, but I'd heard of the Cannes Film Festival because it was the most famous festival in the world. I'd seen photos of the paparazzi lining the red carpet, the glamorous European movie stars in sunglasses on the Croisette, the starlets posing topless on the beach.

Somehow, I'd found an address in Paris of the festival office (this was twenty years before the internet, so it wasn't easy) and on a whim I applied—simply mailing in a handwritten postcard requesting an application.

A few weeks later I got a call from someone in New York asking me to bring my film to a screening room on 45th Street. The Cannes Selection Committee was in town and viewing submissions. I was excited and nervous, then remembered there was a big problem. Although the film was finished, I had not paid my laboratory bill and the only existing print was locked in a storage vault at DuArt Film Lab. The manager of the billing department had a policy that nothing could leave the building until it had been paid for. Fortunately, the president of DuArt, Irwin Young, was a sweetheart and supportive of young filmmakers (Spike Lee and Jim Jarmusch among them). Irwin trusted me to take the print out of the lab without payment. I lugged it over to the screening room, dropped it off at a reception desk, then took the subway home to wait.

A few days later I got a call from a man with a French accent. He told me he had watched *Smithereens* and wanted to meet me for an early breakfast to discuss it. I remember replying, "I'm sorry, I'm not a morning person" (Was I insane!), and asked if we could meet later in the day.

He suggested I become a morning person and said he could meet me at 8:30 a.m. And so it was arranged. We would meet in the lobby restaurant of Le Parker Meridien Hotel on West 57th Street. His name was Pierre-Henri Deleau.

Over breakfast, M. Deleau told me he was in charge of film selection for the *Quinzaine des Réalisateurs,* also known as the Directors' Fortnight. This was the section of the Cannes festival that showcased films by new directors— filmmakers to look out for in the future. This was where many successful directors got their start. He said he wanted to premiere *Smithereens* at Cannes.

Huh?! What?! There's gotta be a catch!

There wasn't a catch, but there was a caveat. An expensive one. In order to screen my film, I would need to blow up the 16mm film print to 35mm because Cannes did not project films in 16mm. This would cost about $20,000! I had not even paid my lab bill—how could I afford another $20,000? He also mentioned that I would need to hire a publicist, make posters, create publicity materials, and subtitle the film in French. That could cost another $5,000, or more. Until that moment, I hadn't realized how expensive taking a film to a major festival was.

There was no way I could come up with another $25,000. My family had been incredibly supportive, but I had squeezed them dry and still owed the money I'd borrowed to finish shooting the film. There was no guarantee I'd ever be able to pay them back. Then luck stepped in.

I've recently heard the expression "Luck is when God thinks you're cool." Did God think I was cool? (I wasn't.) Maybe God thought my movie was cool.

Here's what I really think:

Success is the collision of luck and preparation. Having the right stuff at the right time.

As it turned out, an English man and woman sitting at the next table had overheard our conversation. They happened to be film sales agents who had recently had success selling a small American indie film called *The Return of the Secaucus 7,* made by a first-time director, John Sayles. After hearing my story, they offered to advance the money needed to take *Smithereens* to

Cannes if they could be the film's sales representatives. What they knew (and I didn't) was that if the film premiered in Cannes, they could make foreign sales deals and their advance would be covered—and then some. The movie gods had answered my prayer. I agreed to let them represent the film and we would all go to Cannes together.

The following day I got a Western Union telegram to confirm my invitation—in case I thought it was all just a dream.

But that's not the end of the story. A few days later I got a call from another Frenchman, named Gilles Jacob. He was the president of the entire Cannes Festival and the man who selected the films for the official competition. Those are the films that compete for the Palme d'Or, the most prestigious prize of the festival. Trust me, this was a big deal.

M. Jacob said he watched *Smithereens* and wanted to move the film out of the Directors' Fortnight and put it into the Official Selection, where it would represent America along with two other (Hollywood) movies: *Shoot the Moon* (starring Diane Keaton and Albert Finney) and *Missing* (starring Sissy Spacek and Jack Lemmon).

This was surreal. How could my little 16mm film with a group of unknown, first time actors compete in that spotlight? But this was a once-in-a-lifetime opportunity, so I nervously agreed.

Before I left for Cannes, my new sales agents helped organize a screening in New York for four hundred close friends (most of whom I didn't know), family, cast and crew members, and their guests. It was held in a once-grand Yiddish theater on Second Avenue and 11th Street. This was the first time I was showing the film to an audience of more than four.

As I stood onstage in a spotlight to introduce the film and thank all those involved, I remember squinting out into the audience and spotting Yan with his soon-to-be wife. I had invited him, since he had invested five thousand dollars in the film (guilt money). But also to prove something. I wasn't sure if he would show up and wondered what was now going through his mind. I knew what was going through mine:

See, I'm doing just fine without you.

Go Ask Alice
(Jefferson Airplane)

A month later I showed up in Cannes feeling like Alice in Wonderland. I had fallen through a rabbit hole and landed in a bizarre world of make-believe. The festival had paid for my flight and a three-night stay at the ritzy Carlton Hotel.

On my second day, I returned to the hotel and found Susan Berman, jet-lagged and asleep in the hallway in front of my door. She was clutching a large accordion. The theater producer, Joseph Papp, had generously bought her a plane ticket to France, knowing this was an experience she couldn't afford to miss. Susan had brought along the accordion because she needed to learn to play it for a show she'd soon be performing in at the Public Theater.

We shared the hotel room like a couple of giddy teenage girls at a pajama party who couldn't believe this was actually happening. A few other cast and crew members also showed up in Cannes. We were a ragtag group compared to all the European glamour surrounding us.

The whole experience was surreal, especially walking up the red carpet that led to the Palais, the large movie palace where all the big screenings took place. Midway up the theater stairs, Susan and I were directed by a publicist to stop, look out at the crowd, and freeze so the paparazzi could take photographs. (I'm sure they had no idea who we were, but since we had walked the red carpet, they flashed away.) *Flash! Flash! Flash!* I have a copy of one

Strike a pose!

photo, and we both look stiff and slightly aloof. Privately we were terrified and pinching ourselves to make sure this was really happening.

If I could pinpoint the exact moment when I felt my life change—my *aha* moment—this was it. Standing at the top of the stairs, about to walk into the *Palais* for the world premiere of the little movie I'd struggled to make. The one I edited alone at night in my living room, in my pajamas! Now, looking around at all the paparazzi and a horde of movie fans, I remember thinking for the very first time: *Maybe I really am a director.*

In May 1982, *Smithereens* became the first low-budget independent American film to ever officially compete in Cannes for the festival's highest prize, the Palme d'Or.

Did I feel like a pretender? A fake? Sure, a bit. But I think a little pretending is part of any transition. You need to fake it until you build up the confidence to be the real thing. Although it would take two more years before I could confidently write *Occupation: Film Director* on any official form that asked that question. Was that a female modesty thing? Personal shyness? I know several men who would have confidently filled in *Film Director* after shooting their family's home movies!

My parents and sister showed up in Cannes on the day of the premiere. It must have been surreal for them as well, watching their erstwhile troublesome teenage daughter being lauded by the international press. I wanted them to be proud of me (especially my dad), but none of us were prepared for what a crazy circus Cannes would be. My father spent the next few days spotting celebrities and taking photos of topless women on the beach.

I remember the press conference after the screening. The idea that journalists wanted to ask me questions and bothered to write down my answers was daunting. After my first day of interviews, I lay in the hotel bed, sleepless, thinking up much better answers than the ones I'd given, hoping I could do it again. The next time around, I'd be wittier.

I got calls from agents in LA who had tracked me down at the hotel in Cannes. I was suddenly being pursued by people in Hollywood. They were sending flowers. Showering me with flattery. I knew most of it was baloney, but it felt good to feel appreciated—so I took it all with a pinch of salt.

Success had come quickly, but with its own set of anxieties. Would I be able to live up to expectations? Would I be a one-hit wonder? Was this just beginner's luck?

Smithereens was picked up for distribution by New Line Cinema, which was, at that time, still a small New York company, founded by Robert Shaye, that distributed mainly European art films and B-movie cult flicks. A few years later, New Line would have their first big commercial success with *A Nightmare on Elm Street,* then be acquired by Turner Broadcasting System, merge with Time Warner, and Shaye would go on to produce the hugely successful *Lord of the Rings* trilogy.

The film opened at the Waverly Theater in Greenwich Village in November 1982, two years before Manhattan would be cleaned up by its future mayor, Rudy Giuliani, and apartment rents would start to soar. But already the city was changing, and before long, *Smithereens* would look like a time capsule of a downtown world that had started to disappear.

She was a legend
in her own mind.

SMITHEREENS

STARRING SUSAN BERMAN, BRAD RINN AND RICHARD HELL
MUSIC BY "THE FEELIES" · DIRECTOR OF PHOTOGRAPHY CHIRINE EL KHADEM
PRODUCED AND DIRECTED BY SUSAN SEIDELMAN
OFFICIAL U.S. ENTRY IN THE 1982 CANNES FILM FESTIVAL
FROM N NEW LINE CINEMA

AMERICAN PREMIERE ENGAGEMENT
Starts Friday—November 19th at the
WAVERLY I
3rd St. & 6th Ave. · WA 9-8037

To promote the film, New Line sent me on a press tour to a few cities. It was a no-frills publicity campaign where I was put up on the living room couch, or in the second bedroom, of the local publicist's house. I was then schlepped around to alternative college radio stations and university campuses to do Q&As. Because I was new to this, I was willing to do whatever the publicist asked, although a few of the PR opportunities were pretty cheesy.

Once I was asked to show up at the Manhattan Cable TV studio on East 23rd Street at 1:00 a.m. This was the very same public access studio where, three years earlier, porn star Robin Byrd sang "Baby Let Me Bang Your Box" in her crocheted bikini. I was going to be interviewed by a man wearing a brocade 1940s-style smoking jacket who hosted a live talk show watched only by sleep-deprived weirdos. This is the kind of thing you did when you were young and eager and you didn't want to insult your publicist because you still couldn't believe you actually had one.

The studio was empty except for the host and his current guest, a cabaret singer doing a showtune medley accompanied by a pianist with a candelabra channeling the spirit of Liberace.

The room had about twenty folding chairs for a nonexistent studio audience. The only other guest was a young comedian who had also taken a taxi at 1:00 a.m. for the opportunity of doing his stand-up routine for a live audience of four. We briefly chatted while waiting to go on. It turned out that he was a friend of my friend Joanne, both having gone to Emerson College.

Now, I don't say this to name-drop, just to make a point. The fact that Jay Leno, future host of *The Tonight Show* for twenty years, showed up at 1:00 a.m. to do stand-up on a public-access TV show watched by a handful of insomniacs is testament to the determination you need to end up with a mansion in Beverly Hills and garages filled with Bentleys and Lamborghinis. Every opportunity is a chance to hone your craft. Everything is a learning experience. You never know who or what's around the corner.

St. Marks Place between 1st and 2nd Ave. 1982 *(Courtesy of Susan Seidelman)*

These Boots Are Made for Walking
(Nancy Sinatra)

The next year was an exciting time in my life. It was like my internal stereo was playing just the right song, I was feeling just the right amount of sexy, and the world around me had just the right buzz. Those times don't come often, so when they do, you remember them because secretly you know they will not last long.

The culture in NYC was changing, and so was the music. It had shifted from hard-core punk to something more melodic now referred to as New Wave and popularized by the burgeoning of MTV. These were songs you could sing and dance to.

By 1983, the club scene in NYC had exploded. It seemed like every month a new dance club was opening downtown. A mix of straight and gay, Black and white, rich and poor, uptown and downtown crowds. House music, a direct descendant of disco, was the sound of the night, spun by superstar DJ remixers like Larry Levan, Mark Kamins, and Anita Sarko (influenced by Bronx hip-hop DJs like Grandmaster Flash, who popularized the art of turntable scratching).

Clubs such as Area, Danceteria, Paradise Garage, and the Limelight (located inside a deconsecrated Episcopal church) became hangouts for the art world and its followers, combining video, performance art, design, and fashion with throbbing dance music. A few years later there was the Palladium (with its notorious VIP Mike Todd room) and Tunnel, a club inside a disused railroad freight terminal, with unisex bathrooms and decadently themed party rooms.

Then there were the new trendy restaurants like the Odeon, which defined early '80s downtown cool when Tribeca was still a deserted neighborhood. And tiny, chic (and expensive) Chanterelle, on the southern tip of Soho.

Suddenly, being a foodie was in. Drinking good wine, in. Reaganomics had arrived!

* * *

One of my favorite watering holes was called Caramba!, a large Tex-Mex restaurant on the corner of Broadway and Great Jones Street. They made a killer slushy margarita, served in a glass the size of a small fishbowl. This was long before slushy margaritas were available at TGI Fridays or Applebee's. I don't know what kind of mystery alcohol they put in the drink. It wasn't any brand of tequila I'd ever heard of and was vaguely hallucinogenic, but by the end of the night there would be bodies sprawled out on the sidewalk in front of 684 Broadway. Pedestrians would have to step around them. Even the police would drive by without a second glance.

I went there once with three Japanese film distributors who were in town from Tokyo. They spoke very limited English and came with an interpreter, all dressed in suits and ties. The meeting started out stiffly, but after our first margarita we spent a delightful three hours laughing hysterically, without understanding a word of each other's language. Something in the drink triggered a fit of giggles in even the most serious-minded person. I don't remember if the meeting resulted in a Japanese distribution deal for *Smithereens,* but by the end of the night I didn't care. I just remember everyone laughing, making a lot of wild hand gestures, and one of the distributors sliding off his chair in slow motion.

The restaurant closed sometime in the 1990s and the space eventually became an overpriced tourist clothing store where you can buy Billionaire Boys' Club underwear on an installment plan. (Two pairs of men's boxer briefs for only $70!) But New York is ever changing, so who knows what the building will become next. And I never did find out what they put in their mysterious margarita, but most people who hung out downtown have a funny 1980s Caramba! story to tell.

I spent the next year traveling to film festivals around the world. Sometimes I went alone. Sometimes I went with Turk. It was a privileged nomadic lifestyle, since the festival usually put us up in a nice hotel, gave us meal vouchers, and hosted parties with food and plenty to drink.

At the time I knew an impoverished filmmaker who was always hustling for free booze and a couch to sleep on. He was beginning to wear down the patience of his charitable friends. But he was a charming rogue who had made a very low-budget film that had gotten onto the international festival circuit. He would line up a festival-hopping schedule so he could travel from one festival directly to the next. This kept him on the road for long stretches of time where he was treated like a rock star. It also gave him a bed, meals, booze, and access to festival groupies who liked bad boy filmmakers with New York attitude. What he might have lacked in cinematic skill, he made up for with style, and in a creative universe with quixotic rules, attitude is also an art.

Here's what I remember about some of the festivals I attended:

In Cairo, my film never showed up. I took a beautiful boat ride down the Nile, got laryngitis from all the fine sand in the air, and went on a camel ride in the desert, and the camel driver (with whom I shared the camel) tried to hump me from behind.

In Hong Kong, I was jet-lagged after a very long flight and taken to the hotel, where I fell asleep for many hours. When I woke up, I waited for someone from the hospitality office to contact me and tell me where to go and what to do. No one did. Festivals are chaotic, with hundreds of foreign guests. I don't remember going to my screening and don't know if the print even arrived.

In Rio, the film showed up but the reels were projected in the wrong order, so the story made no sense. But the easygoing Brazilian audience was welcoming and enthusiastic and didn't seem to notice or care.

In Cartagena, we were met at the airport and escorted onto a bus by soldiers wearing military uniforms and carrying automatic rifles. Some of them looked no older than fourteen. At the festival, cocaine flowed more freely than wine. The white powder was presented to guests like a welcoming goody bag. The entire week was a blur.

By the end of the year, I had accumulated a vast assortment of film festival tote bags that still come in handy today for carrying groceries at my local Stop & Shop.

Despite all the traveling, I knew I needed to move on to a new project, and my LA agent was sending me scripts and arranging for meetings with studio executives. This time, I would get to meet with execs higher up on the ladder. They were always on the lookout for who (or what) might be the next new thing. And for a nanosecond, that was me.

Feelin' groovy
(Photo by Robyn Stoutenburg)

Californication

(Red Hot Chili Peppers)

Smithereens had gotten strong reviews in New York (thank you, Vincent Canby!) and LA, where it was hailed as fresh and original, so I was flown out to La La Land, first class, by Warner Brothers and put up at the Beverly Hills Hotel. It was a very different experience than sharing a waterbed with my friend Linda.

My agent set up a bunch of meet and greets, so I rented a car and drove from one studio to the next, crossing six-lane highways, terrified. I called it the dog and pony show. Producers asked me questions about what kind of project I wanted to do next. Sometimes they pitched me a project of their own. There was always a lot of excitement, enthusiasm, and then . . . nothing.

I remember one particular meeting in the office of a senior studio exec. I was escorted into the room by his attractive assistant, who brought me a bottle of expensive mineral water. The office was filled with toys, gizmos, and brightly colored playthings as if to remind all who entered that making movies was fun. (Think *Pee-wee's Playhouse*.) Pinball machines, a barber's chair, guitars hanging on the walls along with kitschy 1950s horror movie posters. His coffee table was covered with bobbleheads and bowls of brightly colored M&Ms. The only other place I'd seen so much candy on display was my grandmother's credenza.

I was given some dopey teen comedies with provisional offers to direct, pending a meeting where I was meant to discuss my "creative vision" for the film. (My creative vision was that these scripts were mostly moronic with little redeeming value.) Several were teen comedies about horny high school girls. Female versions of *Porky's,* a film that had recently been a surprise box office hit, so studios wanted "more of the same, only different." One was a script called *The Joy of Sex,* based on a bestselling sex manual by Alex Comfort. Paramount paid a lot of money for the rights to the book's attention-grabbing title, but struggled to turn it into a cohesive story. The film was produced a year later, directed by another female director who must have seen possibilities in the material I had missed. But she was later fired for wanting to cut out several scenes with gratuitous nudity. Making the film turned out to be a miserable experience, and she considered taking her name off the studio's re-edited version, but eventually left it on. In the end, it was no surprise that the film was a flop. As my outspoken grandmother, Nanny S, might have said: *"You can't put lipstick on a pig."*

However, the LA trip turned out to be successful. One production company offered me a development deal to supervise a screenplay based on an original idea I had pitched. It was called *Ozone,* about a tough girl group from Ozone Park, Queens, trying to make it in the early 1960s music business in New York. The story was inspired by the Shangri-Las, famous for both their bad-ass attitude and their angsty songs: "Leader of the Pack," "Remember (Walkin' in the Sand)." Despite having recorded several hits, the Shangri-Las had no power over their career and never made money. At that time, the industry was controlled by powerful male producers like Phil Spector and Berry Gordy.

Somehow, I was able to track down the Shangri-Las' former record producer in LA, a guy named Shadow Morton. He wore a black eye patch, like a pirate. He was the man who came up with the idea to put sound effects into their songs, like the *vrooming* of car engines, the *screeching* of tires, the *crunching* of metal to simulate a car crash. At first, it was an attention-grabbing gimmick that worked, but by 1968 the music scene had changed, and youth culture had turned hippie and psychedelic. The Shangri-Las' sound was no longer in style. They had legal battles with their record label and there was friction between the girls. Then, poof, they vanished.

I thought that would have made an interesting movie because lots of creative women have vanished from pop culture history, and I wanted to tell that story.

The executive who made the deal was an intelligent, very confident, and (at the time) very large young man named Scott Rudin. He was sharp as a razor and would eventually become just as cutting as his power within the industry spread. He was building a reputation for having good taste and the ability to get films made. Unfortunately, this script, like the majority of screenplays that are optioned, never made it beyond the developmental stage. Later, I would find out that less than .03 percent of the scripts that are developed actually get turned into movies.

* * *

I knew, as a director making the transition from an indie film to a studio movie, I needed to be selective and passionate about what I did next. I'd heard a cautionary tale about another female director, who had made a critically acclaimed small, personal film, then directed her first studio movie with an overbearing male producer. The movie was a box office disappointment, and she wasn't heard from again for a very long time. I didn't want that to happen to me. I realized that picking the right producer was just as important as picking the right screenplay. I'd always been my own boss and feared someone breathing down my neck. I was afraid of losing touch with my intuition, which had served me well in the past.

Alfred Hitchcock once said, "To make a great film you need three things—the script, the script, and the script."

Then, out of the blue, my agent sent me a screenplay called *Desperately Seeking Susan* from an up-and-coming writer named Leora Barish. It had been well over a year since *Smithereens* was released, and I'd read dozens of screenplays about slutty cheerleaders, bitchy prom queens, and babysitters who get stalked by psychos in dark suburban houses. This one was different. It was also a story I felt confident I could direct. Plus, the name Susan was in the title. It was kismet.

To quote the Roman philosopher Seneca: "Luck is what happens when preparation meets opportunity." Fortunately, I'd been preparing to make this movie ever since I was a teenager, lying in my orange bedroom with pink Day-Glo posters, daydreaming about living a more exciting life.

Briefly, *Desperately Seeking Susan* was the story of Roberta Glass, a bored

New Jersey housewife who lived vicariously by following a love affair carried out in the Personals column of a newspaper where a young man, Jim, is "desperately seeking" someone named Susan. Roberta becomes intrigued by this mysterious adventuress and decides to witness Susan and Jim's rendezvous. Through a series of mix-ups, Roberta is mistaken for Susan by a gangster, and in her attempt to flee from him, she runs into a lamppost, gets conked on the head, and wakes up with amnesia. Now believing she really is Susan, Roberta is suddenly liberated to play out her own adventure. Sometimes you have to lose yourself in order to find yourself.

Girls Just Want to Have Fun
(Cyndi Lauper)

Producer Midge Sanford was the wife of my agent's business partner. Midge had formed a production company with Sarah Pillsbury, of the Pillsbury dough family. Sarah had produced an Oscar-winning short, but neither of them had made a feature film before. As a producing team, they optioned their first script, *Desperately Seeking Susan,* in 1981. Apparently, the screenplay had been floating around LA for a few years before it found me. At one point it was in development at Warner Brothers, where it languished in Development Hell for two years and was then put into turnaround.[9]

This was not an easy film to get off the ground in 1984, since the two leading characters were women. Hollywood's thinking at that time went like this: Women like watching movies about men. Men like watching movies about men. So why not just make more movies about men, and throw a little romance into the mix?

I had not been the producers' first choice. They had not yet seen *Smithereens* and originally considered male directors like Jonathan Demme, Hal Ashby, and Louis Malle. (There were so few female directors to even consider.) But in retrospect I'm confident in saying I was the right choice.

---

9. Development Hell is the period of time when creative studio executives give confusing notes to improve the script, thereby stalling the process of getting it made, before abandoning the project totally. The script is then put into turnaround, where it sometimes gets picked up by another studio that might make it. If not, it just disappears.

The script had attracted the interest of a talented young actress named Rosanna Arquette, who was getting attention at the time. She was rumored to be the inspiration for the 1982 Toto song "Rosanna." (She'd dated the band's keyboard player.) A few years later, in 1986, she became the inspiration for another (better) song, "In Her Eyes," written by then boyfriend Peter Gabriel.

Rosanna came from a family of thespians; her parents were actors, and her grandfather, Cliff Arquette, had been a well-known comedian, performing under the name Charley Weaver. I remembered watching him as a regular on the TV show *Hollywood Squares*. Years later, Rosanna's sister, Patricia, would win Oscar, Emmy, and Golden Globe Awards and her brother, David, would have a successful career buoyed by the slasher/horror franchise *Scream,* then marry and divorce his co-star Courteney Cox. Gender-fluid sibling, Alexis Arquette, would sadly die from complications due to HIV at age forty-seven.

I'm told that when Rosanna first read the screenplay for *Desperately Seeking Susan* she thought she was being asked to play the role of the free-spirited, bohemian Susan, not the unhappy suburban housewife, Roberta Glass.

I flew out to LA to meet with Midge, Sarah, and the writer, Leora. The producers were still pitching the script around town, but felt it needed a re-write. I had some ideas about how to give it a spin. Leora's screenplay was a playful story that I could bring my own bag of tricks to. It reminded me of a French movie I'd seen in the late seventies called *Celine and Julie Go Boating* by Jacques Rivette. When I mentioned this to Leora, she said she loved that film, too, and had been inspired by it. Both stories involved transformation, reinvention, and had a sprinkling of *magic*.

What I also loved was that Leora's script had a bad girl and a good girl—but the good girl was a little bit bad, and the bad girl was beguiling. Instinctively, I knew this was the script I'd been waiting for.

* * *

I'd always been fascinated by stories where people get to exchange identities and live vicariously in another person's shoes. I remember as a kid watching Disney's 1961 *The Parent Trap,* where identical twins, separated as babies, meet at a summer camp and decide to switch places. Both are played by the talented young actress Hayley Mills. Why this theme excited me had little to do with the comedic possibilities of mistaken identity confusion or the farce inherent in near-miss situations. It had to do with the excitement of becoming someone different.

Hiding behind a false identity, desperate housewife Roberta Glass gets to reveal something truthful about herself. Many women have another woman living inside them: The cool and confident one we'd love to present to the world, the one who can dance all night without breaking a sweat, charm her way out of a speeding ticket, and tell a good raunchy party joke. As opposed to the self-doubting and insecure one who goes to sleep with us at night and haunts our dreams. The one we want to smother with a pillow.

Desperately Seeking Susan was also a love story between two women—minus the sex.

Roberta becomes obsessed with her more glamorous double, and in the process, Susan becomes curious about Roberta. The women's relationships with the men in the film are secondary.

As a kid, I'd read *Alice in Wonderland,* the tale of the bored young girl who follows a mysterious creature down a rabbit hole and into another world. Roberta, the wistful housewife, would be Alice. Susan would be the White Rabbit, and I would turn downtown Manhattan into Wonderland, where anything was possible.

* * *

The relationship between a director and a screenwriter can be tricky. The writer conceives of the original idea and writes the script, but then it gets handed over to a director, who must make it their own. This is not about ego (although that's sometimes a factor). This mysterious conversion from words on paper to images on-screen is what gives a film life and personality. A point of view. A script is a blueprint for a story the director rewrites on film, and my favorite movies have always been the ones where the director let me peek inside their head. When a director doesn't succeed in doing that, a movie can feel generic or inert. (Although one could also argue that many a good screenplay has been ruined by the self-indulgence, or ineptitude, of its director.)

The script went through a series of revisions over the next few months. The biggest change involved the character of Susan. In the original 1979 draft, Susan was a nomadic hippie, a role that might have been played by Diane Keaton or Goldie Hawn wearing a backpack. At one point, a studio executive even suggested Barbra Streisand. But after making *Smithereens,* I wanted to set *Desperately Seeking Susan* firmly in the world of the Lower East Side. The character of Susan would be a more charismatic and carefree version of Wren. Both were drifters, moochers, and manipulators, but Susan made it look effortless and fun. Finding the right tone for the film would be my biggest creative challenge. I wanted the characters to be real and recognizable, but the atmosphere to feel enchanted. The vulnerability of Roberta needed to balance the cool of Susan.

Orion Pictures, a mini-major studio at that time, was interested in making the movie, pending the casting of the two lead roles. Producers Midge and Sarah had been incredibly tenacious, enlisting the support of an Orion executive named Barbara Boyle, an outspoken 1970s feminist who wore knee-high boots. Barbara was the senior vice president of production, working directly under President Mike Medavoy. I liked Medavoy, although it was rumored he didn't read scripts. He had been a successful LA agent, repping talent like the young Steven Spielberg and Francis Ford Coppola, before joining United Artists, then becoming one of the cofounders of Orion.

Boyle pushed for the film even when other Orion executives doubted her. She was a fan of *Smithereens* and loved that *Desperately Seeking Susan* had women producers, a woman writer, two female leads, and could be made for under $5 million on location in New York. Our budget was $4.5 million.

Orion Pictures turned out to be the perfect home. Their corporate office was in New York and they had a reputation for being director-friendly and hands-off. Woody Allen, Jonathan Demme, James Cameron, and Oliver Stone had made films there. Orion basically left you alone once the key cast and budget were approved. Even though I'd never directed a studio movie before, I felt confident that I had a clear vision for the film, a supportive studio, and trusted collaborators.

Before we started production, I remember driving around LA with Barbara Boyle in her Jaguar. She was giving me a tour of the town. We drove past the exclusive Hotel Bel-Air, the huge mansions on Sunset, the celebrity homes on Beverly Drive and Carolwood. We were taking a scenic route to her house in the Pacific Palisades, and I was gawking at the view out the car window when she turned and said something like: "This could be your future." And I remember thinking, *Wow, could this really be my future?* Followed by sudden panic, *Is this the future I want?* I confess, something about the deserted streets of Beverly Hills reminded me of a far more glamorous version of the homogeneous suburb I'd escaped, but with bigger mansions and more exotic vegetation. Yet I was flattered to hear her say that this was a future possibility—albeit an unlikely one.

Then I remembered that LA is car culture and I hated to drive. Here's one reason why.

In 1969, my senior year of high school, a college boy from Philadelphia invited me on a date to Manhattan. I'd only visited the city twice before, with my parents to see a Broadway show and eat at an Italian tourist trap called Mama Leone's. But for a young girl from the burbs, NYC seemed magical. So even though I barely knew this boy and we had little in common, going on a grown-up dinner date to the "city that never sleeps" was an adventure I couldn't miss out on.

We went to a fancy-schmantzy restaurant called the Four Seasons and for a few hours I felt very sophisticated. But we still found little to talk about, so I spent most of the evening gazing wide-eyed around the elegant dining room at the beautifully dressed people, pretending this was my normal life.

I had read about the Playboy Club on East 59th Street, so after dinner I suggested we try to get in. At the door, I was immediately carded, and since I was only seventeen (and looked fifteen), I never made it past the bouncer. We then headed home. The boy tried to kiss me on the walk back to the parking lot, but I wasn't feeling it, so I told him he'd probably had too much to drink and should sleep it off in the back seat. I then got behind the wheel of his father's huge Lincoln Continental, a car the size of a boat, and drove all the way back to Philly on the NJ Turnpike. I did a pretty good job, too, considering I was an inexperienced driver, having just gotten my license six months earlier, and could barely see over the steering wheel.

I made it safely to the tollbooth in Willow Grove and paid the toll, but as I drove away, I misjudged a curve in the road, impaling the front end of the Lincoln on a guardrail. The boy in the back seat woke up with a start.

Reluctantly, he called his father from the tollbooth phone to tell him the news. I called mine. We then sat in silence for the next hour in the disabled vehicle, waiting for our parents to show up.

Neither father was happy when they arrived at 2:00 a.m. and took us home in separate cars.

That was my first and last date with the boy. The night had ended with a bang and another strike against me in my father's book.

Four years later, I would move to Manhattan, where, thankfully, I didn't need to drive.

One Man's Ceiling Is Another Man's Floor
(Paul Simon)

Once I signed the contract to direct *Desperately Seeking Susan,* I was able to leave my (lonely) Wall Street apartment and move to Soho. I got a loft on Thompson Street between Houston and Prince. It had high ceilings, brick walls, and rustic wooden support columns. It would be the building where Jonathan (my partner, who I hadn't met yet) and our son, Oscar (who hadn't been born) would live with me for the next thirty-five years.

In the nineteenth century, it had been a factory building that manufactured banners and flags. In the 1970s, Soho was still a marginal neighborhood filled with workshops, small manufacturers, and printing plants alongside four-story tenement walk-ups, mostly lived in by Italian families.

In 1978, the building was converted into one of the first loft co-ops in Soho. Half of the building was designated AIR, living spaces specifically allocated for Artists in Residence (back when NYC actually did benevolent stuff like that). By 1983, when I moved in, the neighborhood had started to change, but still retained a funky, down-to-earth feel. It was not yet a Manhattan neighborhood frequented by tour buses. There were no flagship designer stores on West Broadway, no Gucci, no Prada, no downtown megastores on Lower Broadway. Those would come a decade later.

The west side of Soho was Italian. The area used to be called the South Village, until real estate developers and brokers realized they could charge much higher rents if they just called it Soho. Middle-aged wiseguys from the Genovese crime family sat on folding chairs, drinking coffee and smoking cigars in front of small social clubs on Thompson and Sullivan Streets. They watched over the neighborhood like hawks and knew everyone who lived there and everyone who didn't. As a woman living alone, I felt personally protected by the mob. The corner grocery store was owned by an Italian family before the Koreans took it over in the early '90s. I'd seen Vincent "The Chin" Gigante, boss of the Genovese crime family, wandering down Bleecker Street in his bathrobe and pajamas, mumbling to himself like he had dementia—a ploy he supposedly used to avoid jail time for murder. His mother had a modest apartment nearby.

Graffiti art was starting to pop up on the sides of buildings, and looking down, you could see the word *SAMO©* (short for "same old shit") painted on the sidewalk. It was the tag of Jean-Michel Basquiat—still unknown. There were also the unmistakable outlines of the radiant babies, barking dogs, and dancing men that would make Keith Haring famous.

The neighborhood felt like a small village. Pino's Butcher Shop and Joe's Dairy were on Sullivan Street. Raffetto's pasta on Houston. There was the guy who ran the postbox store on the corner of MacDougal who cut keys, sold a few religious tchotchkes, and was a notary public. He had an outdated assortment of holiday greeting cards that were never sold. Everyone assumed he was connected. No one asked. Down the street, there was the mysterious gun club with a shooting range in the basement and a private dining room for big shots from North Jersey and Staten Island.

The center of this world was St. Anthony's Church. My living room windows faced the church directly across the street. Once a year the church had a confirmation ceremony where twelve- and thirteen-year-olds dressed in white marched down the street carrying flowers alongside floats with statues of saints. Everyone on Thompson Street hung out their windows to watch. I had a front-row seat without leaving home.

In the summer was the Feast of St. Anthony, when the street was closed to traffic and the curb was lined with zeppole, calzone, and Italian sausage trucks, along with carnival games where you could win gigantic stuffed animals and goldfish in baggies. If you got in good with the priests, they made sure you never got a parking ticket. I would become friendly with several of the food truck vendors five years later when they became background actors in my mob comedy, *Cookie*.

There was a small neighborhood playground on Thompson Street with a couple of rusty swing sets, a sandbox, and a small outdoor swimming pool that was opened to the public in the summer. When my son, Oscar, was a toddler, this was where I'd sometimes take him to play, but we never set foot in the pool, not trusting what might be in the water. After the day Oscar picked up a used condom next to the sliding board, we switched our playdates to nearby Washington Square Park.

The superintendent of my building was a Californian who had come to NYC to be an opera singer. Everyone comes to New York with a dream. He ran the building with Svengali-like control and you could hear his booming baritone vibrating through the elevator shaft every afternoon as he practiced arias. The lobby had a scrawny rubber plant that someone had discarded, which now sat next to the mailboxes. No one had the heart to throw it out. The old radiators clanged. The door buzzer only worked until midnight, after which time you needed to personally go downstairs to open the door for your guests. There was a fake security camera hanging from the ceiling in the lobby intended as a visual deterrent, but at the time, the camera wasn't connected to an actual video security system. If Jonathan or Oscar were locked out late at night, I'd throw the front door keys out our living room window, balled up in a sock, onto the sidewalk below.

That was life on Thompson Street and I loved it.

Even decades later, when the neighborhood had been gentrified beyond recognition, our Thompson Street building never put in a gym or a rooftop garden like so many of the new Soho condos now had. But its down-to-earth façade has been home to Daniel Day-Lewis and his wife, filmmaker Rebecca Miller, a hideaway for a young Rockefeller, the residence of two well-known *New York Times* investigative reporters (one with a disability callously mocked by then president Trump), and crib to the kid who started Rockstar Games and made a fortune from *Grand Theft Auto*.

Many of the building's original outliers have since moved away. Like much of Soho, the building is now mostly home to lawyers, investment bankers, and money managers.

Ain't Nothing Like the Real Thing
(Marvin Gaye)

In the spring of 1984, when *Desperately Seeking Susan* was greenlit, there was only one actor attached, Rosanna Arquette, who had been brought on board by the producers. To put together the rest of the cast, we hired two young casting directors, Risa Bramon and Billy Hopkins, whose experience up until that point had been casting for the Ensemble Studio Theatre. This would be their first job working on a movie.

Everyone's concern was to find the right actor for the role of Susan. We considered every young actress who was generating excitement in the early 1980s: Ellen Barkin, Jennifer Jason Leigh, Jamie Lee Curtis, Linda Fiorentino, Kim Cattrall, Kelly McGillis, Melanie Griffith. Even singer Suzanne Vega came in to audition. But I knew of another singer, who happened to live only a few blocks away, in a loft on Broome Street, and thought she might be an interesting possibility.

I remember the first time Madonna caught my eye. It was still the early days of cable TV and MTV (launched in 1981) was playing a music video for a newly released single called "Borderline." There weren't many music videos back then, so the early ones were played on heavy rotation. The singer had messy blond hair held back with a big, floppy headband and wore a cutoff denim jean jacket. She came across as self-assured and cheeky. She knew how to flirt with the camera.

I'd heard that Madonna was interested in a movie career and had done a small singing cameo in the film *Vision Quest*. I thought she might give the role of Susan, the downtown grifter, some authentic street cred, so I asked the casting directors to arrange for her to come in to audition.

The day of our meeting Madonna arrived at the production office by taxi. Somehow, she'd managed to get the driver to wait by the curb while she disappeared inside the building in the hope of finding money to pay for the ride. Cynical New York cabdrivers don't usually wait while a passenger disappears, so already that was proof of her persuasiveness. I think she borrowed money from an assistant sitting behind the reception desk. I don't know if the assistant ever got paid back, but I remember thinking to myself—here's this girl coming in to audition for a job and she actually hit us up for cab fare! That's something "Susan" would have done. It immediately grabbed my interest.

Later on, Madonna would admit to sharing a lot with the character of Susan. The role was not so far removed from the persona she'd adopted throughout the 1980s. Both Madonna and Susan used their powers of persuasion to get friends and lovers to do what they wanted. Both were charming con artists who didn't let you know you were being conned. There was an art to seduction, and Madonna had mastered it. She was a flirt who made everyone she flirted with feel a little bit sexier.

Orion had to approve the casting of the lead actresses, and because Madonna was a newcomer, that involved jumping through some hoops. So Madonna flew out to Los Angeles to meet with the Orion executives. Barbara Boyle had never heard of her, but had a fifteen-year-old son, David, who had. Apparently, he was an early Madonna fan and told his mother that she had to hire Madonna immediately.

The following day Madonna walked into Barbara's office, fell on her knees, and said, "I'll do anything to get this part." Barbara responded: "Sorry, I'm heterosexual." And Madonna replied: "How do you know unless you try?" Instantly, Barbara knew Madonna had the sass to play the role and told her to take a seat.

According to Barbara, they had the following conversation:

BARBARA: I understand you're a successful singer and performer. Why do you want to be an actress?
MADONNA: You understand from whom?
BARBARA: My son, David.

Madonna then took a pencil and paper off Barbara's desk and wrote a note: *Dear David, Tell your mother to give me this role.*

And it worked. Barbara spoke to Mike Medavoy, who agreed to pay for a screen test when Madonna returned to New York. The following week, the cinematographer (Ed Lachman), Madonna, a small crew of four, and I went to a nearby park to film the test. I remember while we were filming, a few passersby glanced in our direction but paid little attention. Small crews of NYU students were often filming in the park. But I recall one teenage girl calling out, "Look! There's Cyndi Lauper!"

Fortunately, the test went well and Madonna was hired.

Allowing me to cast a relatively unknown singer was a risk for Orion. But the risk would pay off in spades. Of course, no one could have predicted Madonna's meteoric rise to stardom only three months later. The proof was reflected in her acting fee—about one third of Rosanna's.

* * *

The best thing about working with someone who isn't yet a star is that there are no agents, managers, personal assistants, or an entourage of sycophants hanging around the set. No personal hair and makeup people hovering near the video monitor and making suggestions.

To prepare, Madonna and I talked about screwball comedies of the 1930s and 1940s. Those comedies had strong and feisty heroines: Judy Holliday in *Born Yesterday,* Barbara Stanwyck in *The Lady Eve,* Carole Lombard in *My Man Godfrey,* and Rosalind Russell in almost everything she did. They were bodacious women, often outsmarting their male counterparts. Screwball comedy gave actresses roles to shine in, ones much more exciting than the traditional housewife and devoted girlfriend roles usually available to actresses at that time.

Now that we had our two female leads, we needed to pull together the rest of the cast.

Billy and Risa knew all the best up-and-coming theater actors and brought them in to audition. For many, this would be their first time in a feature film. John Turturro, Will Patton, Laurie Metcalf, Mark Blum, Anna Levine Thompson, Giancarlo Esposito, and poker-faced comedian Steven Wright would all go on to long and successful careers. I also cast some musicians and performers like Ann Magnuson, Richard Hell, Richard Edson, Anne Carlisle, Arto Lindsay, Annie Golden, John Lurie, and Rockets Redglare, in small cameos.[10] They would add the downtown credibility I was looking for.

Mark Blum was quickly cast in the role of Rosanna's suburban, hot tub–selling husband, Gary Glass. Mark had the clean-cut good looks of a leading man, but instinctively knew how to play a comedic foil without turning the character into a cartoon, bringing the perfect degree of self-deprecating humor to the role. He and actress Laurie Metcalf, playing his neurotic sister Leslie, had great comedic timing, and Laurie delivered one of the more memorable lines in the film: "Just take a Valium like a normal person!"

For the lead role of Dez, we hoped to cast a male star opposite Rosanna. The producers and I discussed Kevin Costner and Dennis Quaid, who had both recently made successful films. But it was hard to find a young leading man who wanted to play third fiddle to two leading ladies. Then we discovered Aidan Quinn.

Aidan had recently starred in a movie called *Reckless,* opposite Daryl Hannah, playing a motorbike-riding high school rebel. He was a serious actor, with an understated cool attitude and brooding good looks. *Reckless* had failed at the box office, which now made Aidan available. That's the way it worked in Hollywood. There was a definite hierarchy. We sent Aidan's agents the script and they expressed interest.

During our first meeting, I remember thinking Aidan was very handsome,

---

10. In a strange twist of fate, Rockets Redglare, the sometimes actor, sometimes drug dealer, and bodyguard to Sid Vicious, was supposedly present the night Nancy Spungen was killed in the Chelsea Hotel. I didn't know this when I cast him in the role of Madonna's chatty taxi driver, who improvised one of the film's memorable lines: "Sushi, I hate the stuff. Although I had some the other day. I took it home, cooked it . . . it wasn't bad. It tasted like fish."

but worried he might be too somber for the role. This was a comedy; it needed to stay buoyant. Then I realized that there were already so many quirky, colorful characters in the film, there needed to be someone to ground the story, to keep it from getting too zany. Aidan gave the role the right amount of edge and earthy bemusement to contrast with Rosanna's slightly dizzy amnesiac.

There was another lead role that needed to be cast, the part of Madonna's punk musician boyfriend, Jim. We held auditions where Madonna read against the top contenders to see how their chemistry would work. Some of the auditions got pretty steamy. There was a dialogue scene that called for a kiss at the end, and the next thing I knew the actors were down on the floor, making out. The casting directors and I watched with dropped jaws. It was certainly attention-grabbing and some of the actors left the casting office blushing, but with a juicy story to tell their grandchildren one day.

(Photo montage designed by Anthony Coombs)

An unknown actor-bartender named Bruce Willis was one of the finalists and gave a great performance, but ultimately the role went to Robert Joy. Bruce would turn up again, working as the bartender at our wrap party on the last night of shooting, as cheerful and irreverent as ever. Two years later I would bump into him at a restaurant in LA where he thanked me.

"For what?" I asked.

He said that because he didn't get the part in *Desperately Seeking Susan*, he had moved to LA to try his luck out there and was quickly cast in a TV series called *Moonlighting*. The show turned out to be a huge hit, which led to several action-hero movie roles and mega-stardom. Sadly, thirty-eight years later, at the age of sixty-seven, Bruce would be diagnosed with frontotemporal dementia, ending his long and celebrated career.

A mix of future stars and downtown celebs assembled for a *Vogue* photo shoot
(Photo by Richard Corman)

To *helm* a studio picture (I love that word—*helm*—so *Variety* speak), I needed to join the Directors Guild. In order to do so, you had to be recommended by three current Guild members. My Directors Guild of America application was signed by Woody Allen (this was the early 1980s, before his reputation was clouded by sexual abuse allegations and a dramatic fall from grace), Mike Nichols, and Martin Scorsese. These were the three best directors working in New York (along with Sidney Lumet), although I'd never actually met any of them in person at that time. But they had either liked *Smithereens,* or just wanted to be supportive of a young woman director, given there were so few.

Years later, I would have dinner with Mike Nichols at a restaurant uptown. I went there with Nora Ephron, while we were working together on *Cookie.* Penny Marshall was also at the table. Both women would go on to very successful directing careers. But Nora hadn't directed a movie yet and was just starting the screenplay for *When Harry Met Sally,* and Penny was still editing *Big* and had no idea it would be an enormous hit. A few years later Penny would direct *A League of Their Own,* making her the first woman to direct two films that each grossed over $100 million at the box office.

Mike Nichols was the epitome of charm, wit, and sophistication. His conversation was peppered with just the right amount of self-deprecating humor and irony. Plus, he'd made three of my favorite movies: *The Graduate, Who's Afraid of Virginia Woolf?,* and *Carnal Knowledge* (and would go on to make the wonderful *Working Girl*). That night he gave me some excellent advice. "Be able to identify a good idea, no matter where it comes from . . . then claim it as your own," he said, and gave a mischievous grin.

* * *

I'd met Ed Lachman at the Telluride Film Festival the year before, and we hit it off on the dance floor. He'd been the director of photography on a few small German films with directors I respected, Werner Herzog and Wim Wenders. He had a painter's eye and wanted to paint with light. We were dancing together at a party when Herzog came over and told me I "danced like a Negro." (At that time, he spoke stilted English.) I think that was a compliment, and that's certainly how I took it.

Executive producer Michael Peyser introduced me to Santo Loquasto, who had previously worked with Woody Allen as a costume designer. Since ours was a low-budget studio movie, Peyser wisely hired Santo as both the costume and production designer. This saved the production money and had the benefit of assuring that the costumes and sets would have a unified vision.

Ed, Santo, and I had long conversations about color palette, lighting design, camera movement, costumes, and props. We thought about the various ways we could create two very different and distinct worlds, one for each of the two main characters. We looked through fashion magazines, photography books, and pop culture references. Roberta, the dreamy housewife, would live in a contemporary suburban house that had soft lighting and was furnished in neutral pastel colors. She would dress in beige. Her life was beige.

Susan's world would be sharp, gritty, and vibrant. We would create a hyperrealistic version of the bohemian Lower East Side using boldly colored gels on the deserted streets and alleyways to give the city an enchanted glow. A combination of grit and glamour. Ed's lighting style would become popular (then overused) in MTV videos for the next decade.

We talked about magic and symbols and the importance of the pyramid jacket that Roberta and Susan would exchange during the film. It was a short tuxedo-style, black-and-gold jacket designed by Santo that would be adorned on the back with a pyramid and the Eye of Providence—the all-seeing eye—surrounded by rays of light. It represented divine providence, exotic adventure, and also, money. It's the symbol on the flip side of a dollar bill.

Years later, I learned that Madonna didn't like the jacket when she first saw it, which is ironic, since it would become linked to her '80s persona for decades to come.

There's an expression, "God is in the details." Details may seem small and insignificant, but they can speak volumes about character and atmosphere. I was happy to be working with collaborators who understood the power the right details could have.

Hit Me with Your Best Shot
(Pat Benatar)

The first day at the production office, I should have worn something different. Having seen photos of legendary directors like Alfred Hitchcock, Howard Hawks, and Vincente Minnelli wearing suits and ties on set, I wanted to "dress" for work. There was (and still is) a typical male film director "uniform"—a baseball cap, jeans, sneakers, and a crew jacket with the name of a previously successful film production embroidered on it . . . oh, and a beard.

I wasn't trying to be "one of the guys," so I decided to wear a skirt. I rarely wore skirts and only owned two. One had a flouncy flamenco style that might have looked good on a beach in Ibiza, but was out of place in a no-frills production office with gray metal rental furniture. In retrospect, I think I wanted to set a "Girls Just Want to Have Fun" atmosphere.

That day, like most pre-production days, was long. Every department had questions, and the director needed to answer them all. If you're not good at multitasking, directing is not the right job for you. At the end of the day, I happened to walk past Santo's office. He smiled, then followed me down the hall and gently tugged on the back of my skirt. Then he whispered: "Your underpants are showing."

"My underpants are what?!"

It turned out I had accidentally tucked the back of my flouncy skirt into my underwear when I used the bathroom. (I don't remember what underwear I was wearing, but I hope it wasn't my cotton ones with the days of the week printed across the backside, because it would probably have been the wrong day!) I must have been walking around like that for a while, without anyone mentioning it. Maybe they secretly enjoyed seeing the director's panties. Maybe they thought calling it to my attention would embarrass me. But I'd like to think they were so engaged in their own creative tasks that no one even noticed. Of course, this was one of those small mortifying moments that others won't remember, but has replayed in my head for years.

Eventually I would come to realize that making a movie is like walking a tightrope. You put one foot steadily in front of the other and just keep walking. Never look down! Although something happened that almost made me stumble.

Two weeks before we were about to start filming, I found out I was pregnant. I now remember this as if it were a movie scene. Here's the screenplay:

EXTERIOR. HOT TUB, MOUNTAIN TOWN—NIGHT
(ONE YEAR EARLIER)

A group of happy, slightly inebriated FILMMAKERS relax in a large hot tub in a storybook Western town where a film festival is taking place. Steam rises from the surface of the tub, enveloping the group in mist. Majestic mountains, silhouetted by the moon, are seen in the background.

A petite, dark-haired film director, let's call her SUSAN, catches the eye of an attractive DOCUMENTARY FILMMAKER soaking nearby. He paddles over to her. They flirt, chat about all the movies they've watched that day. Joke about having butt-ache from sitting for so long. Exchange phone numbers. Nothing more. The festival will end tomorrow and they will both return to their respective coasts.

CUT TO:

INTERIOR. SOHO BAR—NIGHT (SEVERAL MONTHS LATER)

The DOCUMENTARY FILMMAKER is visiting New York City. He calls SUSAN and they meet for a drink, maybe two, possibly three, at a cozy neighborhood bar. More movie talk about upcoming projects. More laughter. More flirting.

CUT TO:

INTERIOR. LOFT BEDROOM—LATER THAT NIGHT

SUSAN and the DOCUMENTARY FILMMAKER are in bed, having just had sex.

CLOSE UP on SUSAN'S FACE. She looks worried. If we could read her mind, we'd know it's concern about a broken condom. She reaches down to touch her inner thigh. It's wet. Sticky.

INTERIOR. BATHROOM—NIGHT (ONE MONTH LATER)

CLOSE ON: an EPT (early pregnancy test) kit. The overly complicated kind they made back in 1984.

SUSAN sits on the toilet seat, pours droplets from a chemical solution into a vial, and mixes it with urine. It looks like a science experiment from high school. There are several steps involved and a twenty-minute wait.

DISSOLVE TO:

The solution in the vial has changed color.
The CAMERA pushes in tight on SUSAN'S face. Distressed.

DRAMATIC MUSIC swells as the screen slowly FADES TO BLACK.

No matter how many times I've replayed this movie in my head, the fact remained the same. I was pregnant, and the timing couldn't have been worse. My professional career was just beginning. At thirty-two, I'd been given a rare opportunity to direct a studio movie. I needed to be at the top of my game physically, mentally, emotionally. On the other hand, I wanted to have a child one day and was no longer young. But being pregnant was not an option I could consider. It wasn't the right time. Or the right partner. So I made a decision that was right for me. I did not take this casually. I would have preferred to keep the whole thing private, but felt obligated to tell my producers. I can only imagine what went through their minds. It was a Friday, two weeks before we were about to start filming.

I've debated about editing this event out of my memoir. I've taken it out, put it back in. In. Out. In. Out. But finally I left it in to make a point. I've often wondered how this situation might have played out if my producers weren't women. Or were less understanding. Or if the choice I made had not been a legal option at the time.

The following Monday I was back in the production office, and two weeks later, on schedule, we began shooting on St. Marks Place on the Lower East Side. I did not wear a flouncy skirt. Instead, I wore jeans, a T-shirt, and a jacket with lots of pockets for all my director stuff: viewfinder, shot lists, headphones, lipstick. Nor did I wear a baseball cap or grow a scruffy beard. I did, however, wear a jaunty porkpie hat.

(Courtesy of MGM Media Licensing, photograph by Andrew Schwartz)

As I watched the camera trucks unloading, the crew setting up for the first shot, and Madonna heading into the hair and makeup trailer, I turned to Midge and Sarah and said, "I guess we can now crack open that bottle of champagne." It had been a long haul and we had never been fully confident that the film was actually going to get made. Even during pre-production, we were waiting for a curtain to drop, saying, "Just kidding. Everyone go home." But the camera was now rolling and I watched as Madonna, playing Susan, walked down the street wearing little white gloves and munching on Cheez Doodles. Some pedestrians stopped to watch, but few paid much attention. New Yorkers are cool and hard to impress. We were just another film crew on the streets of Manhattan. Madonna was not yet famous, so there were no movie stars to gawk at.

That evening Midge, Sarah, and I finally popped the cork and made a toast.

Ten shots down. Five hundred and thirty-five more to go.

Ed Lachman, cinematographer. Michael Peyser, executive producer, center. Joel Tuber, 1st A.D., far left. Ira Hurvitz, script supervisor, far right. Count the number of women in the frame. (*Courtesy of MGM Media Licensing, photograph by Andrew Schwartz*)

Big Girls Don't Cry
(Fergie)

First impressions are powerful, so the way you introduce a main character into a story is extremely important. When someone enters a room (just like when they enter a movie scene), you get an instant sense of who they are. You're immediately engaged, or not. I knew I needed to find the right opening image and set a tone to quickly define each leading lady and establish the different worlds they lived in.

Roberta is introduced in the soft, feminized world of a hair salon, a place for transformation. People go there to be changed, made over, renewed in some way, and Roberta was a woman desperate for reinvention. We first see

Introducing Rosanna Arquette (Roberta) and Laurie Metcalf (Leslie)

her being fussed over by her overbearing sister-in-law, Leslie, who knows exactly what Roberta needs to be happy: a better haircut.

But what Roberta really needs is passion and adventure. She's a romantic at heart.

*   *   *

In contrast to Roberta's wistful daydreaming, we meet Susan sprawled out on the floor of a garish hotel room in Atlantic City. She's dressed in black fishnets and a tuxedo-style jacket with a gold pyramid emblazoned on the back. Discarded room service trays, poker chips, and playing cards are scattered on the floor around her and she's taking *selfies* with a Polaroid camera. (Who knew two decades later everyone would be taking selfies?!) There's a man asleep in a bed behind her, but Susan looks bored. Restless. We will later find out he's a gangster with whom she had a short fling.

Instantly, the film sets up that Susan is naughty, adventurous, and narcissistic. Someone who lives life by her own rules. The introduction of the two main characters establishes their differences, but also their similarities. Both are scanning the personal ads in a newspaper. Both are desperately seeking something.

*   *   *

This would be Madonna's first film role, and our relationship was relatively straightforward and stress-free. I liked the little details she brought to the role. One of my favorite moments took place in the bathroom at the Port Authority Bus Terminal.

It was scripted that after arriving on a bus from Atlantic City, Susan goes into the restroom to change her clothes and wash up. While filming, Madonna suddenly flipped the nozzle on a wall-mounted air blower and used it to dry her armpits, turning this improvisation into a memorable movie moment and, years later, a popular internet GIF.

An improvisation that became a memorable movie moment
(*Courtesy of MGM Media Licensing, photograph by Andrew Schwartz*)

* * *

My relationship with Rosanna was more complicated. There was an undercurrent of defensiveness on both our parts. This was the first time I was working with a young Hollywood star who was probably used to more stroking than I was giving. Her on-screen fragility and vulnerability were what made her past performances so moving, and she'd just come off the set of the latest Martin Scorsese film, *After Hours*. He was far more experienced than I at knowing how to make his actors feel special and secure. Also, he was an older man (seventeen years Rosanna's senior). I say that because, in retrospect, I think gender and age were a factor. Young women directing young women was still a relatively new thing, and I would later come to realize that the job involved a lot of cajoling and ego massaging to get performers to do what you wanted (or needed) them to do. I had come from the rough-and-tumble world of low-budget New York indie filmmaking. During *Smithereens,* the actors were newcomers. We were all in the trenches together. There was no power hierarchy, no schmoozing. I was unskilled at hiding my feelings. I'm sure that whatever was on my mind was written across my forehead.

Unfortunately, once tension between an actor and director sets in, every creative decision, every suggestion, is viewed with mistrust and suspicion. That mistrust goes both ways, and when that cycle begins, it's like walking on eggshells. The simplest feedback can become a defensive argument.

That's something they don't teach you in film school. It's not always easy to communicate with actors, which is why so many young filmmakers focus on the technical aspects of moviemaking. Those are the things you can control: the camera, lighting, production design, and editing. Dealing with creative people with egos and insecurities (as well as your own self-doubt) is a tricky maneuver that involves subtle negotiation and intuition. It's also about trust.

I had a clear vision of how I wanted the film to look and feel, but hadn't yet earned Rosanna's trust. On top of that, she had signed on to star in a movie with a relatively unknown co-star when midway through production that dynamic totally changed. Madonna started to get a massive amount of attention, and the press began referring to the film as "The Madonna Movie." In retrospect, I probably wasn't sensitive enough to how Rosanna might have felt.

I still had a lot to learn.

A rehearsal. Can you feel the tension?
(Courtesy of MGM Media Licensing, photograph by Andrew Schwartz)

* * *

Then came the day I cried on set. In public. It's unusual for me to cry in public. I'm not a crybaby and have a pretty high anxiety threshold. It would be the only time in my nearly thirty-five years as a director that would happen.

"Stop it. Control yourself. . . . Directors don't cry!" I said to myself, pressing a fingernail sharply into the palm of my hand as a distraction. Then came that choked-up feeling I get in the back of my throat when I'm angry or upset . . . and I felt my eyes begin to tear. I don't know what triggered this sudden flood of emotion. Anxiety? Exhaustion? Frustration that I didn't know how to communicate with Rosanna?

It was the day we were filming a scene in the Port Authority Bus Terminal, where Roberta finds a key to a locker in the pocket of her pyramid jacket. If you've seen the movie, you'll remember the scene. Roberta, suffering from amnesia, goes with Dez (Aidan Quinn) to the bus terminal to find out what's inside the mysterious locker.

What started the clash was a conversation Rosanna and I were having about amnesia. In real life, a person with amnesia might be terrified and totally disoriented. Amnesia is scary. But this was a comedy, so it needed to be played realistically enough to convey memory loss, but without destroying the lighthearted tone of the film. What began as a private conversation quickly escalated to a public argument in front of forty crew members and a hundred extras standing around watching. (Thankfully this was a decade before the internet. No one had a cell phone or could post a photo online!)

Maybe if I'd been more experienced, I'd have understood her method and been more helpful. Certainly, we should have found a private place to talk. I was stressed. So was she. The assistant director was pointing to his watch and flashing me a cringy "let's get moving" face. The crew and all the extras were in place waiting to shoot, and here Rosanna and I were, sitting on the floor of the bus station, stuck in an emotional loop.

Midge and Sarah were on set that day and eventually joined in the conversation. Pretty soon we were all in tears. (Midge later said: "There should be more crying on movie sets. It's the female version of yelling.") Long hours and a pressurized schedule can cause tensions to flare. But it was also because we all cared. We had worked so hard to get the film made and wanted to get everything right. Besides, crying isn't a sign of weakness. It's a sign that shows you don't give a shit if your nose is running and your eye makeup is smeared down your cheeks, making you look like a rabid raccoon. I wonder, do male directors and actors ever cry together on set? Maybe they just punch the crap out of each other.

Eventually emotions cooled. We all took a deep breath and got on with our work. But sometimes the most exhausting moments on set are the ones that turn out best on film.

* * *

There were fortunate surprises, too. Like the day we were filming on 25th Street and walking down the sidewalk, just by happenstance, were three identical-looking young men dressed in identical clothing. Since *Desperately Seeking Susan* was a movie about mistaken identity and doubles, it seemed auspicious that *triplets* should suddenly wander onto our movie set. I asked if they would mind standing in the doorway of the building where we about to start filming and smile at Madonna as she walked past them in white fishnets and a garter belt. They readily agreed.

Three identical strangers
(Courtesy of MGM Media Licensing, photograph by Andrew Schwartz)

I knew nothing about the triplets' lives or past history, which turned out to be fascinating, but ultimately sad. Twenty-five years later they would be the subject of a documentary called *Three Identical Strangers,* the story of triplets adopted at birth by three different families and unaware of each other's existence until they were twenty.

Unwittingly, they had been part of a secret scientific experiment that studied the development of genetically identical siblings who were intentionally raised in different socioeconomic circumstances. Nature vs. nurture.

They had been used as human guinea pigs.

* * *

It took a little over nine weeks to shoot *Desperately Seeking Susan.* One of our final filming locations was the Magic Club, the set we created inside the Audubon Ballroom, on 165th Street and Broadway. The place had long since gone to rack and ruin and Santo used the ballroom's crumbling texture to create a nightclub that felt magical and timeless. Ed lit the exterior with green and purple gels, giving it an otherworldly Wonderland glow.

I remember seeing Rosanna sitting in a corner of the Magic Club while we were setting up lights for a shot. She was reading a script called *Silverado,* a Western that would become her next movie. I sensed she had mentally moved on. There was now pandemonium surrounding Madonna, since her album *Like a Virgin* was about to be released. In two weeks, she would be on the cover of *Rolling Stone.* A few months later, she would host *Saturday Night Live* and sell out Radio City Music Hall. I had never seen a career skyrocket so quickly. Just eight weeks earlier we'd been filming on St. Marks Place, attracting little public attention. Now the production needed security guards.

I wish I could have told Rosanna that playing Roberta Glass would bring her international fame and kudos. That it would be a film she'd be proud of decades from now. But whatever the cause of the tension between us, the push-pull resulted in a great performance, one of the most accoladed of her career. She would be nominated for a Golden Globe and win a BAFTA (the British Academy Award). But I wasn't to know that yet, so I took a deep breath, preparing myself for a possible argument, then dug my fingernail into my palm and walked toward her to discuss the scene we were about to shoot.

The Way We Were
(Barbra Streisand)

It was now 2010 and I hadn't seen Rosanna in nearly twenty-five years. She was living on the West Coast. I, on the East. But tonight was the twenty-fifth anniversary screening of *Desperately Seeking Susan* at Lincoln Center. Mark Blum and Aidan Quinn showed up. So did the producers and many of the crew members. Madonna did not.

Rosanna looked beautiful and happy and had a new love in her life. Both of our careers had hit a few bumps over the years, but we were still busy working, hangin' in there. And it was genuinely nice to see her and reconnect in a different way. Maybe it was maturity, or empathy, or a simple understanding that came with getting older. (We were both now fifty-ish, give or take.) Or maybe it was the knowledge that we had worked together to create something memorable and unique—a film that had passed the test of time. Not many movies do.

Watching the film again, up on a big screen with an audience, I could see how nuanced her performance was. She was vulnerable and charming, and I appreciated all her quirky little facial expressions and great comedic timing. She was the heart of the movie and I was glad to have the opportunity to tell her so during the Q&A that followed the screening. And again, in private, at the party afterward. Since that night, we've kept in touch sporadically. An occasional email, text, or Instagram message. I've followed her political activism and admired her courage to stand up to bullies, particularly the once-powerful Harvey Weinstein (now inmate number 3102000153).

I wished our relationship had been more convivial during the making of the film, but I'm not sure that would have made a difference. Sometimes a little tension is a good thing. Maybe it kept us both on our toes.

But here I go again, I'm letting my story jump ahead of itself, so let's go back to 1984.

* * *

We filmed our final shot on November 11, 1984. The next week I would go into the editing room for several months to work with editor Andy Mond-shein. The producers would fly back to LA to focus on marketing and promotion. The production had gone relatively smoothly, with only a few minor hiccups. My spirit and confidence were still intact. Plus, I'd learned several important lessons (that apply to life, not just filmmaking), especially from my mistakes.

LESSON #1: Filmmaking is about decision-making. Each shot contains the director's multiple creative decisions, which are then carried out by a large number of people: actors, designers, a camera and sound crew, wardrobe, hair and makeup teams. Be confident in your choices. But here's the thing about decisions. . . . Sometimes you make the wrong one and you can't be afraid to change your mind when that happens. The images you put on film will last a very long time, so make sure they are the ones you intended.

LESSON #2: It's okay to say "I don't know." If you don't know something, don't pretend you do and give a stupid answer. It will only come back to bite you in the ass. Find someone who knows the answer and ask them. In general, women seem to have an easier time saying "I don't know" and realize it's not a sign of weakness. It's simply common sense.

LESSON #3: Make friends with the hair and makeup team. They are your allies. They are the first people to greet the actors in the morning and play a crucial role in the psychological well-being of the production. They serve as therapists. They can calm down an actor who has had a romantic meltdown or been up crying/drinking/self-medicating all night. They can soothe the jitters of a performer having a panic attack. They can make pimples and undereye bags magically disappear. They also give good neck massages.

LESSON #4: Tune out the small stuff. With so many things that can potentially go wrong, there's always an on-set crisis. Don't let it distract you. Stay focused on the big picture. Being a director is like being one of those old-timey plate spinners on *The Ed Sullivan Show*. You need to do a lot of running around just to keep all the plates in motion.

LESSON #5: Have a clear and solid plan for each day, then be prepared to change everything at the very last moment. Preparedness allows for spontaneous discovery on set. And always have a Plan B . . . then a Plan C.

LESSON #6: Don't expect to ever have weekends off.

LESSON #7: Respect your crew. These are the folks who get up at 4:30 a.m. every morning to beat rush hour traffic on the Long Island Expressway to make it into the city, where they work long hours behind the scenes so that the director, producers, writers, and actors can get all the glory. They are the unsung heroes of moviemaking, and you need to thank them every day!

I also realized that directing is a physically and mentally exhausting job that is not at all glamorous, despite what outsiders might think. You find yourself shooting in lots of dirty rooms, breathing noxious fumes from oil-burning smoke machines in order to make a shot look pretty, and your face breaks out in pimples from all the grit and grime. I learned you drink tons of bad coffee, because Starbucks doesn't yet exist and regular coffee is still lousy. You spend a lot of time waiting for lights to be set, cables to be laid down, and actors to get out of the hair and makeup trailer. Then you cram yourself into a tiny crawl space with six, seven, eight other crew members in order to get the perfect camera angle, trying to ignore the silent-but-toxic fart someone just expelled.

There's ego massaging, psychologizing, and on-the-spot problem-solving. There's shouting about "We're losing the light" when the sun is rapidly disappearing below the horizon and day is turning to night and you haven't finished filming the scene.

And I won't say what I know or what was whispered about the personal relationships that sometimes develop on a film set. If there were any rumors floating around, they were just that, rumors, maybe mixed with a little truth and some wishful thinking. All I can say is that I now understood why actors, directors, producers, cinematographers, and various crew members sometimes find it difficult to separate their professional life from their personal life. It's the occupational hazard of a job where the hours are long, the atmosphere is emotionally charged, and the production is shrouded in fantasy. A movie set is a world of make-believe, where adults get paid well to play "let's pretend."

Yet, despite the stress, the commotion, and the occasional battle of egos, I loved almost every minute of it. And I can't describe the euphoria I felt when the lighting was beautiful, the dolly move was perfect, the actors hit all their marks and said their lines with just the right attitude and feeling. When everyone working in front of, and behind, the camera was moving in sync like a beautifully choreographed ballet. You never know how the footage will come together in the editing room, but I hoped the film would have a spark of magic, because I desperately wanted to do it again.

Multitasking on set. A haircut by stylist Werner Sherer while reviewing location photos with Santo Loquasto during a lunch break (*Courtesy of MGM Media Licensing, photograph by Andrew Schwartz*)

Into the Groove
(Madonna)

Our editing suite was in the legendary Brill Building on Broadway and 49th Street. The Brill was a large, beautiful building built in 1932, with a brass plaque over the doorway in memory of the builder's son who had died in a traffic accident as a child. In the 1940s through the 1960s, its heyday, the Brill had been the center of the music publishing business. Each floor was a hive of small independent music publishing offices, some no bigger than a closet with a piano. All the great East Coast songwriters have walked its hallways. Carole King and Gerry Goffin, Ellie Greenwich and Jeff Barry, Leiber and Stoller, Hal David, Burt Bacharach, and Neil Sedaka wrote their early hits there. Songs like "It's My Party," "Chapel of Love," "Be My Baby," "Stand by Me," and hundreds more.

In the late 1960s, the music business shifted to the West Coast, so the offices were slowly turned into film editing suites. By the early 1980s almost every major film production in NYC was edited at the Brill. A big film sound mixing studio was built on the second floor and you never knew who you might bump into in the elevator. Woody Allen, Marty Scorsese, the Coen brothers, Francis Ford Coppola, Mike Nichols, or Elaine May (who had been editing her latest film, *Ishtar,* there for what seemed like years).[11]

---

11. Although *Ishtar* was plagued by massive cost overruns and a raging battle of egos among the three heavy-hitting participants—Elaine May, Warren Beatty, and Dustin Hoffman—it had moments of comic brilliance. But the malicious behind-the-scenes rumors created a negative buzz.

* * *

Andy Mondshein and his two assistants were hard at work on the seventh floor. Back then, movies were edited on celluloid, so there were bins with hanging strips of 35mm film scattered around the room. There was also a large flatbed editing machine (a Steenbeck), and an upright, old-fashioned editing machine called a Moviola.

Our post-production schedule was rushed. The film was originally scheduled to come out in May or June of 1985, but Orion decided they wanted to push for a March release to take advantage of Madonna's rising fame. Secretly, they feared that Madonna's career might be over by the time the movie came out in the summer. That's how it was with female pop stars back then. They came and went in a flash.

One afternoon, I got a message that Warren Beatty wanted to stop by the editing room to take a look at some footage. He was interested in possibly using Madonna in a movie he was developing. Although I wasn't eager to show the unfinished film to outsiders, how could anyone refuse Warren Beatty? (Back then, few people did.) So he arrived at the editing room along with his producing partner to watch some scenes we'd put together featuring Madonna. Of course, he was charming and flirty and movie-star gorgeous. I could see his eyes light up as he watched Madonna on-screen, like a cartoon wolf licking his chops.

I don't know what events followed, because Madonna was now dating Sean Penn and they would soon be married in a wedding splashed across newspaper headlines around the world. But four years later they would divorce, and the following year Madonna would star in Warren Beatty's 1990 film, *Dick Tracy,* and their relationship would become public. Beatty would also appear in her 1991 documentary *Madonna: Truth or Dare,* where she seemed to have turned from a wily wolf into a tame pussycat. Maybe he had met his match—a woman who could out-flirt him and had both youth and unapologetic ambition on her side.

* * *

As a result, the film was predestined to be a box office flop even before it was released. The tainted production took a toll on director Elaine May, who never directed another film.

Meanwhile in Los Angeles, producers Midge and Sarah were meeting with Orion executives to deal with the advertising and marketing of the movie.

Many people know the difference between a director and a producer. But for those who don't, these are two distinct jobs with a little overlap. Here's some clarification for the benefit of my relatives who ask me at every family wedding or Thanksgiving dinner, "So, how's your *producing* coming along?"

A *producer* deals with all the behind-the-scenes managerial aspects of financing, making, and promoting a movie. They may have originally optioned and developed the screenplay and attached the director.

The *director* is focused on all the creative aspects of putting the story onscreen: working with the writers, actors, cinematographer, designers, editor, and composer.

Both the producer and director are blamed if the movie goes over budget or if the dailies look like crap.

If the movie is a hit, they both take full credit.

If the movie flops, they blame each other.

* * *

The folks in Orion's marketing department (mostly middle-aged guys who didn't totally *get* the film and were at a loss about how to market it) suggested to Midge and Sarah that we change the movie's title to something more generic. They proposed the title *The Personals,* afraid that younger audiences (Madonna fans) would not understand what "Desperately Seeking Susan" meant. They were also afraid that the title would sound like a lesbian love story.

Orion had designed some poster mock-ups. One featured Rosanna's face reflected on the side of a shiny metal toaster with Madonna popping out of it like a piece of toast. Thankfully the producers fought against these silly ideas.

As it happened, a young photographer named Herb Ritts had been hired to take some publicity shots of Rosanna and Madonna. They featured both women dressed in black, their messy blond hair pulled back with big floppy bows, wearing the film's signature pyramid jacket. The background was simple—plain white. The women stood arm in arm, looking sexy and exuding attitude. Rosanna is staring defiantly at the camera, Madonna is looking away, too cool to return the viewer's gaze. At the producers' request (and with the support of a young Orion publicity guy), it was suggested that the Herb Ritts photo be turned into the poster. The image would become iconic.

(Courtesy of MGM Media Licensing, photograph by Herb Ritts)

Meanwhile, back in the editing room, Andy had put together a solid cut of the film. We knew it still needed trimming, but we were now focused on the soundtrack.

Months earlier, I had filmed a scene in Danceteria, a popular NYC club in the early '80s, one of the first to play new wave dance music. In that scene, Madonna and Mark Blum (Roberta's hot tub–selling husband) meet for the first time. The scene had originally been scripted as a dialogue scene to take place standing at the bar, but I thought it would be fun to stage it on the dance floor so that the characters danced while they talked. It was also intended as a comedic fish out of water moment to show Roberta's straight suburban husband feeling out of place among the punk, goth, and genderfluid crowd.

The day before the shoot, Madonna and I had a conversation about what music might be playing in the background of the scene. She asked if she could bring in a cassette of the new song she'd written with Stephen Bray called "Into the Groove." At the time, I had no intention of actually using the song in the film, but thought it would help get the background extras up on their feet. The way it works when filming a dance scene is that the music is played loudly to get all the background dancers moving to the same beat, then the sound is turned off right before the actors start their dialogue. That way you can record the dialogue clean while the dancers move in sync, silently, in the background. In the editing room, you can then substitute in whatever music you want.

But Andy and I fell in love with the song. It had a great tempo, and we couldn't find anything else that worked nearly as well, so I called Madonna and told her we'd like to use her new song in the film. Of course, now that Madonna was a star, Orion was willing to pay handsomely for it.

* * *

The film composer, Thomas Newman, came from the renowned musical Newman family. Singer-songwriter Randy Newman is his cousin. His father, Alfred, ran the music department at Twentieth Century Fox for decades and won nine Academy Awards. His uncle, Lionel, a conductor/composer, was nominated for eleven. His older brother, David, would also become a well-known composer and conductor. In fact, the Newmans are the most Oscar-nominated family in movie history, with a collective total of ninety-two nominations.

When I first met Tom, he was at the start of his career. He had scored two teen comedies that I wasn't particularly fond of, but on the urging of our music supervisor, I agreed to meet with him. And I'm glad I did. Music is the glue that holds a film together. It gives the movie an emotional pulse that elevates the story to a whole different level. After Tom played me a few sample riffs, I knew his score had the sense of enchantment and magic I was looking for. He would go on to create a signature sound that would influence several of his future film scores. (Listen to the soundtrack of *The Player* and *American Beauty,* and maybe you'll hear it for yourself.) Tom would be nominated for fifteen Oscars, but as of this moment has yet to win one. Although that doesn't matter when you're as talented as Tom.

*   *   *

A studio's marketing department thinks of movie audiences in terms of quadrants: 1) young men/boys, 2) young women/girls, 3) older men, 4) older women—and by "older" that means anyone over twenty-five. A studio's hope is for a film to play to as many quadrants as possible.

Originally, before Madonna's stardom, the executives thought our movie would play primarily to one quadrant: older women. After all, this was a story about a suburban housewife in a passionless marriage who longs to have an adventure. But then everything changed. Madonna was extremely popular with young teenage girls (the *wannabes*), so that brought in another quadrant. And teenage boys liked her, too—so possibly a third quadrant?

Film studios often depend on market research to gauge an audience's reaction to a movie. Few executives trust their instincts, so expensive "experts" are brought in to run research screenings and focus groups. They put together target audiences and hand out questionnaires. But, keep in mind, these questionnaires are given to a group of four hundred teenagers buzzed on Skittles and Pop Rocks in a multiplex in Teaneck, New Jersey. Yet the results can lead to the reediting of entire portions of a movie, or the reshooting of the movie's ending at a cost of tens to hundreds of thousands of dollars.

Around this time, *Purple Rain,* starring Prince, had a successful box office release. In that movie, Prince plays a struggling musician dealing with his difficult home life as he and his band try to make it in the Minneapolis club scene. The film was filled with Prince's songs from his latest album of the same name. For obvious (but wrong) reasons, the market research company decided to target a test audience that had liked *Purple Rain.*

Other than having pop musicians as stars, the films had little in common. *Purple Rain* was a showcase for Prince's music. *Desperately Seeking Susan* was a rom-com starring two women. There were no concert performances and only one Madonna song in the entire film. We were nervous that marketing our movie like *Purple Rain* would only frustrate audiences who were expecting something different.

The audience response at our first preview screening was, well . . . meh. Our film was not really a "Madonna movie," and aggressively promoting it as such might disappoint her music fans. However, while sitting through that very awkward preview screening, the producers and I had an epiphany.

Our film had the wrong ending. No, I'll rephrase that. Our film had too many endings. Audiences have been programmed to think that a rom-com ends with a kiss, because so many actually do. Once the lovers kiss, and the music kicks in, the audience feels emotionally satisfied and people begin to get up out of their seats. In *Desperately Seeking Susan* there was an end-of-movie kiss, but then the story went on for another five minutes and we lost the audience's attention.

The original script ended with the two women going off together on a new adventure, leaving their men behind, sitting at a bar and pining for their return. The film's final image was of Susan and Roberta riding camels in the Egyptian desert. We actually filmed this scene in a sandpit in New Jersey with two rented camels from a nearby zoo. (One was smelly and uncooperative and rolled over with Rosanna still on top.)

Shooting the final scene that would never appear in the movie
(*Courtesy of MGM Media Licensing, photograph by Andrew Schwartz*)

The producers, actresses, and I loved the idea that the film would end with the two women off on a new escapade together. But reality showed us that romantic comedies (even feminist ones) work best when they tug at the heartstrings.

Ultimately, I think we found a satisfying ending—a romantic kiss that takes place in the projection booth of the art house movie theater where Dez works as a projectionist. I staged the scene so that when the lovers kiss, they lean back against the movie projector, causing the celluloid film to jam and then melt. Their kiss literally burns up the screen. It's a romantic moment, but with a tongue-in-cheek wink. A meta way of saying, "Hey, everyone, this is a movie. Enjoy!"

With our new ending in place, Orion submitted the film to the MPAA to get a rating. The committee in charge gave us an R. We were shocked, since there was nothing R-rated about the film. Orion was particularly upset since this would impact their box office revenue. Because of Madonna's popularity with teenage girls, they wanted the film to be PG-13.

The MPAA gave us a list of changes we needed to make in order to get a PG-13.

Back in 1985 there were much stricter rules about what constituted each rating. For example, using inappropriate language (the F-bomb) more than three times in a film automatically gave you an R. We were told to change the word "fucking" to "frigging." We had to put a dark shadow over a shot of Rosanna Arquette soaking in a bathtub because you could see her nipple through the suds. Interestingly, no comment was made about the shot where Madonna undressed in the Port Authority bathroom and her nipples show through her lacy black bra. Most of the MPAA guidelines referred to language and sexual content, not violence. You could chop someone's head off, riddle their body with bullets, beat their face to a bloody pulp, and still get a PG-13. But God forbid you showed a nipple!

* * *

The film had its premiere on Friday, March 29, in LA at a movie complex in Century City just as Madonna Mania was reaching a feverish pitch. But we kept our fingers crossed. The movie business was unpredictable. We still needed Lady Luck on our side.

(Courtesy of MGM Media Licensing, photograph by Andrew Schwartz)

In the Air Tonight
(Phil Collins)

Anyone see Rosanna's name? *(Courtesy of MGM Media Licensing)*

While Madonna stood outside the theater wearing a white Jean Paul Gaultier dress and white fur stole, surrounded by screaming fans, Midge, Sarah, and I waited in the back room of a nearby restaurant nervously sipping wine. Midge and Sarah were checking in with Orion every half hour to get the latest box office reports from New York, which was three hours ahead of LA. The ticket sales were much better than Orion had expected, and we were all trying to control our growing excitement. Too nervous to say it out loud—that the movie just might be a hit.

Madonna Mania! *(Courtesy of MGM Media Licensing)*

Rosanna didn't attend the LA premiere. Maybe she was working on another film at the time, or maybe with so much media attention focused on Madonna, she chose not to attend. Madonna didn't sit through the screening, but left midway with her entourage and joined us in the restaurant to hear the increasingly encouraging box office reports as they came in.

The movie got strong reviews from the major critics in LA and New York, and what those critics said often paved the way for film reviewers in smaller cities to follow. There were a few snarky comments about Madonna just playing "Madonna," but by and large, both actresses' performances were enthusiastically applauded as being vibrant, fresh, and disarming. And the reviews had not just focused on the stars, but on the movie itself. Praise was given to the supporting cast, the throwaway pop culture references, the script, and the magical atmosphere of downtown NYC. It was also praised for telling a story with two female protagonists and a plot that didn't revolve around men. Although I did sense a whiff of condescension from one or two critics who referred to the film as a "chick flick"—a pejorative label used to devalue female-centric work. Would a film like Quentin Tarantino's *Reservoir Dogs* be called a "dick flick?"

Desperately Seeking Susan had passed the Bechdel test, although the Bechdel test wasn't yet widely known. The test, which first appeared in Alison Bechdel's cartoon strip in 1985, lists three criteria: 1) a work (film, novel, play) that has at least two women in it, 2) who talk to each other, 3) about something other than a man.

Would Madonna have become a huge star if she hadn't been in *Desperately Seeking Susan*? Absolutely. Did the convergence of a hit movie coming out at the exact same time as a hit album help to skyrocket her career? In my opinion, definitely. Madonna proved she could cross over entertainment lanes. That was not something many pop stars were able to do. And the film's release coincided with her 1985 Virgin Tour, which would introduce her to the rest of the world. But, like the character Susan, Madonna didn't look back. She was ambitious and already moving on to her next reinvention.

* * *

As for me, the film's success brought me more attention than I'd imagined. I was suddenly getting calls from big-shot producers, powerful agents, and A-list actresses I'd only seen up on a big screen. Goldie Hawn left a congratulatory message on my answering machine, but I was too shy to call her back.

And the best part of it all was proving that a team of women could make a female-centric movie that could be a critical and commercial success. (Plus, guys liked it, too.) We had succeeded on our own terms in a world where powerful men still dictated the rules.

A few months later I'd return to the Cannes Film Festival to screen *Desperately Seeking Susan* for an international audience. This time when the customs agent at JFK Airport asked for my occupation, I said, "Film director" confidently, because that was what I was.

Life in the Fast Lane
(Eagles)

*D*esperately Seeking Susan wasn't a blockbuster, but it was an unexpected sleeper hit and an international box office success, too. It would be nominated for a Golden Globe and a César Award (the French Oscar) for Best Foreign Film. Rosanna would win a British BAFTA award for Best Actress in a *Supporting* (?!) Role.

Hollywood was now paying attention, not just to me but to several other female directors with stories to tell. Amy Heckerling, Martha Coolidge, Randa Haines, Joan Micklin Silver, and, of course, the multitalented Barbra Streisand. Nora Ephron, Penny Marshall, Kathryn Bigelow, and others would make a splash a few years later.

I signed a three-picture deal with Orion and got an office and a charming assistant with a fancy English accent and a posh name, Zara. I couldn't believe that I was now getting paid to do what, not so long ago, I would have willingly done for free. I also received wonderful letters from people around the world who said the movie had changed their lives. That watching it had inspired them to be their authentic selves. Many of these letters were personal and heartfelt, like the one I received from Brendi, a gay teenage boy in Düsseldorf, who became my pen pal for several years.

* * *

After the movie was released, strangers began ringing my door and phoning my home at crazy hours of the night. (My name was on the buzzer and my number in the phone book.) I suddenly felt like I was being stalked. Many were hard-core Madonna fans hoping I'd give them her private phone number or relay a personal message. Some simply wanted to make physical contact with me because it brought them one step closer to her. Two degrees of separation. Eventually I took my name off the buzzer and unlisted my number.

And I realized that if I had stalkers, Madonna's life could never be normal again, which was weird since I'd only met her the year before when she was still this club kid living down the block. But perhaps she never wanted a normal life. She would now be surrounded by security and managers, sycophants and paparazzi. That's the thing about fame. It's a trade-off—you have to give up a piece of yourself in exchange. Although few people enter into that deal blindly.

Andy Warhol said that in the future everyone would have their fifteen minutes of fame. So, I guess this was my fifteen. I made it onto the cover of *High Times* magazine. My mother put the magazine on display on her coffee table in Florida, alongside the baby photos of her grandchildren and my sister's and brother's laminated wedding albums. I don't think she knew what the magazine was about, or maybe she did and just didn't care because my name was on the cover.

(*Photo by Herb Ritts*)

However, sensing how capricious fame and fortune could be, I retained a healthy dose of skepticism. "Celebrity" was like a drug and just as addictive, so there was always a little voice whispering in my ear: *Have fun, but don't let it go to your head. You might not be as lucky the next time.*

Suddenly I was invited to film screenings and cocktail parties. One was at the home of a well-known agent living in a big apartment on the Upper West Side. I was reluctant to attend because I didn't really know the agent or any of her guests. But I went and Jack Nicholson was there.

"Hi, I'm Jack," he said, then a long pause. . . . "Jack Nicholson." He held out his hand with false (but sweet) modesty, as if I, along with the rest of the world, didn't know exactly who he was.

Of course, I didn't mention that we had met at a Student Academy Award party eight years earlier, where I had been gaga and starstruck. (It had been a thrilling night for me, probably not even a blip on his radar screen.) But that evening, he made me feel comfortable in this room full of strangers. Underneath it all, he seemed like a down-to-earth Jersey guy who just happened to be a movie star.

I spent much of the evening standing near the kitchen, munching on hors d'oeuvres, drinking wine, and dribbling a little on my sweater. Also eavesdropping. I realized that although I was suddenly privy to this alternate reality of the rich and famous, most party conversations were similar to the backyard barbecues at my parents' house in the suburbs. Everyone enjoys small talk, shop talk, and gossiping about friends (even if that friend happens to be Dustin Hoffman).

Now for the first time I felt under pressure to produce. Orion had given me an office and expected a film in return. The bar had been raised, and I never liked people watching over my shoulder. I worked best when there was no burden of expectation. I feared that whatever I did next might be a disappointment. Even though it was technically my third film, it would be my second studio movie, and I was aware of what is called the "sophomore slump."

I was sent other scripts to direct. A few I don't regret turning down, like *Shanghai Surprise,* the movie Madonna would do next with her husband, Sean Penn. Both had strong personalities, and as a newlywed power duo, they would probably make their director quiver. I was sent a screenplay called *Cherry 2000* that was very imaginative, but I didn't have a clue what it was about. I got calls from producers in Europe. I remember meeting a German named Bernd Eichinger. He had a script called *Me and Him,* loosely based on a novel by the Italian author Alberto Moravia. It was about a man with a talking penis and Eichinger was looking for a female director. Granted, this was a unique concept, but I could only think of a limited number of things that a talking penis might have to say, so I declined. (The film was directed in 1988 by Doris Dorrie, starring Griffin Dunne as the man with the talkative dong.)

Over the years, there were some opportunities I missed that I'd later come to regret. For example, the movie *Big,* eventually directed by Penny Marshall. Penny did a great job, probably better than I would have done since her instincts were more mainstream and she recognized the big-screen talent of Tom Hanks. I might have cast someone less likable.

* * *

By 1986, the cultural and economic landscape of the city had shifted. Manhattan was being gentrified under the vigilant (but not yet unhinged) eye of its mayor, Rudy Giuliani. Real estate was soaring and Tribeca became the newest hot neighborhood. Even Dean & DeLuca would expand from a small gourmet store on Prince Street to a huge food emporium on Broadway. Eventually it would become a worldwide chain owned by an Asian corporation, then go bankrupt in 2020, $315 million in debt.

And just like that, the Downtown bohemians were eclipsed by a new breed of coke-fueled yuppie stockbrokers and investment bros. These money movers would become the rock stars of the second half of the 1980s. Artists were no longer making the gritty, political street art that had been a "fuck you" to Reagan-era America. It was now about having enough money to buy that art at exorbitantly inflated prices. The market had exploded. The boundaries between art and commerce were crumbling. Ambition and attitude now counted as much as talent, and in some cases even more. Basquiat, Haring, Jeff Koons, Julian Schnabel, and dealers like Larry Gagosian became multimillionaire superstars. It was the beginning of the worship of wealth and celebrity that would grow even more toxic over the next few decades. Material girls, Masters of the Universe, and the .01 percent ruled!

Young novelists like Jay McInerney, Bret Easton Ellis, and Tama Janowitz were writing books that reflected these seismic changes.

Punk was out. Bohemia was out. Second wave feminism, out.

Designer brands were in. Real estate was in. Balsamic vinegar, in.

Greed was good!

Meanwhile, a growing paranoia was sweeping across NYC and LA.

The gay cancer now had a name, and that made it scarier. AIDS was all everyone, straight or gay, thought about, especially in the movie business, where those worlds went hand in hand. And there was so much misinformation floating around about who could catch it and how it spread. Could you kiss your gay friends on the mouth? Was the virus in saliva? Rock Hudson had just died, and his photo was splashed across headlines around the world. I began to see frail and ghostly men walking around the West Village with the help of friends. AIDS would cast its dark shadow over an entire generation.

I was traveling frequently back and forth to LA, staying at the Mondrian Hotel on Sunset. Occasionally I'd meet up with my old friend Billy, who was living there. He had bought an Art Deco house in the Hollywood Hills that had once belonged to a glamorous movie star, maybe Zsa Zsa or Eva Gabor. His gay greeting card company was going gangbusters and on the surface he seemed his usual, happy, larger-than-life self. But from a mutual friend, I'd learned that his partner was sick, although I didn't know the details. Billy simply didn't want to talk about it with me or any of his old friends from Philly. He must have been terrified.

We went out for dinner one night to a restaurant on Melrose Avenue. I remember the moment we kissed good night. It was just a friendly kiss on the lips, although Billy had always been a juicy kisser. There was a millisecond of hesitation on my part, nothing Billy noticed, but I hated myself for it.

Over the next few years we saw each other occasionally for coffee or dinner when I was in LA, but our relationship was mostly by phone. Billy said he was busy with work, but he had always been mercurial. He never mentioned he was ill, even after I found out that his partner had died. Then he gradually stopped calling. I tried to contact him, but he had moved from his Art Deco house, the phone was disconnected, and there were no cell phones back then.

It wouldn't be until the fall of 1989, while talking with a film journalist from LA who knew I'd been friends with Billy, that I heard the news. He said Billy had hanged himself in a rental apartment in West Hollywood, wanting to avoid the agony his partner had gone through. That's how I found out Billy was gone.

Smooth Operator
(Sade)

There were two new popular restaurants in LA in the mideighties, and I can't recall which one I was at—Chinois on Main in Santa Monica, or City on La Brea. What I remember was sitting at a small table with cinematographer Ed Lachman and another man and woman that I'd never met before. I assumed they were a couple, but maybe they weren't. We were mid-conversation when I felt someone rubbing their foot against mine under the table. At first, I thought it was an accident and casually moved my leg away, but when the stray foot again made contact, I realized it was intentional and tucked both my legs under my chair. I think it was the sheer chutzpah of this shameless game of footsies that both surprised and intrigued me.

That's how I met Floyd, the screenwriter with the roving foot. Floyd was a loquacious rascal with swoopy dark hair and a *Viva Zapata!* mustache left over from his globetrotting hippie days. But it's hard to really know a guy with a thick mustache since you don't know what's hidden underneath. There followed a casual, on-and-off long-distance relationship for about a year.

I'd taken Floyd as my date to Madonna and Sean Penn's wedding in Malibu, and amid the paparazzi, power players, and news helicopters flying overhead (making it nearly impossible to hear the vows), I saw him chatting up Princess Leia. Or maybe she was flirting with him? I don't remember. But it was well known that Carrie Fisher was smart, funny, and charismatic.

Hell, I wanted to flirt with her, too! Either way, it was okay because Floyd and I weren't really a couple. We had fun together, but neither of us had long-term romantic expectations. At least not with each other.

The biggest takeaway from our relationship was that I optioned an original screenplay he had co-written with his writing partner, Laurie.

Another takeaway was a case of crabs picked up on our only vacation together in Zihuatanejo, Mexico.

I noticed a crab in my eyelashes when I was in the airplane bathroom on my way back to JFK. I feared these little critters might be other places as well, so I spent the next four hours squirming in my seat, itchy and miserable. On the taxi ride home, I made the driver stop at an all-night pharmacy so I could buy a bottle of Kwell.

But despite the footsies and the crabs, I liked the premise of his (their) script.

* * *

Making Mr. Right was a sci-fi romantic comedy—a satire about the difficulty of contemporary romantic relationships and the shifting power dynamics between the sexes.

Like many other women of my generation, I had spent the last few years focused on my career. I had also dated my share of Mr. Wrongs. And to quote a popular T-shirt slogan of that time: I'd "become the man I once thought I would marry."

There's a myth passed down from the Roman poet Ovid about a sculptor named Pygmalion who makes an ivory statue representing his ideal vision of womanhood. He then falls in love with his own creation. The goddess Venus brings the statue to life in answer to Pygmalion's prayers. This myth would be the inspiration for movies such as *My Fair Lady* and, later, *Pretty Woman*.

Making Mr. Right was a reverse-gender Pygmalion story. The plot went like this:

Dr. Jeff Peters, a misogynistic and socially awkward robotics engineer working for NASA, has fabricated an android named Ulysses that is his identical twin—albeit sweeter, more attractive, and with a larger penis. (Why Dr. Peters felt an android needed a phallus is open for interpretation.)

Ulysses was created to be sent on a seven-year research mission into outer space, something no human could endure. For public relations purposes (and to generate more government funding for the program), Ulysses's media image needs to be made appealing. A savvy female public relations expert named Frankie Stone is hired to do the job. Her mission is to turn this tabula rasa android into a heroic media darling. A robot with the Right Stuff. In the process, she turns Ulysses into her ideal Mr. Right and falls in love with him.

Floyd and Laurie's original screenplay was set in Manhattan, but having filmed my last two movies there, I was eager to work somewhere new. Since the script had a space travel backdrop, I thought relocating the story to Florida, home of the NASA space program, would be fun. It could give the film a *retro-futuristic* style—a nostalgic version of the future, inspired by the World of Tomorrow exhibits I'd seen as a kid at the New York World's Fair in 1964. Back when people were still optimistic about the future.

In the zeitgeist of the midsixties, the idea of going into outer space was exciting. NASA's space program and our space race with Russia were in full swing. This was a positive time in America. (Our struggles in Vietnam and the mounting death toll weren't yet daily headlines.) We still believed in American exceptionalism and being a space cowboy was a sexy, brave, and heroic profession. Astronauts had the Right Stuff. This was the era of Tang!

In pop culture, robots were presented as friendly and helpful. Cartoon families like the Jetsons had a wisecracking robot maid named Rosie, a hardworking and dutiful member of the household. She solved problems, told jokes, and was a surrogate aunt to the Jetson kids. Then along came Stanley Kubrick's *2001: A Space Odyssey* in April 1968, and things changed. Suddenly AI was threatening, and technology could be dangerous when men created machines they could no longer control.

The real world had turned scary by the end of the sixties. Charlie Manson and his delusional followers epitomized the dark turn the counterculture had taken. Four months later, a Hells Angel would stab an eighteen-year-old Black man to death during a Rolling Stones performance at Altamont, bringing the sixties to a violent close. The seventies would kick off with the invasion of Cambodia, the rise of heroin in American cities, Watergate, and an oil crisis resulting in long lines at the gas pump. The decade would end with the Iranian Revolution and the Jim Jones suicide cult drinking poisoned Kool-Aid in Guyana.

I wanted to set *Making Mr. Right* in an unspecified time in the future, but give it an intentionally low-tech style. It would be the opposite of the early eighties' dystopian films like *Blade Runner* or *Mad Max*. A counterpoint to the mainstream sci-fi teen movies filled with lightsabers and laser beams.

I decided to film in Miami Beach, with its pastel 1920s Art Deco buildings and chroma-color sky. I had sentimental nostalgia for Miami Beach. It was where my parents had honeymooned in 1950. It was where I'd spent childhood vacations at one of the big glitzy Morris Lapidus–designed hotels that lined Collins Avenue—the Eden Roc and the Fontainebleau. Of course, this was back when flying Eastern Airlines to Florida was an occasion for the whole family to dress up and airlines still served edible meals with stainless steel cutlery and cloth napkins.

Ed Lachman came back as the director of photography and Barbara Ling would be the production designer. Thirty years later, Barbara would win an Oscar for designing Quentin Tarantino's *Once Upon a Time in Hollywood*.

With a vision of how we wanted the film to look, I now set out to put together a cast, working again with casting directors Risa Bramon and Billy Hopkins.

Weird Science
(Oingo Boingo)

I met several actors for the dual role of Dr. Jeff Peters and his doppelgänger, Ulysses. I remember auditioning Rutger Hauer (*Blade Runner, The Hitcher*), but worried his menacing aura would make the android too scary. I met a young actor, Jim Carrey, who I instinctively liked, but he was still unknown at the time and the studio wanted someone with more film experience. Crispin Glover (coming off the hit *Back to the Future*) flew into New York to meet me. He was fascinating, but very quirky. Robin Williams's name was proposed. He might have been great in the role, but had played a similar character on TV in the popular series *Mork & Mindy.*

Then I met Malkovich. John had created a stir in the theater world with the Chicago-based company Steppenwolf and had recently gotten a Supporting Actor Oscar nomination for his role in the film *Places in the Heart.* I needed an actor who could play two very different characters: the prickly, antisocial scientist Dr. Peters, as well as his innocent android, Ulysses. Malkovich wasn't your typical romantic leading man. He didn't look like the movie hunks of the mideighties—Harrison Ford, Richard Gere, or Tom Cruise. Nor did he resemble rough-and-tumble macho men like Stallone or Mel Gibson. John was a chameleon who was willing to take risks. He was also an accomplished theater director who I sensed would be a good collaborator.

* * *

I cast Ann Magnuson as Frankie Stone, the PR expert hired to socialize Ulysses and make him camera ready for his media debut. I'd known Ann from hanging around the East Village in the early eighties. She'd been the manager and host of Club 57, a performance space on St. Marks Place that became a playhouse for visual artists (Keith Haring and Kenny Scharf), musicians (the B-52s, Cyndi Lauper), and drag performers (RuPaul, Joey Arias, and Lypsinka). Try to imagine a more upbeat version of Andy Warhol's Factory.

I'd gone to Club 57's "Monster Movie Club," where they took great pride in screening the worst monster movies ever made. I'd seen Steve Buscemi perform an absurd comedy routine with Rockets Redglare (they looked like a punk Laurel and Hardy). At the time, Buscemi was still a struggling actor and professional firefighter.

I'd also worked with Ann in *Desperately Seeking Susan,* where she had a small but flashy role as the cigarette girl in the Magic Club, roaming around the nightclub calling out, "Cigars, cigarettes, Tofutti." An improvised line, typical of Magnuson's droll sense of humor.

With her short-cropped red hair, fabulous shoes, and cool eyewear, Ann made Frankie Stone stylish. She embodied the type of woman I wanted to see more of on film. A modern-day version of the sharp career gals played by Rosalind Russell, Barbara Stanwyck, and Eve Arden in the 1940s. Smart, sassy, tough, but with a touch of vulnerable fluster.

In the film's opening title sequence, we watch as Frankie Stone drives to work in her bright-red Corvair, shaving her legs and putting on makeup while stuck in Miami traffic. Her dress is unzipped in the back, and she's driving barefoot, a pair of black-and-white high heels (designed by Keith Haring) resting on the car floor nearby.

(Courtesy of MGM Media)

Frazzled from an argument with her boyfriend earlier that morning and late for work, Frankie dashes into her office with a metal Rolodex dangling from her arm like a charm bracelet. Carrying on two conversations at once, she takes a quick puff off her assistant's cigarette, he zips up the back of her dress, she steps into the high heels, and with the sudden confidence of a pro, Frankie takes a deep breath, sets her face, and enters the conference room where her clients are already seated. "Sorry to keep you gentlemen waiting. I'm always late . . . but I'm worth it," she says, smiling.

(Courtesy of MGM Media Licensing, photo by John Clifford)

My interest in fashion was not just about decoration. Clothing can say a lot about its wearer—things that can't be said with words alone. Frankie's wardrobe, designed by Adelle Lutz and Rudy Dillon, was like architecture—clean geometric lines and highly structured, reflective of Frankie's serious-minded professional life. It served as contrast to her personal life, which was chaotic and sometimes out of control. I admit, I had a thing for strong women who lived messy lives.

* * *

We filmed several scenes in the Art Deco district of South Beach. The neighborhood had not yet been gentrified and was still filled with pastel-colored motels that had been turned into old-age homes. Jewish *bubbes* and *zaydes* sat on lawn chairs, kibbitzing and enjoying the sun. Across the street, suntanned junkies and vagabonds hung out on the beach. Cubano cafés had window signs that read *Se Habla Yiddish*.

I loved places where disparate cultures blended together in unexpected ways. Five years after the splash made by the cocaine-fueled, MTV-style cop show *Miami Vice,* South Beach would be transformed into a mecca of neon-lit hotels with bars serving fishbowl mojitos and flashy nightclubs blasting Gloria Estefan, Ricky Martin, and Enrique Iglesias. But in 1986, the neighborhood was still relatively quiet, its elderly residents asleep shortly after sundown.

The cast and crew were put up in suites in a high-rise hotel in Greater Miami, overlooking Biscayne Bay, across the 79th Street Causeway leading to Miami Beach. My hotel window looked out on several small islands that the artist Christo had once wrapped in 6.5 million square feet of pink polypropylene fabric floating on the surface of the water and extending out two hundred feet from each island. The art project had taken three years to create (1980 to 1983), but the pink islands would be on display for only two weeks before being dismantled. Yet, the idea that someone had created art by wrapping entire islands in a pink plastic skirt was inspirational. A lesson reminding everyone to enjoy things in the moment.

And I did. I thoroughly enjoyed every moment of filming *Making Mr. Right.* The production had a cheerful and relaxed atmosphere. The South

Florida weather was balmy, not yet too buggy. (By May the swarms of mosquitoes would arrive.) The actors got along well, and that's not always the case on a movie set, where tensions can run high. John was there with Glenne Headly, his wife at the time, who had a supporting role in the film and brought along their fluffy little white dog. I was working again with the enormously talented and versatile Laurie Metcalf. Malkovich, Headly, and Metcalf were all members of the Steppenwolf Theatre Company, so they had performed together multiple times. We were making a comedy and I wanted everyone to be happy. And I believed, for the most part, everyone was.

John had recently taken up needlepoint as a way to relax in between setups while lights were being adjusted. I have a funny image seared in my memory of Malkovich, in his blond wig and orange jumpsuit, seated in a director's chair, doing embroidery. Nearby, Ann is wandering around the set in her tight geometric power suit, held together from behind with silver gaffer's tape. (John's costume also needed gaffer's tape by the end of the shoot. Everyone had eaten well in Miami.)

In the evenings, we gathered in a small makeshift screening room to watch the dailies from the day before. We laughed a lot. But after thirty years, I've come to realize that there's no connection between the amount of fun you have while making a movie and a film's success at the box office.

Me and Malkovich. Good vibes on set
(*Courtesy of MGM Media Licensing, photograph by John Clifford*)

My parents came down to Miami to watch the filming. I'd given my dad a small speaking part in the movie. He would play REPORTER #4 at a NASA-style press conference to introduce Ulysses to the public before he is sent on his mission into outer space.

I've never known my father to be nervous or shy, even in his later years and at his most vulnerable, after he began to suffer from memory loss. We'd had a strained relationship during my rebellious teen years, but he was proud of me now, and as a gesture of my love (and because I could), I gave him a speaking part. Just one line.

REPORTER #4: "Aren't you frightened of going up there all alone for seven years?"

But when the camera started to roll, my father suddenly froze and fluffed his line. Again and again. In a crowd of one hundred and fifty extras and John Malkovich waiting for him to deliver his line so the scene could continue. I could see my dad growing increasingly flustered. Ten takes later, he finally nailed it, and his performance was perfect.

This was the only time I'd ever seen my father frazzled in public.

REPORTER #4–aka "Daddy"
(*Courtesy of MGM Media Licensing, photograph by John Clifford*)

Under Pressure
(David Bowie and Queen)

*M*aking *Mr. Right* had not yet been released when I started to wake up in the middle of the night with panic attacks. *Smithereens* and *Desperately Seeking Susan* had both been surprise successes. I was bracing myself for a letdown. The film wasn't getting the same advance buzz I'd felt with the other two. I worried that viewers would misunderstand the tone, or dislike the message.

The film came out on April 10, 1987, to mixed reviews. There were some good ones, some meh, and a few nasty ones. As a result, the weekend box office was soft, a euphemism for flop.

Here's the way it works. Once the Friday night box office results come in, the studio makes a marketing decision. Is the film a hit or a miss? All those months of hard work boil down to a few hours of ticket sales on a Friday night. This was still when the opening weekend box office results were crucial, before cable and streaming changed the playbook.[12]

If a movie is deemed a miss, the marketing budget is cut and the film's failure becomes a self-fulfilling prophecy. Without great reviews or a healthy

---

12. Before the midseventies, films were not judged by their opening weekend box office results. All that changed after the success of *Jaws* in 1975—the first film to make over one hundred million dollars at the American box office. *Jaws* ushered in the concept of the Hollywood summer blockbuster.

advertising budget, it's hard to keep a small movie afloat, especially one without big-name stars.

Could *Making Mr. Right* have been funnier? Slicker? More romantic? Since I was the film's director and executive producer, I'm responsible for all those creative decisions. Could the film have generated more heat with a more recognizable cast? Maybe, but the casting was my decision, too. At the time, Malkovich was not yet a household name and Magnuson was a relative newcomer. The film needed stellar reviews and a larger advertising budget to compete with the much bigger Hollywood movies that opened that same weekend.

* * *

It's hard to read reviews of your work, especially when a critic's personal opinion is made so public. Back then, most of the top critics were men, and the success of a small film boiled down to the opinions of a few reviewers writing for a handful of influential publications. Intentionally or not, there was a sexist bias. (Decades later, the information-sharing connectivity of the internet would dilute that concentration of power.) As a result, many actors, writers, and directors develop a thick skin. Some say they never read reviews. Or don't take them *personally*. But I suspect that isn't totally true.

Of course I took criticism *personally*! How else could I take it? *As a group?* (That's a line from *Cookie,* written by Nora.) After all, there were chunks of me in all the movies I'd made and the ones I hoped to make in the future.

In the case of *Making Mr. Right,* some critics objected to the idea of a woman abandoning human men to find satisfaction with a programmable "sex-bot." One male reviewer called Ulysses "a walking and talking dildo." David Denby, then the film critic at *New York Magazine,* titled his review "Making Mr. Wrong" and ended with the line: *"Until Seidelman ends her reliance on dopey, pseudo-feminist griping and mechanical farce, she'll never make a good movie."* C'mon! How could I not take that personally?! It felt like a punch in the gut. Having never met David Denby, I hadn't realized he was an authority on feminism—pseudo, dopey, or otherwise. It also revealed a blinkered approach to criticism, not acknowledging the possibility that a woman's response to the film might be different from his own subjective perspective.[13]

Male chauvinistic farce and tits and ass jokes had been a staple of movie comedy for nearly a century (watch Groucho Marx's relentless attacks on actress Margaret Dumont). It was fodder for male stand-up comedians and late-night talk show hosts. The source of inspiration for frat-boy magazines like *Spy* and *National Lampoon*. I've had to pretend laugh at jiggly titty jokes ever since I was a teenager. So, in 1987, when I was given the opportunity to turn the tables by creating a female protagonist with a bawdy sense of humor, I figured, why couldn't Frankie and her gal pal, Trish, crack a few dick jokes?

For example:

FRANKIE and TRISH lounge on Frankie's couch, drinking cocktails and discussing their love lives.

TRISH: I've never tried a ménage à trois, have you?
FRANKIE: With Steve? . . . Oh, God, it was hard enough to get him alone . . . and even then, it wasn't hard enough.

Making Mr. Right was social satire. I was poking fun at misogyny and the gender stereotypes that were baked into our culture at a time when bad male behavior was still considered business as usual. Hadn't I planted my tongue firmly enough in my cheek? And what about all those 1980s movie portrayals of Ms. Right as a fish (*Splash*), a department store dummy (*Mannequin*), a sloppy drunk (*Blind Date*), and an adorable prostitute (*Pretty Woman*)? And wasn't the perfect woman created by connecting a computer program to a Barbie doll in John Hughes's *Weird Science*?

---

13. Until 2015, only 20 percent of the Rotten Tomatoes critics were women. In the '80s and '90s, movie reviews were only available in print, and on radio and network TV. Most of the top film critics (with a few exceptions like Pauline Kael, Judith Crist, Janet Maslin, Sheila Benson, and Molly Haskell) were men. And while some might ask, "Do film reviews matter?" I can tell you they do. Especially for a female-centric film without a large marketing campaign. In 1989, the year I made *She-Devil*, the New York Film Critics Circle and the Los Angeles Film Critics Association (combined) had less than 10 percent women members.

Yes, there were male critics who understood *Making Mr. Right*'s intended tone:

With this film, {Seidelman} hits her stride as a comedy director who would rather be clever than obvious, who allows good actors such as Malkovich to go for quiet effects rather than broad, dumb cliches.
                                                          —Roger Ebert, *At the Movies*

With one eye on contemporary life, and another on life the way she'd like to see it, Susan Seidelman is in the mode of a classic satirist. But she's an amiable one, who kind of strolls along, dropping entertaining observations by the wayside.   —Henry Sheehan, *Chicago Reader*

Success is mercurial, and cultural taste never remains static. What is misunderstood by one generation might be embraced by the next, so I held out hope that one day *Making Mr. Right* would find its audience, even if it took a few decades. I watched as over the past thirty years our personal relationship with technology has radically changed. We now live in a time when AI is diagnosing medical problems, taking over the jobs of service representatives, accountants, psychotherapists, and military personnel—even writing songs and screenplays. A ChatGPT love bot named CarynAI can be your virtual girlfriend for one dollar a minute. Maybe it's no longer science fantasy to make your own Mr. Right.

But the movie industry is ruthless. I was nervous that Hollywood would now consider me too indie, too East Coast, too feminist (even worse, pseudo-feminist), and I'd never work again. Although it's well known that in Hollywood, men can fail upward.

Hey! I wanted to fail upward, too!

Around this time, two new men entered my life. Both would have an impact on my future. One would become my life partner. The other would become my agent.

One loved to cook. The other ate paper.

I'll start with the love story first.

Wishin' and Hopin'
(Dusty Springfield)

Back in 1985, after *Desperately Seeking Susan*'s release, I started to get calls from strangers wanting to pitch me film projects. My phone number was listed in the Manhattan phone directory, so I was easy to find. One of those calls came from a man named Jonathan.

Jonathan is a Hebrew name that means "God has given." And although Jonathan was not Hebrew, he turned out to be a godsend. He was also charming, creative, and neurotic. He might say the same about me (the neurotic part) after thirty-seven years of waking up together in tangled sheets and living with each other's quirks and peccadilloes.

In the late seventies, Jonathan was a young lawyer working at a prestigious London entertainment law firm that represented swanky clients like Sir Laurence Olivier, Richard Branson, and Andrew Lloyd Webber. One day a now-legendary character named Seymour Stein showed up at the office. No one wanted to deal with this eccentric New York record producer who was in London signing unknown punk bands, so they palmed Seymour, and his Brooklyn accent, off to one of the junior attorneys, Jonathan. Evidently, Jonathan and Seymour hit it off, and Seymour offered him a job at his burgeoning punk record label in New York, Sire Records. Eager to check out life in the Big Apple, Jonathan readily accepted and a whole new chapter opened up.

Seymour turned out to be a very savvy record exec, signing bands like

Talking Heads and the Ramones before they became famous. Later, he would sign the Pretenders and, of course, help jump-start Madonna's music career, making him very rich along the way. Being in the record business, with Seymour as his mentor, Jonathan was able to get past the velvet rope at Studio 54 and had a front-row seat to the craziness that was New York City in the late seventies and early eighties. It was an eye-opening adventure for this once innocent British public school boy.

Jumping ahead a few years, Jonathan left Sire and was hired by Clive Davis as his right-hand man at Arista Records. But Arista was a one-man show (Clive's), and gradually Jonathan's interest shifted from music to movies as those two worlds commingled more frequently in the '80s.

Around this time, Jonathan had optioned the film rights to a book called *Jersey Luck,* written by Tom De Haven. A publicist at Sire had seen *Desperately Seeking Susan* and suggested that Jonathan contact me, thinking I might be a good director for the project. So Jonathan looked me up in the Manhattan phone directory and a meeting was arranged. Easy peasy.

When I first saw Jonathan standing in the doorway on Thompson Street, I thought he was cute. He was wearing narrow jeans, a tucked-in blue Oxford shirt, and a navy blue blazer. His shaggy brown hair was cut like Eric Clapton's in the '80s, a style popular with British musicians and actors at the time. He was different from the scruffy bad boys I'd been attracted to in the past. We talked for half an hour, and he had a lovely accent. Years later, he would mention that he thought I was rude because I had not offered him a cup of tea. Or a *biscuit*. (British for cookie.)

Two weeks later, we had a follow-up meeting, a lunch that lasted well into dinner. It was ostensibly a business meeting, although I hadn't yet read *Jersey Luck,* so we really had no business to discuss, but I sensed a vibe of mutual attraction. After he walked me home, I took the elevator upstairs, entered my loft, and my doorbell rang. It was Jonathan down below. Through the intercom he said there was something he'd forgotten to give me. I went back downstairs and saw him standing in the building's fluorescent-lit doorway, looking adorably awkward. I opened the lobby door and he kissed me. It was a nice kiss that caught me by surprise. But, unfortunately, the timing was off. I was not interested in getting romantically involved with anyone since I was about to leave for Miami to start prep on *Making Mr. Right*. I would be out of town for the next three months, so I pushed the thought of Jonathan to the back of my mind.

Two months passed and I was in the middle of filming when, out of the blue, I received a five-page handwritten letter. Somehow, Jonathan had tracked me down at the hotel in Miami. It was a chatty letter, and I wish I'd saved it, but I stashed it in a desk drawer along with all my other notes and scribblings and never found it again.

When I returned to New York, Jonathan called and invited me to dinner. This time, there was no pretending it was a business meeting. Instead, we spent the entire evening telling childhood anecdotes and revealing personal details about our lives. He told me he had gone through a complicated divorce and had two beautiful daughters, Hannah and Samantha, aged ten and eleven. Thankfully they were both Madonna fans, so when we eventually met, they thought I was cool. I thought they were cool, too.

On our next date we went to a Cuban restaurant in the West Village where Jonathan told me a story about how, as a young London lawyer, he had bailed Bob Marley out of Notting Hill police station. Apparently, Marley had been arrested on a cannabis charge and someone needed to get him released in the middle of the night. The job went to Jonathan, the only junior attorney willing to get out of bed at 2:00 a.m. Marley had refused to take off his Rasta hat for a mug shot, and tempers at the police station were beginning to flare.

DESK SERGEANT: What's your address?
MARLEY: Buckingham Palace.

Jonathan had used his charm to ease tensions and eventually convinced Marley to remove his hat, sign some autographs, and take a few photos with the arresting officers. Bail was set and Marley was freed. This would be a story that Jonathan would tell—and embellish—at dinner parties for decades to come.

After dinner (and a few too many mojitos), we wandered past a body-piercing shop on Greenwich Avenue, and, intrigued by a large sign in the window that read "Piercing with or Without Pain," we impulsively went inside. Jonathan left with a painful double-pierced right ear, only to realize the next morning that he had pierced the "gay ear." (Back then, wearing an earring in your right ear signaled you were gay.) His ear got infected, so after a few days he took out the earrings and let the holes close up. I think he had been trying to impress me with his non-lawyerlike spontaneity. In any case, I thought the gesture was sweet and oddly romantic, and many more dinners followed, but none involved impulsive tattoos.

Jonathan's WASP British background couldn't have been any more different from my Jewish suburban one. He had been sent away to a Dickensian boarding school with only a suitcase and a teddy bear at the age of eight. My childhood looked straight out of *The Brady Bunch*. His great-grandfather had been the silent movie star Eille Norwood, the first actor to play Sherlock Holmes on-screen and a personal acquaintance of Sir Arthur Conan Doyle. His grandfather attended Cambridge. My great-grandfather sold trinkets from a pushcart. My grandfather quit school at thirteen.

But we had this in common: We had both left other lives and come to New York to become someone different.

I thought: maybe he could be *The One*? Granted, I had once thought Yan was The One, then realized I had twisted myself up into a pretzel trying to fit into his life. But now I had a life of my own, one that I liked, and had met a man I could imagine sharing it with. Plus, he liked to cook (and not just pasta). The first meal he made for me was osso buco and polenta, sprinkled with gremolata (chopped parsley, lemon rind, and garlic). He won over my heart, my head, and my stomach, and I felt secure enough to let down my guard. Sometimes you just have to go with an instinct. Wishing and hoping. Jonathan wasn't easy, but I'd never been attracted to men who were.

Secret Agent Man

(Johnny Rivers)

QUESTION: What's the difference between an agent and a fly?
ANSWER: Flies get back to you.

For a while, I had the most powerful talent agent in New York. I shared this agent with a bunch of very famous actors, directors, and writers, although I sensed I might have been on the lower end of his callback list, which included Mike Nichols, Miloš Forman, Woody Allen, Meryl Streep, Paul Newman, and Nora Ephron, to name-drop a few.

Sam wore glasses (sometimes clear frames, sometimes tortoiseshell), rumpled khaki trousers, and loafers. His blue or yellow cashmere sweaters were expensive, but had food stains and holes. He looked more like a disheveled Ivy League professor, or a New York intellectual—a character sitting around the table at Elaine's in a 1980s Woody Allen movie. Not the puppet master he really was.

Sam Cohn had helped to create ICM Partners, one of the three big talent agencies that controlled the entertainment industry at that time. (William Morris and CAA being the other two.) He was a law unto himself. Everyone knows that actors, writers, and directors (referred to at an agency as *talent*) are insecure, vain, and neurotic. This is what made Sam Cohn different. He was as neurotic as his talent. Maybe even more so.

Sam ate paper. Literally. At lunch, he would sneak little balled-up bits of napkin or tissue into his mouth and chew. And he was powerful enough to get away with it.

But let me rewind to the fall of 1986.

I was at the Brill Building working with Andy Mondshein, editing *Making Mr. Right,* when I got a call from Sam Cohn's office suggesting we meet for lunch. After *Desperately Seeking Susan,* I had been thinking about leaving my small talent agency in LA and was flattered Sam wanted to meet me. He had a reserved corner table at the Russian Tea Room on 57th Street. This is where the New York power players and producers "in from the coast" met for lunch. Sam ate there practically every day and usually ordered the same meal. I think the waiter slipped whiskey into his coffee.

I was sitting across from Sam when I noticed him rolling little scraps of white tissue paper into balls and discreetly slipping them into his mouth. It's hard to remain straight-faced when you're in the middle of a serious conversation with a man who is eating his tissues. I tried not to smile, laugh, or comment because I wanted him to be my agent. Sam was smart, and despite his outwardly sweet (but sly) smile, he had a killer instinct. Plus, I was feeling anxious that *Making Mr. Right* would be a letdown after *Desperately Seeking Susan* and I'd need a powerful agent on my side moving forward. So, I ignored the paper wadded in his cheek and signed with ICM.

Sam was a maestro at putting together film packages bundled with his clients. After I signed with him, he sent me a script that two of his top clients had written. Nora Ephron and Alice Arlen, the Oscar-nominated team behind *Silkwood.* Twentieth Century Fox was interested in possibly producing the film, but wanted a director attached to supervise a rewrite. The script was called *Cookie.* The producer, Larry Mark, a former NYU film student, was now an executive at Fox in LA. Larry sent me a beautiful tin of gourmet chocolate chip cookies as an enticement. But what really sealed the deal was that I wanted to work with Nora.

Once again, timing would play an important part in my career. A few months later, *Making Mr. Right* was released with a whimper, but by then, I'd signed with ICM and was already in development on *Cookie.* Proof that I was succeeding in a man's world.

Like many of my male colleagues, I had failed upward!

Respect
(Aretha Franklin)

I remember my first meeting with Nora and Alice. We met at my eclectically furnished loft in Soho. They both lived uptown—Alice on the East Side, Nora on the West. They arrived wearing mink coats with their hair professionally blown out. They obviously hadn't dressed up for me; I think they were going to a formal event later that evening. But I didn't know anyone who wore real fur at that time and I couldn't help thinking about that Blackglama ad campaign of the 1970s. The controversial one that featured another celebrated author, Lillian Hellman, posing with her craggy "don't fuck with me" face, holding a cigarette and wrapped in a sleek, black mink. The slogan at the top of the ad posed the question: "What becomes a Legend most?" (Answer: Beautiful little animals raised on farms to be turned into expensive coats.)

Alice was bright, with a dry WASP reserve. Nora had not yet directed a movie, but her reputation as a sharp wit was already widely known. I remember being nervous before our first meeting, apprehensive that she might be intimidating and I'd come across dull by comparison. But Nora was different than I'd expected. She was smart, funny, opinionated—also down-to-earth and respectful of me, her director. And I learned a few interesting things from both of them:

—That you could walk into a creative meeting wearing a little black dress, with perfectly coiffed hair and manicured nails, and be taken seriously.

—That it was possible to age with grace and be respected in an industry that worshipped youth.

—That you could be a full-time creative film professional and also a mom.

I knew very few women in the movie industry who juggled work with a busy family life, so I paid particular attention to the way they did it. Nora had two young sons at the time, about nine and ten, and I remember script meetings at her big Upper West Side apartment in the Apthorp, when her boys casually wandered in and out of the room. Her older son, Jake, was an avid Madonna fan and occasionally joined in our conversation.

We sometimes sat around the kitchen as Nora cooked spaghetti carbonara (she loved bacon) while discussing story points, effortlessly doing both things simultaneously. Sometimes, she reheated leftovers of a dinner party from the night before. Food was often a part of the meeting. To this day, I still remember her advice about ordering white wine at a restaurant: "Don't order an expensive bottle, ask for the coldest."

It was no surprise when a few years later, with both her sons now almost teenagers, Nora would become a successful director, a job that involved a lot of multitasking. But I remember thinking, as I watched her putter around the kitchen, that this seemingly effortless blend of personal and professional life was something I might want, too.

* * *

There's a T-shirt someone once gave me as a joke. The kind of thing you could buy at a souvenir shop on the Jersey Shore boardwalk. It had a Roy Lichtenstein comic strip image of a tearful woman with a thought bubble that said: *I can't believe it. I forgot to have children!* Funny, maybe, but true for a generation of women who, like me, had spent the last decade focused on their careers.

I was now almost thirty-six and the thought crossed my mind, with more and more frequency, that one day I'd like to have a child, but film directing was a physically demanding, full-time job. The hours were crazy, unpredictable, and zapped 100 percent of my energy. Then I remembered a great quote from Betty Friedan: "You can have it all, just not all at the same time."

I didn't know any working women directors with young children. This was not a topic discussed at DGA meetings or Women in Film seminars. Women were still struggling to break into an industry that had excluded them for far too long. That was hard enough without adding more ammunition to be used against them: They want babies. They get pregnant. They have raging hormones. They will be torn between work and children.

After spending several months working on script revisions, Nora, Alice, and I flew to LA to meet with the executives at Twentieth Century Fox. The meeting had been arranged by our producer, Larry, a likable guy with powerful friends.

Gathered in the Fox conference room was an intimidating group of male power players. These were tough businessmen, not cinephiles. Chairman Barry Diller had created the ABC Movie of the Week. After stints at Paramount and Twentieth Century Fox, he would go on to launch the Fox

Network, USA Network, and QVC before becoming a billionaire media mogul. Sitting across from him was Leonard Goldberg, president of Fox and former head of programming for ABC. He had been the business partner of Aaron Spelling, producing enormously popular '70s kitschy TV shows like *Charlie's Angels, Starsky & Hutch,* and *Fantasy Island.* Then there was Scott Rudin, whom I'd met (and liked) years before. He was now a feared film producer prone to temper tantrums who allegedly threw hard objects (phones, a baked potato) at his assistants.

In the past, there have been times when I was aware of my small stature. I was short. Big deal. Sometimes I used it to my advantage. But being small is different than feeling invisible. And in this room of formidable men, that was how I felt. Invisible. I wondered if Nora and Alice felt the same. I knew after three minutes that Twentieth Century Fox was not going to make our movie. And it was true. They didn't. The script was put into turnaround, which meant it was now available to be picked up by another film company—assuming we could find a buyer—or it would disappear like hundreds of other projects in development did every year.

The company that came to the rescue was Lorimar Pictures, then run by a successful talent manager named Bernie Brillstein. Bernie had a white beard and a mischievous twinkle that made him look like Burl Ives playing Santa Claus. Bernie ran a very successful company, Brillstein-Gray Entertainment, that managed all the top *Saturday Night Live* comedians and produced many of the movies those comedians starred in.

Sam Cohn was friendly with Bernie and knew a deal could be made. Bernie was interested in making the movie if it could be produced for a *reasonable* budget and star one of his clients. This turned out to be Peter Falk.

That's the way things worked. It was sometimes more about the deal than about the movie. It's a "who you know" business, and personal relationships counted for a lot. For a cutthroat industry, there was honor among thieves. There's an industry saying: "Be nice to people on the way up, you'll probably meet them again on the way down." And it's true. This is the same reason many insiders never reveal their true opinions at industry film screenings. Hollywood is a tight-knit community, and you never know who you'll need to do business with the next time around.

I remember going to lunch with Sam when he scribbled a number on a scrap of paper. It said eighteen, meaning that if we could make *Cookie* for that budget, he could get the film financed. This was more than double the budget of anything I'd worked on in the past! Of course I could make the film for *only* $18 million! He said he'd start out by asking for $22 million. The folks at Lorimar would say no, then they would settle at $18 million, and everyone would think they won. Sam called the process "dancing the gavotte."[14]

Sam then discreetly slipped the piece of paper into his mouth and chewed.

---

14. The gavotte is an old French folk dance that involves kissing—and everyone in show business learns the art of ass-kissing as they climb up the ladder and stumble back down.

She Drives Me Crazy

(Fine Young Cannibals)

Peter Falk was a genuinely idiosyncratic person. You know how Columbo mumbles to himself, looking bemused while solving a crime on TV? Well, that was Peter in real life. At least that's how he came across during our first meeting in LA. Charming, scattered, disheveled. Then he caught me off guard with his sharp, sly intelligence.

Peter would be playing the lead role of a mobster named Dino Capisco—a fictional character modeled on the real John Gotti, known in the press as the Dapper Don.

Around this time, Gotti, reportedly the head of the Gambino crime family in New York, was making daily headlines, wearing $3,000 Brioni suits and hand-painted silk ties. After having orchestrated the murder of his former mob boss, Paul Castellano, outside Sparks Steak House on December 16, 1985, Gotti was treated by the press like a movie star. Suddenly, Mafia movies became even more popular. Every New York actor with dark Mediterranean looks found steady employment on a film set.

With Peter onboard, we opened a production office in New York and hired some key crew members. Ellen Chenoweth was brought on as the casting director. Our biggest challenge was to find a wonderful young actress to play the lead role of Cookie.

I often think about all the different versions of a movie that could have been if the casting had been different. Imagine *Gone with the Wind* if Bette

Davis, Lucille Ball, or Katharine Hepburn played Scarlett O' Hara, instead of Vivien Leigh. (All three had wanted the role.) Or if Harvey Keitel, instead of Dustin Hoffman, played Benjamin Braddock in *The Graduate*. (Apparently Keitel had auditioned for the part.)

I met with several young actresses who, in retrospect, would have been interesting choices for Cookie. I don't remember now why they weren't cast, but they weren't, and I can't rewrite that part of the story. One was Jodie Foster, who was at an in-between stage in her career. No longer a child star, she was super smart and had taken time off to go to college (Yale, no less), but hadn't yet transitioned to the award-winning adult roles that would follow. Another was Molly Ringwald. She was at the height of her John Hughes fame but looking for more adult material. She no longer felt pretty in pink.

Ellen Chenoweth auditioned nearly a hundred actresses, putting their performances on videotape. A few years ago, I came across an old VHS casting tape and, lo and behold, there was Julia Roberts! (Back then she was still known as Eric's younger sister.) Later that year she would star in *Mystic Pizza*, her breakout film. Two years later, *Pretty Woman*, and the rest is movie history.

I had recently seen a terrific British movie called *Wish You Were Here*, written and directed by David Leland, that starred a first-time actress named Emily Lloyd. Her performance blew me away (along with most of the film critics in England and America). She was raw, cheeky, and unpredictable. I decided that for the role of Cookie, we should try to find an American Emily Lloyd—and then I met the British one.

Emily had just turned seventeen and was getting a lot of media attention for an actress who had made only one small British film. Talent agents were vying for her attention with offers of signing gifts. One agency even offered to buy her a horse! I can only imagine the heady whirlwind this teenage girl from Islington suddenly found herself in.

When I met Emily, there was something raw and unspoiled about her. Although we all worried that her accent might be a problem and had some reservations that her Englishness was what had made her performance in *Wish You Were Here* so special. Could she be believable as the Italian American daughter of a mobster? But, in the end, Emily was hired and sent off to Brooklyn to live with an Italian American family for a few weeks to study the accent, the attitude, and eat a lot of pasta loaded with "Italian gravy." We also hired the best dialect coach in the business, Tim Monich, who would be on set every day with headphones to monitor her accent.

Before the start of filming, Emily, along with a chaperone, moved into the Mayfair Hotel, overlooking Central Park. At first her chaperone was a no-nonsense middle-aged woman hired to make sure Emily arrived on set on time and didn't run wild in the big city. Later, upon Emily's ardent request, this woman was replaced by someone younger and more fun. Emily enjoyed NYC nightlife. C'mon, what seventeen-year-old with thousands of dollars of petty cash stashed in her hotel drawer wouldn't?!

Cookie was a Mafia comedy. Peter Falk played a mobster hoping to go straight and reconnect with his longtime mistress, Lenore (Dianne Wiest), and their illegitimate daughter, Cookie, after being released from thirteen years in jail. During his absence, Cookie had grown from a baby into a rebellious teenage troublemaker. Dino also finds out that while he was in prison, he'd been swindled by his old partner in crime, Carmine (Michael Gazzo). Now that Dino is out, he wants what he's owed so he can walk away and live the rest of his days in peace with his mistress and daughter.

Pressured by Lenore, Dino reluctantly hires Cookie as his personal limo driver to keep her busy and out of trouble. Both father and daughter are stubborn and constantly banging heads. (*"I knew a guy in prison named Billy Blue Nose who put a hit on his own kid!"* Dino threatens Cookie.) Being Dino's driver, Cookie is now in a position to eavesdrop on mob business and learns that her father is in danger of getting offed by Carmine. She concocts a plot to save his life, retrieve his stolen money, and keep her family together, thus proving that she's a pretty smart cookie.

During the course of the movie, Cookie goes from being a bratty teen to a wannabe Mafia Princess to a genuine Mafia Queen, earning her father's love and respect along the way. I related personally to the theme of a reprobate daughter trying to prove her worth to her tough-guy father. I'd knocked heads with my own tough dad many times as a teenager.

* * *

I liked bending traditional movie genres. *Desperately Seeking Susan* put a spin on a screwball comedy. *Making Mr. Right* was a twisted sci-fi movie. So the idea of telling a Mafia story from a female point of view was exciting. What made me nervous were the action sequences. The script had car chases, explosions, gun fights, lots of locations, lots of extras, and plenty of macho posturing. I would be working outside my comfort zone, but that would be the challenge.

Mob movies were back in style and there were a group of New York Italian American actors who got cast regularly to play wiseguys in films. One of them was a former felon named Tony Sirico, who'd been arrested for extortion, assault, and robbery and had spent time in Sing Sing. He would hang around our set schmoozing with the stars and eventually worked his way into the background of a few scenes. Finally, he was given a small speaking role even though technically only Screen Actors Guild members are allowed speaking parts, but I think everyone was afraid to ask him to leave the set. Personally, I liked Tony. So did the camera. He had a distinctive look, two wings of white hair on the sides of his head, set against his dark, slicked-back coif. A few years later, he would become a successful TV actor, and if you watched *The Sopranos,* you'd know him as Paulie Walnuts.

My favorite scenes involved Dino's relationships with the women in his life: his smarty-pants daughter, Cookie; his foul-mouthed wife, Bunny (who ran a pet shop selling stolen dogs), brazenly played by Brenda Vaccaro; and his sweet and sly mistress, Lenore. Nora and Alice were at their best when writing sharp, colorful dialogue for strong female characters. Why Nora chose to write a Mafia comedy might be in part explained by her recent marriage to Nicholas Pileggi, author of the enormously successful book *Goodfellas,* soon to become an enormously successful Scorsese movie.

The women of *Cookie*: Bottom row (from left to right): Alice Arlen, Emily Lloyd,
Brenda Vaccaro. Top row: me, Dianne Wiest, Emily Wiest, Nora Ephron.

In the 1970s and '80s there were three directors who worked regularly
in New York: Woody Allen, Martin Scorsese, and Sidney Lumet. Each had
their own loyal crew and production team. At the time, Lumet was the
most prolific, known for his fast and efficient way of working, blocking out
his shots and camera moves well in advance, on a rehearsal stage. He often
did only two or three takes, then moved on to the next setup. There was no
wasted time with Sidney.

On *Desperately Seeking Susan,* I'd worked with cinematographer Ed Lachman and Woody's more relaxed crew. But on *Cookie,* I had Lumet's team—
guys with an "I've seen it all before" attitude (and they probably had!). I was
also working with a new cinematographer, an Englishman named Oliver Stapleton. Between the mobster characters (real and fictional) and the macho
Lumet crew, there was a lot of testosterone on set. I'm sure for several of the
crew members, I was their first woman director, and most of the guys were

respectful. But there's often an asshole in every group. This particular guy was a troublemaker with a secure union job and a chip on his shoulder. I could feel waves of aggravation radiating from him as he grumbled incessantly under his breath. Being the director, I could have had him replaced, but I knew the other crew members would be unhappy because despite being a cantankerous a-hole, he was good at his job, having done it for twenty years. So, I put on blinders, bit my tongue, and let his snarky attitude roll off my back. Nothing pisses an instigator off more than being ignored.

*　*　*

Peter Falk had a glass eye due to a childhood illness, so we needed to be mindful when filming him. This involved designing the shots so as not to have the camera lens pointed for too long at the side of his face featuring his lifeless eye. Peter was also a method actor who could get lost in a role. I'd often spot him wandering around the set alone, mumbling to himself, practicing his lines and punctuating them with animated hand gestures.

One afternoon, during the rehearsal of a heated father-daughter argument, Peter grabbed Emily by the head and slapped her across the face. This was not in the script. It was an improvisation that went too far. Emily looked stunned, then . . . slapped Peter back. Hard. The scene had somehow heated up and slipped beyond an ordinary acting rehearsal. I was startled (so was everyone else on set) and stepped in to stop the rehearsal. Understandably, Emily was shaken and didn't want to continue filming. I could see that Peter was upset, too. He knew his behavior had unintentionally crossed a line. His method acting had gone too far. I tried to calm everyone down and we wrapped for the day, hoping that tensions would cool by the morning. And they did, after threatening calls were made to the producer by Emily's agent.

The next day Peter sent a gift to Emily's trailer. It was a large bouquet of mylar helium balloons with a sweet note. An apology, but perhaps also a symbolic gesture intended to remind Emily that she was still a kid and kids are supposed to respect their elders. Emily would have preferred an adult bouquet of roses, or maybe a bottle of perfume, but after that incident they got along better.

Under the Boardwalk
(The Drifters)

Midway through the shoot, we went to Atlantic City to film some scenes that took place on the boardwalk. That's when I met Jerry Lewis.

I'd watched many Jerry Lewis comedies as a kid: *The Nutty Professor, The Patsy, The Bellboy.* He was a master of physical comedy, a director much loved by the French, and the inventor of the video assist. This was the device that connected the movie camera to a small video monitor several feet away, enabling the director, producers, script supervisor, agents, studio executives, and assorted guests to squeeze around a tiny video screen to watch the shot being filmed and offer their (mostly unwanted) opinions.

By the time I was a teenager, Lewis was hosting Muscular Dystrophy Association telethons that raised millions of dollars for people living with this disease. Starting in the midsixties, these telethons were the TV event of the Labor Day weekend. A quasi variety show that went on nonstop for twenty-one hours. It signaled the end of summer and back to school. Everyone took bets on how many hours into the show it would be before Jerry started to sweat and removed his tie, or took off his jacket, or unbuttoned his shirt.

Contemporary history would not be kind to Jerry's reputation as a humanitarian or a comic genius. Allegations of sexual assault and harassment would be made public by some of his female co-stars, actresses now in their eighties who had kept their mouths shut for decades for fear of Hollywood's retribution and loss of employment. Dirty laundry would be aired only after

Jerry passed away in 2017. But back in 1988, when I heard that the legendary Jerry Lewis was willing to play a small but pivotal role in *Cookie,* I was excited. He had recently given a terrific performance in the Scorsese film *The King of Comedy.*

I met Jerry on the morning of his first day on set. He was in his camper with his wife and two yappy little dogs. He greeted me warmly, with a white towel around his neck. He was in the middle of putting on his own makeup, having refused the services of the film's professional makeup artist. I had heard that Lewis was a control freak, so I guess that's why he wanted to put on his own makeup. He'd even brought his personal wardrobe to wear in the film. But what surprised me most was that his face was a deep shade of orange.

The character Jerry was playing was a shifty Atlantic City real estate mogul with a year-round suntan. (Sound familiar?) But his face was very, *very* orange, covered with a thick coat of Max Factor pancake. It was the kind of makeup they used back in the 1950s on Hollywood soundstages with heavy lighting, very different from the more naturalistic makeup actors used today. Frankly, it looked weird, and I didn't know what to say. I had just met this legendary star and felt uncomfortable asking him to wash his face. So, I took the cowardly approach. I said nothing, crossed my fingers, and hoped for the best. I would find out the results the next day when we watched the dailies.

If this photo was in color, you'd see Jerry's orange face.

* * *

I was excited to be filming in Atlantic City. It was no accident that this was the town where we first see Madonna/Susan in *Desperately Seeking Susan*. Atlantic City held special personal significance for me. A place I associate with my innocent (and not-so-innocent) childhood summers.

In the 1920s and '30s, the Seidelman family had a pharmacy in West Philadelphia, which gave them access to medicinal alcohol. During Prohibition, that alcohol was transported to Atlantic City to be turned into booze by my great-uncle Mike in a false-bottomed car driven by my teenage grandmother Nanny S. My aunt Elaine had grown up there in the 1940s and went to Atlantic City High. Her parents ran an old boardinghouse for "entertainers" (a euphemism for showgirls, barmaids, and escorts). As a child, my mother had spent summers fishing in the bay for fluke with her father. In the 1950s, my parents frequented Skinny D'Amato's 500 Club, where they'd seen Jerry Lewis performing with Dean Martin and Sammy Davis Jr.

I also had fond memories of Atlantic City in the 1960s, when it was a family-friendly resort town popular with Philadelphians. Every summer, we spent one week at the Hotel Ambassador on the boardwalk, where my father took the American Plan (breakfast and dinner included). As a kid, I'd seen a horse dive into a tub of water off the high diving board on the Steel Pier and gotten a stomachache eating an entire box of James Salt Water Taffy. As a teenager, I'd spent hours on the beach in the midday sun, slathered with baby oil (a decision I'd come to regret once I turned forty). The weekend after Labor Day, we'd join the cheering crowds lining the boardwalk to watch the Miss America pageant parade and hope to catch a glimpse of its famous host, Bert Parks. That is, until the pageant was disrupted by feminist protesters in 1968 carrying signs that read: *Welcome to the Miss America Cattle Auction.*[15]

---

15. Fun facts: The first and only Jewish Miss America, Bess Myerson, was crowned in 1945, right after the end of World War II. She was told to change her name because it sounded too Jewish. She didn't. The first Black Miss America, Cheryl Browne, Miss Iowa, was chosen in 1971. In 1994, Heather Whitestone, Miss Alabama, was the first Miss America with a disability (deafness). It wasn't until 1985 that contestants' body measurements were no longer listed in the event's program guide.

By the end of the '60s, Atlantic City was falling apart. There was massive unemployment, the hotels were half empty, and the boardwalk had become shabby. The real estate was now dirt cheap, so by the mid-seventies, investors and developers like Donald Trump started to buy up the dilapidated oceanfront properties at rock-bottom prices with a plan to turn the city into a mini-Vegas. Within a few years, many of the grand 1920s brick and stone hotels were knocked down and replaced with cheaply built concrete and tinted-glass casinos like the Taj Mahal, Sands, and Resorts International. Then came the busloads of geriatric gamblers. Smokers with oxygen tanks, wheelchairs, and walkers clamoring for a spot at the slot machines. Anyone who could afford a five-dollar round-trip bus ticket (which included a free drink voucher) made their way to AC. By 2015, many of those casinos would go bankrupt. Gambling was now available online and several of the big hotels were boarded up, home only to rats. But Atlantic City is a survivor, and the city is constantly in the process of reinventing itself.

* * *

Jerry turned out to be pleasant to work with and, around me, he was always a gentleman. He had asked for a cast and crew list on the day he arrived and memorized the names of every single crew member on set: "Hi, Dave," he'd call out to the dolly grip. "How's it goin', TJ?" to the boom operator. But unfortunately, he was unable to memorize his dialogue with the same accuracy, and whenever he fluffed a line, he would turn it into a comedy routine, mixing in silly made-up words, Yiddishisms, and the vocal sound effects he was famous for, making everyone laugh. He finally got through his scenes with the help of cue cards held up alongside the camera.

And about the orange makeup . . . well, Jerry was right. The Max Factor pancake looked fine on camera and worked perfectly for the sketchy sun-tanned real estate developer he was playing. I was glad I'd kept my mouth shut.

* * *

Andy Mondshein was back onboard as the editor. This was the third film we'd worked on together, and post-production went smoothly. But there are missed opportunities on every film production.

Because of Jonathan's connection to the music industry, he was hired to put together the movie's soundtrack album. One day he brought in a song that a music manager had slipped him in advance of its commercial release. Jonathan thought it would make a strong opening title track and was able to negotiate a cheap licensing fee, since the song "She Drives Me Crazy" by Fine Young Cannibals was still unknown. I thought it would be a great way to introduce the character of Cookie because she was a limo driver who drove everyone crazy. Unfortunately, others involved in this discussion didn't agree. They thought the song would never be a hit, that it wasn't catchy and lacked a strong musical hook. I was outvoted and the song never made it into the film. A few months later "She Drives Me Crazy" was released, soared to the top of the Billboard charts, and has since been voted one of the best fifty songs of the 1980s.

I think the Oscar-winning screenwriter William Goldman was right when he said: "Nobody knows anything." Maybe success really does boil down to luck and timing. But timing doesn't always work in your favor.

Cookie had been financed by Lorimar, but in the never-ending game of Hollywood musical chairs, Lorimar had recently been sold to Warner Brothers, so when the film was ready for release, it no longer had the support of its original production company. It was an orphan and its release was delayed by a full year. By the time the movie finally came out, there were three other Mafia comedies that covered similar territory, and *Cookie* no longer tasted quite so fresh. Despite strong performances by Falk and the lead actresses, the film didn't stand out in this now-crowded marketplace.

I guess that's just the way the cookie crumbled.

LIGHTS! CAMERA! COOKIE!
Filmmaker Susan Seidelman Brings Home The Bakin'
By Lisa Schwarzbaum

Cover of the *New York Daily News*. Unfortunately, the bakin' was burnt.
(Photo © Deborah Feingold)

Meanwhile, Nora had moved on to her next project, having started work on the script of *When Harry Met Sally* while we were still in pre-production. Little did she know that movie would change her life and launch her career as a writer-director after its huge box office success.

I had moved on, too. I'd already begun pre-production on my next film, *She-Devil*. Meryl Streep had agreed to play the lead role.

* * *

I lost touch with Emily shortly after *Cookie* was released. Years later, I began to hear rumors that Emily had mental health problems and had lost several prominent film roles as a result. Perhaps it was too much, too soon. Or maybe there were some deeper psychological, or biochemical, factors involved. It was sad to read the disturbing news stories because I remember Emily's vivacious teenage personality with great affection.

Two decades later, Peter would be diagnosed with Alzheimer's, and in 2009 there would be a legal battle over his care. Sadly, he no longer remembered playing Columbo.

You're the Devil in Disguise

(Elvis Presley)

I was waiting in the lobby of a posh hotel on the Upper East Side for my meeting with Meryl Streep. Maybe it was the St. Regis? Or it could have been the Carlyle or the Mark. I don't remember. But it was understated and elegant, like Meryl.

Meryl was finishing up a meeting with another director, who had also come to pitch her a project. I watched as the other director, Lawrence Kasdan, got off the elevator and walked through the lobby. I knew who he was because I liked his films *Body Heat* and *The Big Chill*. Now it was my turn.

At thirty-nine, Streep was already one of the world's most celebrated actors. Thus far, she'd gravitated to serious dramatic roles, often involving characters with complicated foreign accents. She'd never done a comedy film before, but as a student at the Yale School of Drama, she'd performed in some of Chris Durang's outrageous plays and was very funny. And isn't comedy really tragedy seen through a fun house mirror?

Sam Cohn, who was both of our agents at the time, had set up the meeting at my request.

I was nervous as I headed up to Meryl's hotel suite, not just because it was *the* Meryl Streep, but because I hated pitching projects. "Pitching" was like public speaking mixed with self-promotion and triggered the same anxiety I'd felt when I was forced to read aloud in Mrs. Kirschbaum's fourth-grade reading group. But I knew how important first impressions were and wanted to make a good one. I was passionate about the film's story and hoped my enthusiasm would shine through.

I wish I could tell you more about that first meeting, but what I remember most is that we talked in the living room of her tastefully appointed suite for about an hour. She wore little makeup and was very down to earth. I hadn't expected that. She was also funny, and that put me at ease. It turned out that Roy Helland, Meryl's personal hair and makeup artist, was familiar with the novel *The Life and Loves of a She-Devil,* written by British author Fay Weldon. It had been made into a four-part BBC drama in 1986. Perhaps having Roy's seal of approval on the source material worked in my favor.

Me and Fay Weldon, 1989. Fay died on January 4, 2023, at age ninety-one.
(Courtesy of MGM Media Licensing, photograph by John Clifford)

The *She-Devil* that I envisioned was a dark comedy about an ungainly and unappreciated homemaker who vows revenge on her husband after he dumps her for a rich and glamorous romance novelist. The ultimate revenge fantasy of every wronged woman. The screenplay, by Barry Strugatz and Mark R. Burns (the writing team behind *Married to the Mob*), would be more comedic in tone than the novel, but with a similar satiric edge.

I'd come to ask Meryl to play Mary Fisher, the hyperfeminine romance novelist. This was a very different character than Streep had ever played before and that's what made the idea exciting. I thought she could bring her intelligence, impeccable timing, and some wicked humor to the role, which was exactly what was needed.

Mary Fisher was the epitome of shallow pretentiousness. She lived in an enormous pink mansion by the sea, decorated in pastel-colored silks and satin. It was a fantasy world of her own creation that she used as source material for the bodice-ripping romance novels she wrote, read by millions of women in need of escape from their own dreary lives.

Mary dressed in pink, wore big hats, and spoke with an affected upper-crust accent. She had a pampered poodle and a hunky Latino butler who wandered around her mansion bare-chested. She spent her days in the estate's beautiful garden, typing steamy romance novels on her pink keyboard, without ever ruining her perfect manicure. She paid to keep her elderly mother tranquilized and locked away in an expensive nursing home so the old bat wouldn't embarrass her.

On the surface (and this is a comedy about surfaces and what's hidden beneath), Mary seemed to be living a *fantabulous* fairytale life. That is, until she stole Ruth Patchett's husband.

Ruth's husband, Bob, was Mary Fisher's accountant. When Bob dumps Ruth to move into Mary's mansion, Ruth decides to get revenge. On the night that Bob storms out of their suburban house, he bitterly calls Ruth a "she-devil," and so that is what she becomes. She makes a list of all Bob's assets: 1) his home, 2) his family, 3) his career, and 4) his freedom—and systematically sets out to destroy each one. But Ruth is not diminished by her wrath; she's rejuvenated by it, and she embarks on a mission to empower other downtrodden women along the way, unraveling Mary's superficial lifestyle in the process. In the end, both women end up someplace better than where they started.

This was also a film about contemporary culture's obsession with beauty, fame, and glamour. Ruth and Mary are both victims of the beauty myth. Ruth is powerless because she is ungainly and unattractive by conventional standards. Mary is losing her power because she is getting older and becoming desperate. The lines on her face have begun to show, her eyelids are starting to droop. And once Bob and his kids move into her mansion, she has the added burden of being a surrogate mother and caretaker—a job that all women know takes time, zaps energy, and doesn't pay well.

I hoped Meryl would like the script's subversive themes, because underneath all the pink frivolity, there was a serious feminist message.

I left the hotel feeling slightly more confident than when I'd arrived.

* * *

I waited three weeks to hear back from my agent, jumping every time the phone rang, nervous that Meryl had chosen the other project. Then I got a call from Sam telling me Meryl had agreed to sign on. (CUE SFX: Huge sigh of relief.) I later found out that after first reading the script, Meryl had considered playing the role of the housewife, Ruth, then decided that the narcissistic Mary Fisher would be more fun. It turned out that *She-Devil* would be the first in a long line of comedic roles that Streep would play in movies like *Death Becomes Her, Defending Your Life, The Devil Wears Prada,* and *Mamma Mia!*

* * *

I was not just directing the movie but also co-producing it with Jonathan. It would be the first time we worked together as producers, and I valued his opinion and trusted our personal relationship wouldn't get in the way of our professional one. It turned out we worked well together. Sometimes getting along even better on set than at home.

Finding the right actress for Ruth Patchett wasn't easy. It was important that Ruth was both physically and emotionally the opposite of ultra-feminine Mary. Plus, we needed someone who could convincingly play a downtrodden housewife, then transform herself into a strong, vengeful she-devil.

I don't remember who first mentioned Roseanne Barr. I think it was Ellen Chenoweth, our casting director. The *Roseanne* TV show was finishing its first season and had become an enormous surprise hit. The former stand-up comedian and self-proclaimed domestic goddess became a household name.

I met Roseanne in a suite at the Four Seasons Hotel in LA, where Jonathan and I were staying courtesy of Orion. Despite never having acted in a movie before, she seemed unintimidated by the idea of co-starring alongside one of the world's most accoladed actresses. I remember she got down on her knees and told me how much she wanted the part. She said she would fuck me to get it. I assumed she was kidding. At least I hoped so. I told her that wouldn't be necessary and we both laughed.[16]

I liked Roseanne's lack of pretense. She had an authenticity that felt right for the role. She had been a midwestern housewife doing stand-up gigs in local comedy clubs in Denver who had made it into the big time in the very cutthroat, very macho TV sitcom business. I admired people who were self-made. Writer Barbara Ehrenreich said it best when she called Roseanne a working-class spokesperson representing "the hopeless underclass of the female sex: polyester-clad, overweight occupants of the slow track; fast-food waitresses, factory workers, housewives, members of the invisible pink-collar army; the despised, the jilted, the underpaid."

Roseanne was an underdog who gave hope to all the women who couldn't see a way out of their circumstances. And, needless to say, the most acclaimed movie actress in America starring opposite the most popular TV housewife seemed like a perfect match of opposites. In a reversal of expectations, Roseanne, the comedian, would play the dramatic role and Meryl, the serious thespian, would be funny.

To round out the cast, we hired Ed Begley Jr. as Bob, the philandering husband of Ruth and the accountant-turned-lover of Mary Fisher.[17] Ed had a wry, self-deprecating sense of humor and the good looks of an unconventional Ken doll with his tall, athletic build and swoopy blond hair. He would play the comedic foil.

---

16. I know this story sounds similar to the one Barbara Boyle told about meeting Madonna. Clearly there was a "we all know how the casting couch works" joke going around town, highlighting what every actress already knew to be true.

17. We had originally considered actor Charles Grodin for this role, but his agent demanded far too much money and blew the deal. This is not uncommon in the film business.

Burning Down the House
(Talking Heads)

I was working again with production designer Santo Loquasto, and, as in *Desperately Seeking Susan,* we wanted to create two visually distinct worlds— one for each main character. Ruth Patchett's suburban home was messy, chaotic, filled with children and pets, and decorated in a hodgepodge of patterns (stripes, plaids, prints); wood-grain paneling; brown, orange, and mustard yellow earth tones.

Mary Fisher's world was pink—lipstick pink, ballet slipper pink, Barbie Dreamhouse pink. The color most associated with femininity.

It was scripted that Mary lived in a pink mansion by the sea. But where would we ever find a pink mansion? Santo went out location scouting and lo and behold, there in Port Jefferson, overlooking the Long Island Sound, was the mansion we'd been dreaming of. Not only was it huge and pink, it was perched on a cliff overlooking the water. It had wrought iron and gold entrance gates, a long sweeping driveway, a marble foyer with a circular staircase, plus an indoor swimming pool. And it was owned by a countess. A real Hungarian countess, who was thrilled to have Meryl Streep filming in her home.

* * *

Samuel Goldwyn, the legendary movie producer, once said: "Pictures are for entertainment. If I wanted to send a message, I'd use Western Union." But I believed you could send a message on film. I wanted to make people laugh, then make them think.

The opening scene of *She-Devil* could be the thesis statement for the entire film. Imagine this:

A long tracking shot that moves dreamlike along the cosmetics counter at Bloomingdale's, as hypnotic harmonies play in the background. The camera glides past the shimmering surfaces of perfume bottles, atomizers, expensive face creams, powders, mascaras, lipsticks—objects of glamour intended to make women look and feel beautiful. The camera now rises to reveal the faces of the gorgeous women studying their loveliness reflected in mirrors, reflected in each other . . . until the camera arrives at RUTH PATCHETT. A woman who will never live up to these culturally imposed standards, but is a prisoner to them.

(Courtesy of MGM Media Licensing)

That is, until the day Ruth frees herself by burning down her house.

(Courtesy of MGM Media Licensing)

Roseanne, who had never worked on a film set before, got the hang of things quickly, even though shooting a feature film was very different from taping a half-hour sitcom in front of a live audience. She was willing to go beyond her comfort zone and I admired that. I sensed some part of her still couldn't believe she was starring in a movie opposite Meryl Streep.

I didn't get to know Meryl very well off set. She was extremely professional, incredibly prepared, and very private. When Meryl wasn't filming, she'd spend time in her trailer with Roy, her personal hair and makeup artist. He was a fiercely loyal confidant who had worked with Streep since 1975 and would work with her for another forty years.

On the other hand, Roseanne liked to hang out on set. She enjoyed a live audience and had little hesitation sharing the intimate details of her personal life with everyone, whether it was about her morning bathroom habits, or her sexual escapades of the night before with her new beau, Tom Arnold—a (then) unknown comedian she would marry the following year and divorce four years later. It was clear that Roseanne operated without a filter. Over the years, her outspokenness would be both a blessing (the source of her best comedy material) and also a curse, resulting in her abrupt fall from grace after a racist late-night tweet in 2018 about Obama advisor Valerie Jarrett.

It was a different experience working with each actress. Roseanne thought like a comedian in terms of jokes and punch lines, but she was now playing a dramatic role. Ruth Patchett was a victim of emotional abuse. Her character was not funny. Over the course of the story, she would need to evolve from a powerless underdog to a powerful manipulator. My job was to make sure there was a believable emotional arc and that Roseanne's performance felt honest. And I believe it did.

From left to right: Linda Hunt, Meryl, Sylvia Miles, Roseanne, and me
(*Courtesy of MGM Media Licensing, photo by John Clifford*)

* * *

You don't really "direct" Meryl Streep. She knows exactly where her performance needs to go in every scene, so I found myself directing *around* Meryl, making sure all the other characters and elements needed to support her performance were working. I'd make suggestions to dial her performance up a notch, or tune it back down. But mostly, I focused on the blocking and kept track of the storyline and its various twists and turns since (as is often the case) we were shooting the film totally out of sequence.

There were a few times while watching Streep's performance that I'd break into uncontrollable giggles. It was an involuntary reaction, like hiccups, and the more I tried to repress it, the more the laughter had to erupt. If we were in the middle of filming, I tried desperately to hold it in so as not to ruin the take, but my shoulders would shake and tears would stream down my cheeks. Maybe it was nervous energy, or perhaps it was the ghost of that suburban teenage tramp, watching from another time zone and laughing as she witnessed her adult self directing a scene with Meryl Streep writhing around on pink satin sheets and jiggling her booty.

I think Meryl was having fun, too. I saw it on her face and felt it in her no-holds-barred performance.

Watching playback with screenwriters Barry Strugatz and Mark R. Burns
(*Courtesy of MGM Media Licensing, photo by John Clifford*)

* * *

After the filming ended, I returned to the Brill Building to work with a new editor, Craig McKay, who had edited *Something Wild* and *Married to the Mob* and would go on to edit *The Silence of the Lambs.*

Meryl was off to LA to star in *Postcards from the Edge,* a movie based on Carrie Fisher's semiautobiographical book, directed by Mike Nichols.

And, to my surprise, I was off to have a baby.

Oops! . . . I Did It Again

(Britney Spears)

There's something I neglected to mention.

While I was filming *She-Devil,* I'd missed my period. I was also gaining weight, which should have been a clue, but I just racked that up to binging on Pringles and Oreos at the craft service table.

In the past, my menstrual cycle had sometimes been irregular during production. This was nothing to be alarmed about, but clearly something I needed to check out. I was looking for a new gynecologist and figured that since Meryl was so smart, she'd know the best doctors in town, so I asked her for a recommendation. She gave me the name of a doctor, but it turned out it wasn't her doctor—it was a referral from one of her New York theater friends.

I went to see the doctor in his cramped office on the ground floor of a modest brownstone in Yorkville. He did an exam, took a test, and said I was not pregnant. He told me it was most likely a hormonal imbalance given my hectic schedule and the stress of my job. But I didn't feel particularly stressed and I wasn't nauseous or sick. Since I knew so few women directors, I had no one to ask about the effects of a crazy production schedule on your hormonal system. With no stories to compare and no free time, I trusted the doctor's diagnosis. After all, he was a gynecologist and knew about these things. I figured my hormones would adjust once shooting was over.

Here's the thing about film production—it's like a roller-coaster ride.

Once it starts, it's impossible to get off until the ride is over. In between, there's no time to think about anything other than solving the day-to-day problems that constantly arise, getting through the day's shooting schedule, and dropping off into a comatose sleep at night.

When production ended three months later, I finally had the chance to catch up on much-needed rest while I waited for Craig to finish the first rough assembly of the film before joining him in the editing room.

One night, while lying in bed, I felt a sharp pain in my lower abdomen. Having ruled out pregnancy early on, I was worried I had some sort of internal blockage. Something was clearly wrong that could no longer be ignored, so I went to the gynecologist the next day.

As I lay splayed out, feet in stirrups, I saw the doctor's face backlit in a halo of fluorescent light. He looked shocked as he broke the news. I was entering my fifth month.

I was in shock, too. So was Jonathan.

Okay, I know what you're thinking . . . and I know this sounds crazy! I, too, have scoffed at those stories about a teenage girl who didn't know she was pregnant, then had a baby in the girls' lavatory during her senior prom. How could she not have known? How could I, a well-educated woman with an MFA from NYU who had just helmed a $20 million motion picture, not realize I was pregnant until my fifth month?!

Here's the truth. I honestly didn't. When I analyze this, I come up with five possible scenarios:

1. I was so myopically focused on my work that my head was totally out of touch with my body.
2. I had blind faith in my doctor because he had a medical degree and I didn't. He said I wasn't pregnant, so I wasn't.
3. I was in total denial, given the unusual timing.
4. I subconsciously really wanted a baby.
5. None of the above. I'm just a numbskull. Or, maybe there was some karmic thing going on that was beyond my control.

Had I been given a correct diagnosis four months earlier, I don't know what decision I might have made.

234 | SUSAN SEIDELMAN

I'd never been one to *goo goo* or *gah gah* over babies. I thought babies were cute but demanding little humans who needed to be fed, washed, and coddled until they were old enough to become interesting mini-people. Most of my similarly aged relatives already had children. Most of my NY friends did not.

I was scared and thrilled. Scared because I'd done things a pregnant woman shouldn't do: drank, smoked, taken medication. But so had my mother and all my aunts during their pregnancies in the 1950s, and my siblings and cousins were all relatively normal. Thrilled that at thirty-seven I was having a baby.

In my imagination, the baby was a little girl, and I daydreamed about all the mommy-and-me things we would do together. I was determined to be a nonjudgmental, loving, and encouraging mother. I would see that my daughter had the confidence to be whoever she wanted to be. She would grow up a genuine "city girl," taking advantage of all the opportunities New York City had to offer.

A few weeks later I had another sonogram. The baby had shifted position. It was a boy.

STOP! PAUSE! REWIND!

The mommy-and-me movie that had been playing in my head now zips back to the beginning and I recast it with a boy. It's a different movie, but a good one, and I was over the moon. So was Jonathan. He had two lovely daughters, Sammy and Hannah, from his earlier marriage and I think he was secretly hoping for a son.

A name sticks with you for your entire life, becomes part of your identity. And because you never know the person your child will turn out to be, we wanted to choose a name with some flexibility. We decided to call him Oscar, not just because we were in the movie business (okay, that had some ironic appeal), but because Oscar was a family name. My father's favorite uncle was Uncle Ockie, brother of beautiful Uttie and whiskered Tootie. Plus, the name Oscar can sound artistic and sophisticated, as in Oscar Hammerstein and Oscar Wilde. Or funky and rock 'n' roll, like Ozzy Osbourne. We didn't realize it could also trigger third-grade embarrassment, as in Oscar the Grouch.

Changes
(David Bowie)

My belly was getting bigger, and the editing of *She-Devil* was going well. Howard Shore had composed a terrific orchestral score. Lush, with a hint of dark humor. At the same time, we were working on all the other post-production tasks: creating the opening title sequence, putting in special effects, music, and a voice-over narration. I was also making up for lost time. Taking nutritional supplements, going to regular doctor's appointments, reading the baby classics: Dr. Spock and *What to Expect When You're Expecting* (skipping over the chapters for months one through five) and signing up for Lamaze class.

Orion had organized a publicity photo shoot for Meryl and Roseanne with the famous fashion photographer Patrick Demarchelier. It was fascinating to watch him work; he moved around his studio effortlessly, like a cat. Artists make it look so easy. Occasionally he would whisper a direction to his assistant to move a light this way or that. He knew exactly when to click the shutter and did very few setups. At the end of the shoot, Demarchelier had some film left in his camera and asked Jonathan and me to step into his lighting. By now, I was very pregnant, and he positioned me with Jonathan sitting slightly in front, blocking my big belly. He made a small hand gesture to his assistant to tweak a light, said something that made us both smile, and clicked. The whole thing took less than a minute.

(Photo by Patrick Demarchelier)

About a month before the film's scheduled release, Jonathan had a meeting with Orion's marketing and distribution teams. He had heard that Twentieth Century Fox had a domestic revenge comedy scheduled for release on the exact same day as *She-Devil.* He didn't think it was a good idea to release two revenge comedies on the same weekend, knowing how important opening weekend box office results were. The other film was *The War of the Roses,* directed by Danny DeVito and starring Michael Douglas and Kathleen Turner. A proven comedy trio with two big hits already behind them.

Orion's distribution team didn't think *Roses* would be a threat. Plus, they had already booked the film into over two thousand theaters for opening weekend. Getting screens was competitive and Orion didn't want to lose any bookings. Advertising and marketing campaigns were already underway. Trailers had been sent out to theaters. With so many moving parts, it was hard to change gears now. But still, I wished those films hadn't been released on the exact same day and *She-Devil*'s poster had been less cheesy.

Original movie poster   Video cover

For the video release, the studio's marketing department added in Ed Begley Jr. with
Meryl and Roseanne cat-fighting over him. Go figure? Unfortunately, neither poster
reflected the tone or intention of the film. (*Courtesy of MGM Media Licensing*)

*　*　*

She-Devil had its premiere at Radio City Music Hall in early December,
followed by an after-party at the Museum of the Moving Image. I was three
weeks away from my due date, so I shuffled around all evening, sipping
sparkling water, wearing an oversized '80s Versace men's shirt in lieu of a
maternity dress.

A few days later, I was invited to a Muse Award luncheon hosted by New
York Women in Film & Television. The event was held in a hotel ballroom
in midtown Manhattan. I was to receive an award along with two other
muses. As I sat on the dais, waiting for Glenn Close to finish her acceptance
speech, I glanced around the room, packed with women of various ages.
Some were film professionals, some were women trying to break into the
industry, others NYWIFT guests and supporters.

When it was my turn, I waddled over to the podium, looked out at the
audience, and broke into a gigantic grin. I'd never seen so many women-in-
film sitting in one place, and that made me genuinely happy. I hoped there

were some young aspiring film directors in the crowd. I wanted them to see that *this* was what a movie director looked like. At four feet, eleven and a half inches with a big pregnant belly and stretchy black leggings, I presented a very different picture than the role models I'd grown up with: macho men in suits or hippie guys with baseball caps and beards. A sign that times were clearly changing.

That night, Jonathan and I went to our country house in western New Jersey. We figured it was our last safe weekend to leave the city before the baby was due. We drove down at night, stopping along the way for Szechuan food (not a good idea when you're entering your ninth month), then arrived at the house around ten o'clock and got ready for bed.

We both weren't tired, so we put on a VHS tape of our favorite movie, Billy Wilder's *The Apartment*. Somewhere in the middle of the scene when Jack Lemmon realizes that the woman he loves, Shirley MacLaine, is having an affair with his married boss, Fred MacMurray, I felt a *pop* and liquid started running down my leg.

My water had broken and I was going into labor. It was after midnight. We were in the middle of nowhere. My ob-gyn was in Manhattan, two hours away. It was December and had just started to snow.

Jonathan woke up our doctor in New York to ask what we should do. He said get to the nearest hospital. Fast. There was a county hospital about twenty-five minutes away and we rushed over. By now my contractions had started and I was trying to remember what they told us to do in Lamaze class—if only Jonathan and I had paid more attention! Was it deep breaths in? Puffing breaths out?

At the small local hospital, I was the only one in the dark maternity ward. The night nurse on duty called a neighborhood doctor, who drove over to check me out. I hoped we had enough time to make it back to Manhattan. The doctor said he thought we could, but no guarantee. The decision was ours. We decided to make a run for it, but the thought of giving birth on the side of the New Jersey Turnpike flashed through my mind.

It was 2:00 a.m. and the snow was getting heavy. I was lying on my back across the rear seat of Jonathan's Jeep Cherokee, distracting myself from the contractions with a phone call to my mother, giving her a moment-by-moment replay. At the time, we had one of those big, chunky car phones—

the kind that came in a carrying case the size of a briefcase. Jonathan was driving, giving me location updates since I couldn't see out the window. It turned out he was fibbing so I wouldn't panic. "We're only twenty miles from the Holland Tunnel. . . . I see Exit 14C up ahead. . . . I see the Twin Towers. . . . We're going through the tunnel. . . . We're heading up Park Avenue. . . . I'm pulling up in front of Lenox Hill. . . ."

After we made it to the hospital, I was given a room and examined. But Oscar/Ozzy wasn't ready to arrive. The contractions would continue for another twenty-eight hours. By this time, any thoughts I'd had about a mellow, natural childbirth had flown out the window. I wanted to do it the good old-fashioned way—unconscious, exactly as my mother had given birth to her three kids in the 1950s. Anesthesia! Forceps! Drugs!

Night turned to day and back to night again. By now I had been given Pitocin to induce labor, so the contractions were coming fast and furious. I was exhausted. The television in my room was on in the background as my doctor checked my cervix. Gene Siskel and Roger Ebert's *At the Movies* happened to be playing, and Gene and Roger were quarreling, as they often did, over the week's latest releases.

But . . . wait! . . . what? . . . they were reviewing *She-Devil*! This had to be one of the more surreal moments in my life. (Believe me, I couldn't make this stuff up!) Talk about a bizarre intersection of private and professional.

In between pushes, I watched as the two critics debated the merits (or lack thereof) of my movie. I was hyperventilating and in pain. My legs were spread wide apart. My doctor's hand was up my vagina, and he was telling me to "take a deep breath and push!"

I pushed; Uhhhggg! But my eyes darted back to the TV screen.

Roger Ebert gave the film an enthusiastic thumbs up. Gene Siskel, a critical thumbs down.

My mind was now in the Twilight Zone, and I started to scream.

"Screw you, Siskel! Owww . . . You pompous . . . Oowww . . ." and I let out a yelp.

"Roger! . . . This one's for you . . . uuhhhhggg!" And pushed.

The maternity nurse thought I was delirious, talking back to people on TV.

After thirty hours of labor, Ozzy/Oscar still didn't want to come out.

Maybe he knew it was a tough world out here, where film critics get paid to say snarky things, and he wanted to stay inside where it was nice and cozy. So the doctor decided that a C-section was needed, and by now that sounded good to me, too.

As I lay numb from the breast down, with my lower abdomen cut open, I felt a tugging, followed by the strange sensation of a body being pulled from my own, and a wave of joy swept over me. Jonathan was standing next to me, dressed in scrubs, beaming down and stroking my hand, taped with an IV. And there he was. Our beautiful baby boy.

Bibbidi bobbidi boo, I was a mother.

Oscar at three weeks. The T-shirt is from the Pedro Almodóvar film *Women on the Verge of a Nervous Breakdown*. I don't remember if I was wearing it ironically. (*Photo by John Clifford*)

Don't Let the Sun Go Down on Me
(Elton John and George Michael)

I knew I was walking on thin ice. *Making Mr. Right* had been a box office miss. *Cookie* had gotten lost in the Hollywood shuffle. Unfortunately, *She-Devil* wouldn't live up to the studio's expectations. The film had been released during the Christmas holiday season, a competitive time when studios put out their top movies. Expectations were high (it starred America's most prestigious film actress opposite America's most popular TV star), but just as Jonathan had predicted, on the opening weekend, *War of the Roses* got the lion's share of the box office. *Roses* was a good movie, directed by Danny De-Vito (see how things circle around), with a powerful marketing campaign, so I understood why. And it was a date-night movie. Both male and female audiences enjoyed seeing a sexy leading man and beautiful leading lady battling it out on-screen, even if they were beating the shit out of each other.

It turned out that *She-Devil* wasn't a *flop* flop. It was more like a commercial disappointment. And with a disappointment you hold out hope that the film will sell in foreign territories (it did), do well on video, and that sometime in the future it might be rediscovered by a new generation of filmgoers. In any case, Meryl would be nominated for Best Actress in a Comedy or Musical at the 1990 Golden Globes for her first comedic film performance.

* * *

Everyone knows Hollywood is ruthless. Three strikes, you're out.

So, for now, I was in movie jail, but I wasn't ready to roll into a ball and disappear. I'd worked nonstop throughout the 1980s. It was now 1990 and I had a newborn baby, so this felt like the right time to press PAUSE.

Stop. Reflect. Rejuvenate.

I loved making movies. I had other stories to tell. New stories. Maybe about motherhood? Maybe about getting older? Maybe about the changing zeitgeist of the nineties? And if Hollywood wasn't going to make them, I'd figure out another way. I was tenacious. I'd done it before.

I wanted an Act Two.

ACT TWO

Landslide
(Stevie Nicks)

For the first half of 1990, I hung around at home. Motherhood was a lesson in selflessness. Making movies seemed relaxing by comparison. I was exhausted and looked like a blob. My hair went unwashed, my clothes were covered with baby goo, my breasts hurt, and several times while changing diapers, I was pissed on—right in the face. But every time that little ET-like creature made a goofy toothless smile, or looked up into my eyes, my heart turned to mush.

Jonathan and I started to call him Oskie. That was the nickname that stuck until he could choose another he liked better.

I was used to organizing projects, so I made up lists of various household tasks to keep myself busy while Oskie napped. I color-coordinated the clothes closets, organized bookshelves by category, alphabetized the VHS tapes, rearranged spice racks. When Oskie turned ten months old, I joined a Mommy and Me class at Gymboree to be part of a group. I was still figuring out how to be a mommy. Motherhood wasn't something that came naturally, although other women made it look easy. I didn't want to be an Obsessive Mom, a Doting Mom, or a Competitive Mom. I wanted to be a good mom, but knew that eventually, I needed to go back to work.

* * *

In the summer of 1990, *She-Devil* had its video release. Video stores were popping up like weeds on every street corner across America and Blockbuster was going gangbusters. The movies that people hadn't seen in theaters were getting a second chance on VHS. (DVDs wouldn't appear until 1997.) Lots of copies of *She-Devil* had been preordered by the major video chains because of the star power of its cast.

However, I could not have predicted that on July 25, 1990, the same month as *She-Devil*'s video release, Roseanne would screech the national anthem at a nationally televised baseball game—the San Diego Padres and Cincinnati Reds doubleheader in San Diego. She put her fingers in her ears while singing and (Oh no! Please don't!) grabbed her crotch. I'm sure this was intended as comic relief, to make fun of her bad singing voice (everyone knows it's impossible to hit that high note on "land of the freeeee"), but Americans take their patriotism seriously, especially at baseball games, and the crowd was outraged. The event made national headlines, even eliciting criticism from (then) President Bush.

Thankfully, this didn't hurt *She-Devil*'s video sales, since the preorders were already shipped. However, it hurt Roseanne's reputation. She went from sympathetic to toxic. And she would do it again in 2018. After making a spectacular comeback twenty-five years after her TV debut, she would shoot herself in the foot by posting a racist tweet, and ABC would quickly cancel her new hit show. It would return five months later, retitled *The Conners,* but without Roseanne.

Some people thrive on controversy. Roseanne was one of them. In that way, I guess she had something in common with Madonna. Both were self-made celebrities instantly recognizable by a single first name. (Not many women can claim that.) Both were outspoken provocateurs with a personal brand. Both knew their audience and spoke directly to them. One used her voice to support LGBTQ+ rights. The other, to support Donald Trump.

* * *

During that first year at home with Oskie, Jonathan wrote a screenplay for a film he hoped to produce in Wales. Jonathan had grown up in Cardiff, where the Welsh poet Dylan Thomas was considered a national treasure. Jonathan's script, *Dylan,* was the story of this brilliant but irrepressible poet and his volatile relationship with his fiery wife, Caitlin. Jonathan had shown the script to Gary Oldman, still an up-and-coming actor at the time, who was interested in playing Dylan, provided his new bride, Uma Thurman, played the role of Caitlin.

Getting any movie made is a battle. What follows is a war story.

The warning bells should have gone off when I accompanied Jonathan to a coffee shop near 57th Street where he was meeting Gary for their initial script conversation. We waited and waited, but Gary was a no-show. I forget the excuse Gary would later give, but since this was 1990 (pre–cell phone), we gave him the benefit of the doubt. In retrospect, this should have been a warning sign. DANGER AHEAD!

Gary and Jonathan finally met a week later, and Uma came along. She was young and charming and everyone was on their best behavior.

Trying to raise four million dollars to make a movie is not easy. And for the next few months, Jonathan traveled back and forth to London, sleeping on couches of old friends, as he went about searching for a director and pulling together the financing. Director Mike Newell (*Four Weddings and a Funeral*) expressed interest, but wanted to cast the film his own way (understandably; most directors do). British actress Miranda Richardson read the script and wanted to play Caitlin. But Jonathan didn't want to lose Oldman, and Oldman only wanted to work with Uma as his co-star.

After many meetings, Jonathan found an experienced BBC director and financing from a large Welsh media company—provided he could get an American distribution deal. That's what led to the meeting with Harvey Weinstein at Miramax.

Jonathan and his British producing partner, Paul, were in New York scouting locations for the Manhattan portion of the film. They would get permission to shoot at the White Horse Tavern, Dylan Thomas's favorite watering hole in Greenwich Village, where he drank over a dozen straight whiskeys the day before he went into a coma. They even got permission to film at the Chelsea Hotel, in the same room where Dylan Thomas had collapsed from acute alcoholic encephalopathy (brain damage) mixed with pneumonia, before being taken to the emergency room at nearby St. Vincent's Hospital, where he died at age thirty-nine.

Weinstein liked the script, thought it had Academy Award potential, and agreed to pick up the North America distribution rights. He gave Jonathan and Paul a contract to look over, then exited the conference room, leaving them alone to discuss the deal among themselves. Harvey already had a reputation as a masterful manipulator, and Jonathan and Paul grew paranoid that the room was bugged and Weinstein was listening in on their conversation. Paul put his finger to his lips, and they communicated by passing written notes back and forth.

Meanwhile, Harvey arranged for a limo to drive them to the airport, insisting that the deal be signed before they boarded their plane. And it was. Back then, Harvey always got what he wanted. A production start date was set for January 1991.

* * *

The filming would take place in the small Welsh Village of Laugharne, in the stone cottage where Dylan, Caitlin, and their young children had actually lived in the early 1950s.

I was thrilled that Jonathan had gotten his dream project off the ground. I would take a back seat. *Dylan* was Jonathan's baby, and I was glad to tag along for emotional support and to keep our little family together.

* * *

Right after Christmas 1990, we all headed to Wales. We would be there for three months and moved into a rental apartment in the dockland of Cardiff. A decade later this would become a fashionable neighborhood filled with chic restaurants, luxury condos, and a modern opera house. But in 1990, gentrification was only just beginning. The Cardiff docks were still pretty deserted, reminiscent of Soho in the 1970s.

My involvement in the film was only as a casual observer, so my recollection of events is secondhand and possibly distorted. I was rarely on set and spent most of my time wandering around Cardiff pushing a baby stroller. It was a beautiful old town, but in January and February it was cold, wet, gray, and lonely.

At first, the filming went smoothly. Oldman had astonishingly transformed himself into Dylan Thomas and his performance was lively and authentic. But the work hours were long, and for the first nine days there was little time off.

Long story short, on the morning of the tenth day, Gary had a nervous breakdown in his makeup trailer. He started crying and couldn't stop. He said he couldn't continue filming and needed to be driven back to a hotel in London, three hours away. Immediately! And that was what happened. A car came and drove Gary away.

I remember Jonathan calling me from the film set in shock to tell me that Gary was on his way back to London. I feared that once they let Gary leave, they would never get him back.

Meanwhile, the entire film crew waited in Wales, unsure of what to do next. It's true, the schedule had been exhausting and the weather was cold and damp, but Gary's breakdown came as a total surprise to everyone.

Needless to say, Jonathan was devastated. It had been a yearlong struggle to pull together the actors, the financing, the production team. Usually on the first day of shooting, once the camera begins to roll, there's a sigh of relief knowing that even though there is no guarantee the film will be successful (or even good), at least it will get made! It's rare that a movie collapses during the second week of filming, unless there's a tragedy on set—an accident, a death, a national disaster. Infrequently, directors and actors get fired and replaced, causing a delay in production, but the movie usually goes on since so much time and money have already been invested. Various middlemen from the financing company and Miramax were brought in to try to get Gary to return to the set. Even the insurance company got involved since over a million dollars had already been spent and this would now turn into an insurance claim. But whatever was going on could not be fixed. Gary's doctor said he was suffering from nervous exhaustion, and after two weeks spent unsuccessfully trying to get Gary to return, the film officially shut down. The cast and crew were told to go home.

I don't claim to understand all the outside factors involved, but a month later Gary was on a plane heading to Dallas to work with director Oliver Stone. He had been offered the role of Lee Harvey Oswald in Stone's film *JFK* and had moved on to another movie.

Why Gary suddenly had a nervous breakdown is a question I can't answer.

Was it marital tension or something else? Working as newlyweds on a film might have been stressful. All I know is that Gary and Uma were divorced in 1992, the year after *Dylan* collapsed.

And here's another thing I know: talent doesn't excuse everything.

I hope if Gary writes a memoir one day, he'll fill in what happened. This was just a blip in his long and esteemed acting career, but it took a toll on Jonathan, who had worked hard to pull the film together. It also left sixty cast and crew members out in the cold, without a job. In the end, all that remained was one third of an unfinished movie in metal film cans.

At some point, Jonathan asked a friend to edit those scenes together. I've seen the edited version, and Gary is very good. So is Uma, in a role totally unlike any she would play in the future. And just maybe, had the film been finished, Gary Oldman might have received his 2018 Academy Award for Best Actor twenty-four years earlier, for playing Dylan Thomas, not Winston Churchill. But that wasn't to be.

What's Up?
(4 Non Blondes)

We returned to Manhattan deeply disappointed. No, that's putting it mildly—Jonathan was miserable. All he had was a VHS tape with thirty minutes of roughly edited scenes from a never-to-be-finished movie. But there was one upside. We returned home with Penny, Oscar's Welsh nanny.

Oskie had fallen in love with Penny when she came to work with us in Cardiff. She was twenty-one and from the town of Caerphilly (famous for its cheese). She'd rarely traveled outside of Wales. I'm not sure she'd even been to London. When we left Cardiff, I asked if she wanted to come to New York and she jumped at the opportunity. Living in Soho would be eye-opening for her, just as it had been for me twenty years earlier.

Oskie was now a year and a half, up on his feet and toddling. I was getting itchy to go back to work. I needed a project, something creative to focus on, and having Penny living with us made that possible.

But there was something else I worried about. Something that went beyond work. I wondered if motherhood and a certain degree of creature comfort had blurred my vision, dulled the edge I'd had when I was younger, hungrier, and eager to take risks. Had I become content? Oh shit! Isn't contentment the killer of creativity?

Creativity is selfish and ruthless, qualities opposite the ones I wanted to cultivate as a mother. And creativity doesn't like to play second fiddle to anyone or anything. But it's hard to feed your inner *art monster* when you also want to nourish your child. How did other women do it? With limited time and only so much emotional energy, women are constantly forced to make choices.[18]

Two months later, out of the blue, I got a call from a producer at BBC Scotland who was putting together a TV series called *The Directors Place*. He had asked various directors from around the world to make a film about a place or a time that had had an impact on their work. Each director was given the same budget, and each film would be fifty minutes long. It was a manageable project and something personal I could sink my teeth into.

My fortieth birthday was rapidly approaching, which felt like a turning point. I'd put off contemplating middle age throughout my thirties, but now it hit me like a ton of bricks. I was no longer young. There was a new generation of creative kids out there, starting to make their own cultural mark. Times were changing. It was no longer the eighties!

Every storyteller knows this: setting informs character. It's the source of all the influences you have subconsciously absorbed, or consciously rebelled against. The stuff that makes you *you*.

I thought about growing up in the suburbs outside of Philadelphia in the 1960s and the impact that had on my films. How my teenage fantasies of escape and reinvention had influenced *Smithereens, Desperately Seeking Susan,* and *She-Devil*. My umbilical connection to the suburbs had given me a point of reference, but also something to push back against. So, I returned to my hometown to interview four of my old high school friends, women I hadn't seen in many years. Each of our lives had taken a different path. I wanted to ask them how their expectations as teenage girls growing up in a protective bubble differed from their adult reality. *Confessions of a Suburban Girl* was part documentary, part dramatic re-creation, mixed with film clips and home movies. The title was inspired by the scandalous *True Confessions* magazines that fascinated me as a girl.

I worked with my first female cinematographer, Maryse Alberti. Maryse would make a name for herself in a career nearly impossible for women to

---

18. It came as no surprise when I read that Patti Smith—musician, poet, author—dropped out of the creative spotlight for sixteen years to raise her kids in the outskirts of Detroit, only to return after her husband died and her kids were grown.

break into at that time. She would go on to shoot movies like *The Wrestler* (Mickey Rourke) and *Creed* (Michael B. Jordan and Sly Stallone). Pretty impressive for a girl from a small district in France who had come to America at nineteen to work as an au pair.

Confessions of a Suburban Girl. Front row: me and Cindy Mullock, playing the 1960s version of myself in the film
(Courtesy Susan Seidelman)

For several days my old friends and I lolled around in a suburban bedroom with flower-print wallpaper like a bunch of teenagers at a pajama party, playing a grown-up version of Truth or Dare. What was clear from our conversation was that the world had shifted in ways we'd never expected. We'd all lived through the innocent fifties and early sixties, the hippie years and social revolutions of the '70s, the coke-fueled yuppie materialism of the '80s. The '90s had just begun, and we had no idea what changes that decade would bring.

The truth was, life had not been what we were brought up to think it would be. Had we been tricked by the images we watched on TV? The

254 | SUSAN SEIDELMAN

Prince Charming fairy tales we'd read as little girls? The fake advertisements in fashion magazines? Surprisingly, out of the five of us, not one had a traditional, married-with-children lifestyle even vaguely resembling our mothers'.

One was a divorced mom, working long hours to raise two young kids on her own.

One was married to a man she later learned was gay and divorced.

One was in a traditional marriage, working full-time as a banker, and had chosen never to have children.

One was single, struggling to support herself with a low-paying waitress job, but as America reshaped itself in the 1990s, she would slip out of the middle class. Two decades later, she'd be living in her car.

As for me—I was a working mom in a domestic partnership with no future plans for marriage. In case you're wondering, here's why: Most of the married people I knew were divorced by forty, or on their second or third marriage. I figured our relationship stood a better shot at survival if Jonathan and I didn't officially tie the knot. I'm sure this was mixed with some rebel-girl instinct having grown up at a time when a woman's value was so closely linked to her marital status.

Were my friends and I outliers? A statistical glitch? Or was this the new normal?

The Long and Winding Road
(The Beatles)

It's never easy for two people with creative aspirations who work in the same field to have a balanced relationship. Ask any actress married to an actor. Or any director married to a writer. Or watch *A Star Is Born* in any of its three remakes. Same story. One person's career is always in a different place than the other's. And there is some degree of competition, or tension, even when you're in love and want to be supportive. That's just human nature.

I had hoped *Dylan* would be Jonathan's personal success, but it hadn't worked out that way.

On the other hand, Jonathan and I shared something in common: perseverance. The belief that there will be something good waiting around the corner if you just hang in. And we weren't afraid to explore new paths when old roads reached a dead end. Besides, there was nothing else we wanted to do other than make movies. We had no backup plan.

So, while I was in the cutting room with editor Mona Davis, working on *Confessions,* Jonathan was busy in a nearby office writing a new screenplay for a project we could collaborate on.

* * *

The next two years were filled with professional ups and downs. Projects in development that never got made. Screenplays written that weren't produced.

I was traveling back and forth to Europe, collecting frequent flyer miles, speaking at movie seminars, and serving on international film festival juries—a fun but exhausting job—watching three or four subtitled movies a day for a week, then negotiating with the other jury members about which films should receive prizes. This involved a lot of politicking.

My reputation in Europe was still pretty good, so I was hoping to get a new film going with a European production company. I was taking pitch meetings and business lunches with foreign producers, but it seemed like I was always one lunch away from getting a new project off the ground. That's when I met a German producer named Regina Ziegler.

* * *

Regina was larger-than-life. Slightly under six feet, big-boned, with flaming orange-red hair. She had a pretty, delicate face and the theatrical flair of a drag queen. She often dressed in red with scarves draped around her neck and donned hats with veils. She was the kind of person who made a strong impression when she entered a room. Maître d's at chic restaurants usually gave her a good table, right up front, even before they knew she was a generous tipper.

Regina was the president of a successful production company based in Berlin and was now producing a series of short films for German TV called *Erotic Tales.* She planned to approach sixty-nine directors (69! Get it?!) from all over the world and ask each to make a thirty-minute film about something erotic. When I asked her what she meant by "erotic" (not sure if that was just a euphemism for "porn"), she answered elusively: "Make a movie about whatever *erotic* means to you."

Hmm. What *did* erotic mean to me?

* * *

Around this time, Jonathan and I went to Paris to work with a French producer named François, who had optioned a script Jonathan had written and I planned to direct. François had extravagantly flown us over on the Concorde and rented us a spectacular three-bedroom duplex apartment on the Place des Vosges, the oldest square in Paris, once home to royalty and the nineteenth-century writer Victor Hugo. Of course, Oscar and Penny came with us. Paris was child friendly. The parks had pony rides, beautiful old carousels, and playgrounds where sanitation workers in green uniforms raked the sandboxes every morning searching for bits of debris that might harm the fingers of the lucky children who played there. This was a far cry from Oscar's playground on Thompson Street, where I constantly scanned the ground for discarded hypodermic needles.

While we waited anxiously to see if François could pull together the financing, we found ourselves with a lot of unexpected free time on our hands. Everything moved slowly in Paris, especially in the summer when Parisians take off the entire month of August to sunbathe on beaches down south and the city is overrun by tourists. So to keep from pacing the floors, we went out sightseeing. We visited churches and flea markets, and ate our way across Paris, arrondissement by arrondissement. We also frequented the Louvre. Looking at art had always been an escape from the anxieties of the movie business.

One day, as we wandered through the museum, Jonathan was struck by a seventeenth-century Dutch Master painting hanging on the wall. It was painted by Pieter de Hooch and titled *Woman Drinking with Soldiers*. The thing about seventeenth-century Dutch art is its detailed portrayal of urban life of that time. The painting was set in a rustic room with wooden rafters and showed a young woman seated at a table with two men in fancy dress. One is smoking a clay pipe; the other, smiling as he refills her wineglass. By the expression on the woman's face and her relaxed body position, she's pretty tipsy already. An older female servant stands nearby, concerned, her hand to her chest, perhaps telling the man to stop pouring. Through an open doorway, you can see part of another room in the background, presumably a bedroom.

We were both intrigued by the mysterious story within the painting and thought it might make an interesting starting point for a film. Who was this woman? What was going on in that back room? What if someone could magically enter the painting to find out?

That would become the inspiration for our erotic tale, *The Dutch Master*.

Woman Drinking with Soldiers by Pieter de Hooch, 1659.

* * *

Meanwhile, with our Paris movie still on hold, we held dinner parties. We were living in a gorgeous apartment in the most beautiful city in the world, so why not make the most of it? Jonathan loved to cook, and one night we invited a French talent agent over for dinner. She arrived with her new British client, a charming young actor named Hugh Grant. Hugh had just made a film with Roman Polanski in Paris and was about to star in a new movie called *Four Weddings and a Funeral*. He didn't have a clue that night that this film would turn him into an international rom-com star and change his life.

I don't remember all the blurry details of the evening, other than Jonathan's delicious seafood risotto, lots to drink, and Hugh's wickedly funny, self-deprecating stories about being hit on by one of Britain's top directors. But in the photo I took, everyone looked happy and shit-faced.

More champagne, please!

* * *

In the end, our French film never materialized. François had been overly confident about his ability to pull the financing together, so we had no choice but to move on. We would make an *Erotic Tale* instead.

For the next two weeks Jonathan and I sat at a café on the rue du Temple and pounded out a script. Yes, we had arguments—but the productive kind. We each brought different strengths to our collaboration. Jonathan thought in broad strokes and big concepts. He approached stories like architecture. I focused on creating distinctive characters and how to make their emotions and motivations feel real, even when the situations they found themselves in were fantastical.

By the time our apartment lease was up, we were ready to go home and get to work. This time around we would make sure our producer really had the money. (She did.) Ironically, the day we left for the airport, there was much hoopla in all the French newspapers that Madonna had arrived in Paris to unapologetically promote her new, controversial book *Sex,* a collaboration with photographer Steven Meisel. The backlash from the book would nearly torch her career but wouldn't diminish her determination.

Our paths didn't cross.

Wildest Dreams
(Taylor Swift)

I'd always loved stories about women looking to escape their mundane lives. That theme exists in several of my earlier films, played out by Wren in *Smithereens,* Roberta Glass in *Desperately Seeking Susan,* and Ruth Patchett in *She-Devil.* It was my own story as well.

The Dutch Master was about a bored New York dental hygienist named Theresa, who works in a sterile dentist's office on Fifth Avenue, across the street from the Metropolitan Museum of Art. Theresa spends her days hidden behind a hygienic mask, cleaning people's teeth. One afternoon, during a lunch break, she wanders inside the museum, where she is struck by a handsome man in a Dutch painting hanging on the wall. She returns to the museum day after day, even dragging along her hygienist girlfriends, to gaze at the painting and daydream about the man within it. Then one day, the man suddenly smiles at her, the painting comes to life, and she miraculously finds herself transported inside the painting where she has an erotic adventure.

The star of *The Dutch Master* was a then-unknown actress named Mira Sorvino. Three years later she would win a Best Supporting Actress Oscar for her role in Woody Allen's *Mighty Aphrodite.* Mira played the wistful hygienist, nervous about her upcoming marriage to her high school boyfriend—a neighborhood cop—and looking to escape a predictable humdrum future.

I asked Maryse Alberti to be the director of photography. The set, a life-size re-creation of de Hooch's painting, was built in an empty warehouse on West 14th Street and Ninth Avenue. The space is now an Apple store, but back then it was a derelict warehouse in the Meatpacking District. This part of 14th Street, near the waterfront, was deserted at night and had the stench of rotting meat in the air. It was also a prominent cruising strip for transvestite prostitutes. Since we were shooting all night, we would have to navigate our way through a gathering of outrageously dressed (or undressed) hookers to enter our film set.

Back in the early '90s, there was only one place to eat late at night in the Meatpacking District. It was an all-night diner called Florent, on cobblestoned Gansevoort Street. It was frequented by artists, club kids, night owls, drag queens, and a loyal gay clientele going to, or coming from, the Mafia-owned sex clubs nearby. The owner was a Frenchman who had been diagnosed with HIV in 1987 and reportedly posted his T-cell count on the chalk wall menu along with the restaurant's daily specials. The only other places in the area that were open at this hour of the early morning were the nearby slaughterhouses, where men were busy hacking up sides of beef.

Florent was one of the establishments that led to the popularity of the Meatpacking District in the late 1990s and turned the neighborhood into a fashionable and expensive tourist destination. In 2008 Florent would close, priced out of the luxury real estate market it helped to create. This same area, where bloody sides of beef had been butchered and deviants paid to be spanked or pissed on, was now officially listed on the National Register of Historic Places and rebranded the Gansevoort Market Historic District.

But isn't that how it often works in big cities? A neighborhood is cheap and marginal, the gays move in and fix it up, the real estate developers arrive, prices soar, then the original inhabitants can no longer afford the skyrocketing rents and are forced out.

New York City is constantly in flux, which is both its blessing and its curse.

My life was also in flux. Oscar had turned three and it was time for him to have a real bedroom. He'd outgrown the crib in the walk-in closet we'd converted into a nursery after the surprise of finding out Oscar was on the way. So, after finishing *The Dutch Master,* we moved into a bigger loft, a duplex in the same building, to give everyone more space. Penny, our nanny, moved back to Wales, missing her family and boyfriend. Oscar was enrolled in nursery school, and I was working from home, reading scripts, books, plays, and trying to figure out what to do next.

Then we got some good news. *The Dutch Master* had been nominated for an Academy Award for Best Live Action Short Film. This was certainly a boost to my and Jonathan's spirits after the last few years of roller-coaster ups and downs.

A few weeks later, we were invited to a reception at the Russian Tea Room for all the East Coast nominees. I was seated at a long table across from a young actor with a baby face who seemed genuinely excited to be there. At nineteen, Leonardo DiCaprio was the youngest person in the room, having been nominated for Best Supporting Actor in a film called *What's Eating Gilbert Grape.* He came across as charming, shy, and totally unassuming as veteran actors crossed the room to shake his hand, offering congratulations and words of advice. They already sensed that Leonardo was destined for stardom. Three years later, he would be in *Titanic,* one of the most successful movies of all time and the first to gross well over a billion dollars at the box office. *Gilbert Grape* would be DiCaprio's first of seven nominations. He would finally win a Best Actor Oscar twenty-two years later, in 2016, for *The Revenant.*

As we left the restaurant, all the nominees were given a swag bag with a gray sweatshirt inside printed with the words *66th Oscars* and embossed with a little gold statuette. A souvenir for all those who wouldn't get the real thing.

The following week, Jonathan, Oscar, and I flew to LA for the ceremony.

* * *

Plane travel with Jonathan had never been easy. What made it worse was that for the past year he'd been writing an action-adventure script called *Turbulence,* about the hijacking of a 747. All the research he'd done about airplane disasters and mechanical failures only fed his anxiety. Every clang, creak, and groaning engine noise (sounds and vibrations regular passengers ignored) was a sign of imminent disaster. We clenched hands during takeoff and landing.

We were staying at the Sunset Marquis in West Hollywood. It had been a funky rock 'n' roll motel in the 1970s, a place where B-level bands were put up while in LA. (A notch better than the Tropicana Motel on Sunset, where the really raucous bands threw TV sets out the window and puked on the carpet.) The Sunset Marquis had recently been given a facelift, but still retained some of its original rebel rocker vibe. When we arrived, I spotted Bruce Springsteen at the café by the pool. He too was in town for the Oscars, having been nominated for his song "Streets of Philadelphia."

Regina, her husband, Wolf, and a group of German TV executives who had flown in for the event were also staying at the hotel, and so on the afternoon of the awards ceremony, Regina arranged for a stretch limo to take us all to the Dorothy Chandler Pavilion. I'd gone to Henri Bendel a few weeks earlier and spent far too much money on a woman-tuxedo with a low-cut *V* in the front and little gold military-style buttons. It was sexy in an androgynous way, but slightly tight, bought as a motivation to lose a few pounds before the trip.

The Dorothy Chandler Pavilion looked smaller in real life than on TV. We took our seats in the area designated for people nominated for short films and documentaries (in other words, the section off to the side). I noticed there were seat savers waiting in the wings. These were young men and women, dressed in formal black, who hurried to take the vacated seats of invited guests when they left for the bathroom or went outside to smoke, so TV viewers wouldn't see any empty seats.

Whoopi Goldberg was the host and made history by being the first woman to host the Oscars on her own, and the first person of color. The nominees in the Best Dramatic Short Film category were announced by Rosie O'Donnell. Jonathan and I touched fingers nervously, imagining our names being called out . . . imagining our march down the aisle to thunderous applause . . . imagining our walk up the steps onto the stage . . . then slipping on a cosmic banana peel and landing flat on my face.

But, we didn't win, so we were spared that humiliation. (Hey, we still had our Oscar souvenir sweatshirts!)

I could say we were relieved, but that would be a lie. We wanted that sexless little gold man! He would have looked great sitting on our living room bookshelf. Or in our powder room, where we could discreetly position him in plain view of a captive audience and pretend like it was no big deal.

Schindler's List won for Best Picture, and there were many emotional speeches about the horrors of the concentration camps, the six million Jewish lives lost (almost two out of every three European Jews), victims of Nazi Germany's racist ideology, referred to frighteningly as the Final Solution. There was thunderous applause as some of the Holocaust survivors walked onstage and gave impassioned accounts of their personal experiences.

Listening to Steven Spielberg's acceptance speech about the strength and resilience of the survivors, I felt my Jewish pride swell. I had never been traditionally religious. I'd taken my Judaism for granted, yet I knew it played a part in the way I viewed the world. I recognized it in my father's ironic sense of humor, my dislike of pretentiousness, and my interest in bodily functions.

I glanced over at Regina, trying to gauge her reaction to the speeches. I knew little about her German background, her politics, or what her parents did during the war. She looked vaguely uncomfortable, but I think that was disappointment about not taking home an Oscar.

Following the ceremony, there was a big party called the Governors Ball—drinks and hors d'oeuvres under a big tent behind the Dorothy Chandler Pavilion. It was a Hollywood crowd, and Spielberg was clearly the man of the hour, having received his first Oscar. I'd now spent enough time in LA, so I knew some people there, including my old *Smithereens* collaborator Ron Nyswaner. He had been nominated for his screenplay for *Philadelphia* (starring Tom Hanks, who got the Best Actor Oscar that night, as did Springsteen for Best Song). Although Ron didn't win, it was great to see him again and know his career was doing so well. Nora was there, too, nominated for co-writing *Sleepless in Seattle*.

After the ball, people headed off to different private parties, some a hotter ticket than others. I was hoping to tag along to a hot one, but Regina suggested we all go back to her German producer friend's house in one of the Hollywood canyons. Jonathan and I didn't really want to go, but my inner good girl took over. Regina was our producer; she financed the movie that got us here. Plus, it was her limo.

As we waited in line for our car, I realized we were standing next to Deborah Kerr. She was now in her midseventies and had received an honorary Oscar that evening for the many great films she'd starred in over the years: *From Here to Eternity, The King and I, An Affair to Remember,* just to name a few. Apparently, she'd been nominated six times, but had never won. I noticed a group of young starlets and their dates, with Tenaxed Luke Perry–style hair, passing by Kerr without even a glance. They probably didn't know who she was. Old age makes you invisible.

The party turned out to be at the home of Bernd Eichinger,[19] the producer I'd met several years earlier who had asked me to direct the movie about the talking penis. It was a large midcentury house with about twenty people milling around. Jonathan and I didn't know the other guests, and most were chatting in German. We stayed for an hour, then returned to the Sunset Marquis to pay the babysitter.

Oskie was sound asleep across the middle of our bed when we got back, and we didn't have the heart to wake him up and move him onto a cot. So, we quietly took off our dress-up clothes and, not having eaten all night, raided the minibar for overpriced junk food. Then we slid into bed on either side of our son and fell asleep hugging the edges of the mattress, with Oskie sprawled horizontally across the middle. His head snuggled into my hip, his toes jabbing Jonathan in the back, like a big letter *H*.

* * *

The next day, Jonathan and I were invited to lunch by an Italian producer. I felt a little guilty leaving Oscar at the hotel with a babysitter, but he wanted to go swimming. The business lunch would only last two hours, then we would hurry back to the hotel. What could go wrong in two hours?

We went to a nice Italian restaurant in the Hollywood Hills. Charlton Heston and his family were eating at one table. Warren Beatty and Annette

---

19. In 2004, Eichinger would write and produce a film called *Downfall,* about the final days of Hitler in his Berlin bunker, starring Bruno Ganz and nominated for a Best Foreign Film Oscar. It would also become the source of many Hitler Rants video parodies that would go viral.

Bening at another. Our meeting was going well until midway through the panna cotta, there was a rumble, and the table began to shake. Now the entire building was vibrating. People began running for the exit, some crouched under tables. Total pandemonium.

Not being a Californian, I was unsure what was happening at first. Then I realized—it was an earthquake! And now I was freaking out about Oscar. I tried frantically to call the hotel, but, of course, cell service was out.

In the ensuing mayhem, we spotted Charlton Heston calmly leaving the restaurant with a group of people following behind him. He looked like Moses leading the Israelites to safety. I figured if we followed Moses, we would be fine. So, Jonathan, the Italian producer, and I followed Heston over to a safe spot on the lawn to wait things out. Finally, ten minutes later, someone inside the restaurant gave the all-clear signal.

The traffic was heavy heading back to the hotel, but we made it there in a little over an hour to find Oskie in the swimming pool, wearing floaties, unaware that anything dramatic had happened. He did mention that the pool had big waves and it was fun.

* * *

There's another story I want to mention about *The Dutch Master*. This took place two months later, when the film premiered at Cannes. This would be my fourth visit to the festival, so I now knew how to navigate through the circus.

The Dutch Master was screened in the Palais on a double bill with another of Regina's *Erotic Tales*. That one was directed by Bob Rafelson (*Five Easy Pieces, The Postman Always Rings Twice*). The screening went well; Regina was happy with the enthusiastic response and made some lucrative European distribution deals. She had now produced twenty of her *Erotic Tales* and took us all out to dinner to celebrate.

The next day, I was asked to stick my hand in wet concrete for a handprint that would be put in the sidewalk along the Croisette—a French version of the celebrity handprints outside of Grauman's Chinese Theatre on Hollywood Boulevard. They gave me a block of wet cement and a sharp stick and asked me to write my name. There followed a moment of indecision.

Should I sign in cursive or block script, aware that this signature would be permanent? I started to write my name, but the letters came out jagged and my hand looked like a child's. I immediately wanted a redo, but was too embarrassed to smooth out the concrete and ask to do it again.

Then I thought about returning to Cannes one day as an old lady and seeing my wonky signature and small handprint on the sidewalk. I imagined putting my now arthritic hand alongside it to see how I had changed over time. Hopefully my cement block would still be there—not replaced by someone with better penmanship or a more illustrious career.

Don't Stop Believin'
(Journey)

I t had been five years since I'd directed a feature film, and although I enjoyed making the shorts, I was itchy to make a long movie again. I felt like
an out-of-shape boxer who needed to get back in the ring—even if it was
just for practice.

Around this time, I was sent a script for a Disney TV movie that was
shooting in LA.

It was a comedy about the television business, with a goofy premise,
but a healthy dose of satirical humor. It was unlike anything I'd ever
directed before. There were no female protagonists, no themes of transformation or reinvention. It wasn't a story I felt passionate about, but the
script was funny. I could think of it as a job. It would get me back on a
film set to exercise my directing muscle. (Plus, the film's opening logo
would feature the Disney castle and Tinkerbell's magic pixie dust. Oscar
would like that.)

The producers made me an offer and gave me a start date. I'd never
filmed in LA, so that would be a new experience. I'd never directed a TV
movie before, which had a much faster production schedule than a studio
feature film. I'd also never directed an animal. . . . Oh, did I mention—it
featured a chimp! No joke.

It was called *The Barefoot Executive,* a remake of a Disney movie from
1971 that had originally starred the young Kurt Russell. The plot revolved

around an ambitious mailroom clerk trying to get ahead at the TV network where he worked. Unfortunately, none of the network executives wanted to hear a mail boy's opinion about which TV shows he thought would be hits. But it turned out he had a pet chimpanzee named Archie (an out-of-work chimp actor rescued from a canceled TV series) who liked sitting on the couch, eating bananas, and watching television—and Archie had a knack for predicting which new shows would be successful.

Archie's ape instinct was superior to the highly paid network boobs who relied on market research to justify their creative decisions, having no real opinions of their own. Basically, the film was a satirical commentary on the TV business and the ridiculous way that programming decisions are made. The message: a chimp could do a better job.

Still, I had to ask myself the following question:

Susan, what the fuck are you doing!? You've made three films that played at the most prestigious film festival in the world. You made a hit movie with Madonna and Rosanna. You directed Streep and Malkovich. You have an Oscar nomination. Why are you making a Disney TV movie with a CHIMPANZEE?! The optics don't look good.

And the answer: I missed being around actors and designers and cameras and crew. I wanted to get back on a big movie set. Creativity is something you need to work at and the more you work, the more you hone your craft. Plus . . . it would pay some bills. However, the irony of going from directing Meryl Streep to directing a chimpanzee was not lost on me.

* * *

The year 1995 was a stressful one in my relationship with Jonathan. He was working on rewrites of *Turbulence,* his airplane disaster movie that had been optioned by veteran Hollywood producer Martin Ransohoff. But its production status was in limbo.

Jonathan didn't want me to go to LA with Oscar and refused to accompany us. I tried to persuade him that living in LA for a few months would be good for him too, since that was where the film industry was centered.

But Jonathan was still stinging from the collapse of *Dylan* and the uncertainty of his new script. He said going to LA would jeopardize our relationship. He said I was being selfish.

Traditionally, women have been more likely to adapt to their male partner's career than the other way around. But there was nothing traditional about our relationship. I needed to get back to work.

So I said yes to the offer and hoped Jonathan would change his mind.

A few weeks later, I left for California to find an apartment. Oskie would fly out the following week, chaperoned by my mother. Jonathan remained in New York.

I've edited out the scene where we argued as I left in a town car for the airport, alone, my stomach churning. I've omitted the angry long-distance hang up, call back, then hang up again phone calls that followed. There were other things, too. Incidents I've left out that might make you hate me. Or hate Jonathan. During this time, we were not our best selves.

*   *   *

I rented a two-bedroom apartment at the sprawling Oakwood Apartments. It was a huge complex of modest short-term apartment rentals near the Burbank studios. The apartments were bland and impersonal, but the complex had a big swimming pool and was located near the film's production office. I met a lovely Belgian au pair named Valerie, who moved into the second bedroom and made delicious *mousse au chocolat* from scratch.

Because it was summer, it was TV pilot season and the Oakwood was overrun with hopeful moms and precocious children who had come to LA for a shot at the American dream. These kids were on display around the swimming pool, laughing, splashing, and doing jazz-hands routines. Many of the moms had saved their money and driven here from parts unknown with the hope that little Jimmy, or precious Jenny, might become the next Leonardo DiCaprio or Drew Barrymore. I felt a little anxious for them, knowing the road ahead wouldn't be easy. A few might make it, and for those who did, the life of a child star wasn't always easy. (I thought about Corey Haim and Gary Coleman, and flashed back to my childhood actress friend, Rona Gail, dead at twenty-eight.) But the dream was potent and the carrot at the end of the stick was seductive.

* * *

Working on a TV movie felt different from working on a theatrical film. Everything happened so much quicker. Pre-production was only four weeks long, compared to ten (or more) on the feature films I'd directed. The shooting schedule was twenty days. (On *She-Devil* and *Cookie* I had sixty.) On a positive note, working at a TV-movie pace forced me to think fast and be decisive. My focus during the week needed to be on location scouting, script revisions, shot lists, pulling together a cast. Weekends I spent with Oscar, who was now five. It was a tricky balancing act, being a mother and a film director, and wanting to be good at both.

* * *

Jason London, the movie's lead actor, was a likable newcomer. The film was also peppered with a bunch of funny comedians: Chris Elliott (who would go on to star in *There's Something About Mary*), Jay Mohr (*Jerry Maguire*), Julia Sweeney (from *Saturday Night Live*), and Willie Garson, whom I'd work with three years later on *Sex and the City* playing Sarah Jessica Parker's gay friend, Stanford. And there were cameos by veteran actors Eddie Albert and Yvonne De Carlo. Both had been movie stars in the 1940s and 1950s, then TV stars in the 1960s. (Eddie starred in *Green Acres.* Yvonne had starred in *The Munsters,* playing Lily Munster.) Both were now past seventy and doing small cameos to stay active or pay bills.

Work is work.

* * *

On the first day of shooting, we filmed the last scene of the movie—which is never desirable, but sometimes a necessity, when decisions are based on budgetary concerns, not creative ones. We were at the LA zoo, which doubled as an animal sanctuary. It was a scene where Archie is returned to the wild so he can once again be a *normal* chimp.

After finishing the last shot of the day, I walked back to my car and was shocked to see Jonathan standing by the entrance to the zoo. Without letting me know, he had flown to California and come to the set. He'd always been full of surprises. We walked toward each other . . . and hugged. It was like one of those schmaltzy slow-motion shots in a 1970s romantic drama. But I was really happy he was here. Oscar was, too.

And it turned out that *Turbulence* had been picked up by a studio and looked like it was actually going to get made. The studio had flown Jonathan to LA and put him up in a much nicer hotel than the Oakwood Apartments so he could work on a rewrite. We would both be in LA for the next month. Jonathan, staying (mostly) at his hotel. Me, staying (mostly) at the Oakwood with Oskie and Valerie, but we would spend family weekends together at the hotel, taking advantage of room service and breakfast in bed.[20]

* * *

It was three months since the start of filming and *The Barefoot Executive* had already been edited and aired on ABC. The film got a good review in *Variety,* but the entire process felt like eating fast food. Momentarily tasty, but it left you feeling hungry and wanting more.

People are often put into boxes, labeled, and squeezed into convenient categories. So, now that I'd directed a TV movie, I was labeled a TV director and started to get offers to direct other television movies and series. I directed a few random episodes of network shows, but without the passion, vision, or enthusiasm I had for making movies. Television was a writers' medium, and for me, a director, it felt like a job.

* * *

In the 1980s and '90s, the worlds of film and television existed in two separate universes. Actors and directors might start off working in TV, but if they were successful or created a big enough splash, they quickly moved

---

20. *Turbulence* was produced the following year, starring Ray Liotta, and would go on to three sequels. This would be a boost to Jonathan's spirits, our relationship, and our finances.

on to a prestigious movie career (think of George Clooney or Will Smith). Granted, you could make a shitload of money working on a hit TV series (think *Seinfeld* and *Friends*), but being a TV star didn't have the same cachet as being a movie star. At least that's the way it was until HBO reinvented the game.

It was now 1997, the early days of pay cable, and HBO was primarily known for broadcasting movies that had played in movie theaters six months earlier or boxing events. With the exception of *The Larry Sanders Show* and *Arli$$,* HBO's original programming had not yet generated much heat. But all that was about to change.

Living for the City
(Stevie Wonder)

'd never watched *Beverly Hills, 90210* or its spin-off, *Melrose Place,* so I only had a vague notion of who Darren Star, their creator, was at the time. I'd seen clips from both TV shows on *Entertainment Tonight* and knew they were popular with young audiences and had a cast of attractive dudes with gelled hair and blow-dried babes in designer jeans. But I was a forty-four-year-old New Yorker with limited interest in the soap opera shenanigans of privileged kids in Beverly Hills.

I don't remember exactly who sent me the script for *Sex and the City.* It might have been my agent at the time. I'd moved from ICM to the William Morris Agency after I was no longer on Sam Cohn's callback list. So in the spring of 1997, when I was sent the screenplay for a new television series, I was not particularly excited. I was hoping to make a feature film. However, I was told that the show would be shot on location in New York City and that this was the pilot episode, which definitely made the project more appealing. There would be no template to follow, no preexisting style to mimic. I would get to help create the look and feel of a new series. And because it was on HBO, the language could be bolder and the subject matter more adult than what typically played on network TV. Plus, it starred four women in their thirties.

The script hooked me with the very first line:

CARRIE (VOICE-OVER):
Once upon a time . . .

It read like a modern-day dark fairy tale about life, love, and sex in the city I loved. (Admittedly, it was a vision of Manhattan that *Smithereens'* Wren would no longer recognize and probably disdain.)

As I read Darren's script, I watched the story play out in my head and I knew I wanted to spend time with these characters. So a phone call was arranged and we had a very friendly, relatively short conversation. I basically said, "I'm onboard if you want me." Darren said "yes" and a deal was quickly struck with HBO. My goal was to make a show that was not just about the four main female characters but about the city itself.

The series was based on a weekly newspaper column in *The New York Observer,* written by the wickedly clever Candace Bushnell (the real-life Carrie Bradshaw), who had genuine NYC cred. She was writing about herself, her friends, and their actual lives. It had authenticity. And that's what the series needed, too. I wanted to capture Bushnell's world with all its idiosyncrasies, jigs and jags and *fabulosity*. Also, its phonies, creeps, and wannabes. It was the world of aspirational urbanites seen through the lens of a fractured fairy tale and set against the backdrop of a big, chaotic city.

The other thing that made the show appealing was the age of the characters. A group of single women in their midthirties, living in a city that made it complicated for single women after a certain age.

Thirty-something life in Manhattan is different than twenty-something life. That's when reality kicks in and you realize that your cool job as an unpaid intern at Miramax isn't going to cover your rent and Mommy and Daddy have stopped subsidizing you. That's when sharing a small one-bedroom apartment on Bleecker Street with three roommates is no longer fun.

Yet . . . if I could pick one stage of my life to play on repeat, it would be my midthirties. That's when a woman is at her best. When she's the most confident, kick-ass version of herself. When she's finally figured out who she is and young and fearless enough to enjoy it.

* * *

I didn't want the pilot episode to look like a typical network television comedy. It needed the texture of a New York indie film, and Darren encouraged me to hire a movie crew. I brought in Stuart Dryburgh, the director of photography who had shot Jane Campion's film *The Piano,* and production designer Mark Friedberg, who would go on to design Todd Phillips's *The Joker.* We would make the lighting a little darker, the framing a little off-balance, the transitions between scenes sharper, and the locations real. The tone I was going for was this: gritty and magical. As in *Smithereens* and *Desperately Seeking Susan*—that was the version of the city I liked the best.

Sarah Jessica Parker and Kim Cattrall were already attached to the show before I came onboard, and Darren had worked with Kristin Davis on *Melrose Place,* but I was part of the casting conversation for Miranda and Mr. Big. I recently found an old casting list with names of other actors who had come in to audition. Not famous names you'd recognize, but good, solid working actors, like Cynthia Nixon had been before being cast as Miranda. It's now hard to imagine any other actors in these iconic roles.

Of course, the pilot introduced the first batch of Toxic Bachelors, the original villains of the show. They would be joined by other Terrible Men in future episodes to help the audience understand the world of toxic masculinity these women were living in.

TOXIC BACHELOR: When you're a young guy in your twenties, women are controlling the relationship. By the time you get to be an eligible guy in your thirties, you feel like you're being devoured by women. Suddenly, the guy's holding all of the chips. I call it the midthirties power flip. The problem is expectation. Older women don't want to settle for what's available. Why don't these women marry a fat guy? Why don't they just marry a big fat tub of lard?!

Mr. Big was a combination Toxic Bachelor and Prince Charming. A Master of the Universe with swoopy dark hair, who looked good in expensive suits. Big could be funny, generous, but also cruel. A mystery man with no name, until it was revealed in the last episode that he had the very ordinary

Mr. Big in a dress in *Smithereens*

name, John. I knew the actor who played him, Chris Noth, from *Smithereens*. He had a small role in that film playing a transvestite hooker sitting in the back of a van in the final scene of the film. He wore a dress and had one line of dialogue: "Say hi, bitch."

One of my favorite characters introduced in the pilot, who pops up a few times in Season One, was named Skipper Johnston, played by Ben Weber. In a sea of toxic bachelors, Skipper was a nice guy, a web designer with a childlike innocence and geeky charm. For a few episodes he was Miranda's boyfriend, although he liked her way more than she liked him, and followed her around like a puppy. I was sorry to see him vanish without explanation in Season Two because he was one of the sweetest male characters in the show. Maybe that's what happens to men who come across as *too* nice? They disappear.

* * *

My goal was to present a time capsule of single life in NYC in the late '90s. We would film in fashionable restaurants and trendy clubs. The characters would wear fantastic clothes they could never afford in real life. It would have style and glamour, but mixed with a healthy dose of dirty truths about single life in your thirties.

In the pilot episode, the lead character, Carrie, lives in a small studio apartment on Madison Avenue in the East 70s. Her apartment is illuminated by a flashing neon sign from the coffee shop below. It's on the third floor of the nondescript building, probably a walk-up. You can see her bedroom nook in the background, separated from the living area by just a fabric curtain. You can hear traffic outside. She's introduced, sitting on her bed, cross-legged, typing on a laptop. Her hair is brown, curly, and barely shoulder length. Her makeup is dark and smudgy. She wears lots of black and smokes lots of cigarettes. (In other words, she looks like a real NY writer.) She's writing a column called "Sex and the City" for a local newspaper, and since journalists don't get paid much, her apartment reflects that. There are Chinese take-out cartons and fashion magazines scattered around the room. It's clear she's not very domestic. A single woman always on the go. A frazzled, modern-day version of Mary Tyler Moore.

I liked that Carrie was struggling. I liked that she was aspirational and worried about paying her electricity bill, yet would buy a pair of shoes that cost as much as a month's rent. She was relatable and endearingly irresponsible. Stylish, but not yet the fashionista she would become in later seasons.

The very first scene we shot was at the Gramercy Tavern. It was a scene where Carrie is eating lunch with her best friend, Stanford, a dandy who runs a modeling agency with only one client who also happens to be his boyfriend. (Hey, it was the '90s—every unmarried leading lady had a gay best friend. In this case it was Stanford Blatch, played by Willie Garson, an actor I'd worked with previously in the chimp movie, who sadly died of cancer in 2021.) At the bar, Carrie spots her ex-boyfriend, Kurt, having a drink, and decides to try a little experiment, posing the question: "Why can't a woman have sex like a man?"

Candace Bushnell came to the set that day. I'd never seen someone so genuinely and unabashedly excited. She probably couldn't believe that the newspaper column she'd written in her modest one-bedroom apartment was now a TV series. She didn't yet know how famous she and her fictionalized friends would become. There were a dozen film equipment trucks parked on the street outside of the restaurant. Inside, a crew of forty were scurrying around, setting up lights, laying down dolly track, doing last-minute touch-ups. There was a room full of sixty background extras sitting at tables, getting ready to *pretend* to eat.

I watched Sarah Jessica Parker studying Bushnell, since she was playing a version of Candace in the show. But to me, in person, they projected different vibes. Candace had an open, unfiltered quality that made her seem vulnerable, even slightly *daffy*. (She wasn't.) Parker was a talented and skillful actress who seemed tougher and more in control. Maybe you had to be tough to survive in this business, and Parker had learned the ropes early, having starred on Broadway in *Annie* when she was fourteen. But underneath Parker's easygoing veneer, there was an exacting *girl boss* who would one day be running the show.

On the surface, the four actresses appeared to get along well, at least while I was around during Season One. I think everyone knew they were working on something special and were thrilled to be a part of it. Although, many years later when the rift between Parker and Kim Cattrall went public, I was not totally surprised. Cattrall, who played the outrageously confident, sex-positive Samantha Jones, seemed, in some reversal of persona, the more fragile of the two in real life. But on-screen, Samantha was the most fiercely independent of the foursome, and the most unapologetically promiscuous. Miranda, the intelligent and cynical workaholic. Charlotte, the traditional good girl and privileged princess.

Sure, they were character types. And watching as they walked around the set, or rehearsed a scene, I wondered if these four women would be best friends in real life. Maybe not. But the magic of the show was that it captured our desire to have friendships as tight as the ones portrayed on-screen, and the actresses successfully pulled that off. They made you believe that friends are family.

* * *

So in the end, what was my contribution to *Sex and the City*? I mean, what is it that the director actually does? I didn't write the clever dialogue. Those words came from Darren, Michael Patrick King, and their team of writers. The original characters came from Candace. The actresses were all talented pros.

My contribution was the creation of a world in which those characters could come to life. I tried to set a style, a rhythm, an atmosphere, and conjure up a vision of the city that would make this show stand out from others of that time. I hoped it would be vivid and sharp, with just enough grit and genuine emotion to make in resonate. I wanted the pilot to be fun, but with a pinch of sad.

Here's an example. Take a look at the very last shot of the pilot episode. It was filmed at night, with a wet down (fake rain), using a Steadicam (a stabilized moving camera contraption worn by the operator). When Carrie emerges from Mr. Big's limo after asking Big if he's ever been in love and he responds with certainty, "Abso-fuckin'-lutely," there's a film noir reflection of blue neon on the rainy street behind her as she watches the limo drive away (her back to the camera). Then the frame slightly tilts to capture the vulnerable look on Carrie's face as she turns into a medium close-up—and the frame freezes.

It's an off-balance image that reinforces the unsettled emotion Carrie must be feeling at that moment with enough tension to make the ending feel bittersweet and real.[21]

That's what a director does. Finds ways to visualize what is emotional.

(Courtesy of HBO)

---

21. It's no coincidence that this freeze frame resembles the final freeze of Wren in *Smithereens*. Both women are standing alone on a city street, looking rattled and confused. (Both are also wearing animal-print tops.)

Material Girl

(Madonna)

In June 1997, after finishing the pilot, I went to the country with Jonathan and Oskie for the summer. I was waiting to hear whether HBO would commit to making the series. These were happy times. We had dinner parties with friends, delicious Jonathan-created meals with good wine. We spent days lounging around our old 1950s kidney-shaped pool. There were barbecues with packs of little kids running through open fields, chasing fireflies and waving sparklers. And quiet family evenings reading Alvin Schwartz's scary stories while swinging in a hammock—just the three of us. At the end of August, we heard the shocking news of Princess Diana's death in a car crash in Paris.

A few weeks later, I got a call from Darren. HBO had picked up the series and committed to shooting twelve episodes. Sets would be built and the production would resume filming sometime in the early spring of 1998.

Once the show went to series, several changes were made. Carrie Bradshaw's apartment was rebuilt at Silvercup Studio, a soundstage in Long Island City. It would morph from a funky Upper East Side studio apartment above a coffee shop to a quiet one-bedroom in a Greenwich Village brownstone with a walk-through closet. Her world would not be quite as gritty. Her hair would be longer and blonder. Her wardrobe would become increasingly more eclectic and expensive, due in large part to the vision of Patricia Field, who was brought in by Parker as the costume designer. By the end of Season One, Carrie would no longer talk directly to the camera.

By Season Two, Parker would become one of the show's producers. By Season Three, Carrie would stop smoking (well, almost).[22]

* * *

Patricia Field owned a funky clothing store on 8th Street in Greenwich Village for many years and is credited with popularizing the wearing of women's leggings in the 1970s. Her shop, along with a few others in the East Village—Trash and Vaudeville and Manic Panic—were ground zero in the late '70s and early '80s for punk fashion. And of course, there was Love Saves the Day on Second Avenue if you wanted vintage.

Once Field came onboard, she brought fantasy to fashion, turbocharging Carrie's wardrobe and turning it into an eclectic blend of wearable art and haute couture. The show would become as much about clothing as it was about sex.

I understand why women (some men, too) are obsessed with fashion. It allows you to live out a personal fantasy. Just by slipping on new threads, you can become someone different, if only for a brief period of time. And it's a fallacy to think that women dress for men. They don't. They dress for other women. The characters in *Sex and the City* were dressing for the women watching them on TV. Clothing tells a detailed story about the wearer, and Pat Field knew that. It can tell you a character's social status, their fantasies and aspirations, as well as their emotional state. You just need to read the clues. Clothing is a way of instantly telling others who you are and how you want to be perceived.

* * *

Okay, a confession. I hate high heels. I can't walk in strappy stilettos, certainly not more than two or three steps, without tripping. I would rather

---

22. In the 1950s and '60s, it was not unusual for characters on TV to smoke and drink alcohol. It was considered sophisticated. Even cartoon characters like Fred Flintstone and Tom and Jerry smoked. By 1969, tobacco companies were the largest product advertisers on TV—until April 1970, when President Richard Nixon signed legislation to officially ban cigarette smoking on television. But smoking would make a comeback and Carrie would pick up her Marlboro Lights again in the show's reboot twenty-five years later.

have my feet bound by an ancient Chinese foot binder. I know how lovely a woman's leg can look in four-inch Jimmy Choos in a glossy magazine spread. Or on the red carpet at an awards ceremony. Or worn by a very attractive drag queen. But give me a pair of $199.99 black ankle boots with a nice two-inch heel, and I'm happy as a clam.

Try walking across Soho's cracked sidewalks in a pair of $800 Manolos without twisting an ankle. See how many subway grates and wonky metal ramps you encounter on Prince Street. And forget about wearing stilettos in the Meatpacking District. You're dead meat. I've witnessed many a young fashionista lying splat on the street after her pinpoint heel got caught between cobbles. Trust me, Soho's uneven sidewalks are better suited to Doc Martens or Converse All Stars. So, I have to give all the actresses credit for making it look easy, but I've witnessed all of them rubbing blisters on their feet in between shots.

I would go on to direct two more episodes in Season One. One was titled "The Power of Female Sex." It's the episode where Carrie has a romantic fling with a sexy Frenchman who's in town for one night. In the morning, she wakes up alone in his hotel room and discovers he has left her $1,000 on the bedside table. She's upset that she's been mistaken for a hooker. Samantha explains the situation in terms of power:

SAMANTHA: Money is power, sex is power . . . therefore getting money for sex is simply an exchange of power.

The other episode was called "The Baby Shower" and is a personal favorite. The four bachelorettes show up for the baby shower of their formerly wild and crazy friend, Laney, who is now pregnant and has settled down to a conventional life in the suburbs, but still misses her riotous party girl days.

Filming the episodes was a very different experience from shooting the pilot. The director of photography was now a guy with television experience who knew how to shoot fast. I, like all the other directors, was given ten days to film two episodes, which were shot simultaneously. For example, we'd film a scene from "The Baby Shower" in the morning in Carrie's living room, then a scene from "The Power of Female Sex" in the same room later that afternoon. There's a lot of back-and-forth costume changing when you're shooting two different episodes on the same day.

The scripts were cleverly structured, and the actors' performances were great, but the environment was more factory-like. That's just the nature of episodic television production. Once a show gets rolling, the schedule is fast and furious, and you need to be decisive. On set, there's no time for reflection and little time for rehearsal. (The lessons I'd learned from the chimp movie came in handy.)

The majority of the show's first season was directed by women. There were three of us. Nicole Holofcener, Alison Maclean, and me. Over the next few decades, television would give many more women this opportunity. It would no longer be unusual to find a woman's name following the credit "Directed by."

* * *

When *Sex and the City* started airing on June 6, 1998, I was surprised by the cultural reverberations the show would have, not just in the US but all around the world. Over the next two decades, it would influence the taste, attitudes, and shopping habits of a generation of women.

Suddenly everyone wanted cupcakes from Magnolia Bakery. Every cocktail bar across the planet served cosmopolitans. Jewelry stores couldn't stock enough name necklaces, like the one that Carrie wore. And the desire for a Birkin bag went through the roof. Even at the obscene price of $8,000 to $200,000 a bag, there was a five-month waiting list! And the show would change the lives of all the actresses more than they could have imagined. They would see their faces on coffee mugs, notebooks, key rings, tote bags, and T-shirts with slogans like: *I'm a Carrie. I'm a Samantha. I'm a Charlotte. I'm a Miranda.* Like the characters in Harry Potter, they were merch.

Years later, the show would be criticized for its lack of diversity. It's true, the main characters were all privileged white women, but, on some basic level, the characters were spirited enough, aspirational enough, and with just enough sympathetic quirks and vulnerabilities that women of all ethnicities and socioeconomic groups could relate. And for a brief moment, every fan of the show, regardless of age or color, fantasized they were some version of Carrie Bradshaw. But more importantly, it showed single women over thirty enjoying each other's company. They were not portrayed as losers who couldn't get a man. The show made it cool to go out to a restaurant on a Saturday night with a bunch of girlfriends, laugh and get silly.

As the seasons went on, the tone began to shift. More traditional romantic plotlines replaced the sharp social observations of the earlier seasons and financial reality flew out the window. (Not to be a killjoy, but the average writer of a newspaper sex column would make about $50,000, pre-taxes, in a good year. Rent for a large one-bedroom apartment in a West Village brownstone would easily eat up most of that.)

I watched the first four seasons, then got busy with other projects— although I'd check in from time to time to see what the gals were up to. But the series that had started out with grit and funky glamour had gradually morphed into something different. Originally, Carrie and her BFFs were independent women, having relatable adventures while navigating their way through the big crazy city. Their stories were now increasingly defined by the privileged lifestyle they were living. As fine-tuned to the rhythms of modern life as the original series had been, the two feature films that followed and the show's reboot twenty-five years later (*And Just Like That*) seemed tone-deaf.

Yet, through it all—even amid rumors of behind-the-scenes fighting among the actresses—their on-screen camaraderie prevailed. That was the heart and soul of *Sex and the City*.

The power of female friendship.

Celluloid Heroes

(The Kinks)

've always identified as a New York indie filmmaker despite having directed four studio-financed movies. New York City isn't an entertainment company town, like LA, and living in Manhattan has probably spared me from some of the industry's more blatant sexism.

In the early nineties, the independent film movement exploded. There was a rapidly growing audience for auteur-driven films with a distinctive voice that could be made for only a fraction of the cost of a studio movie. One of the New York indie production companies that paved the way was Killer Films, founded in 1995 by Christine Vachon and Pamela Koffler. They introduced the public to the work of two talented Todds: Todd Haynes and Todd Solondz, as well as many other innovative filmmakers.

But it was Miramax, along with its formidable founder, Harvey Weinstein, that would eventually rule this world from the mid-'90s through the mid-2000s.

Miramax was founded in 1979 by the Weinstein brothers, Harvey and Bob, and named after their parents, Miriam and Max. The company started out distributing low-budget indie fare (rock concert docs), but by the early 1990s began to gain prestige and make money. Among Miramax's early successes were the distribution of Steven Soderbergh's *Sex, Lies, and Videotape* (1989); Neil Jordan's *The Crying Game* (1992), their first Oscar-nominated film; and, most significantly, Quentin Tarantino's *Pulp Fiction* (1994), a film that grossed over $200 million at the box office, made on a budget of only $8 million.

It's hard to imagine now, but back in the '90s, indie films had enormous cultural clout.

By 1993, Miramax had been bought by the Walt Disney Company, but Harvey and Bob continued to maintain control over their company. Harvey now had much more money at his disposal, a great instinct for picking good material, and knew how to mount lavish promotional campaigns. As a result, by the late 1990s Miramax's *Shakespeare in Love* would win the Oscar over the presumed front-runner, Spielberg's *Saving Private Ryan*. Weinstein became the reigning king of Hollywood, as well as the Cannes Film Festival, and Miramax's so-called "indie" films were now prestigious and profitable.

Seeing there was a lucrative and growing independent film market aimed at a more selective audience, the major Hollywood studios now wanted to develop their own indie subsidiaries—Fox Searchlight Pictures, Universal's Focus Features, Paramount Vantage, Fine Line Features—all looking to make commercial hit films that could win awards, but be produced at a much lower cost. The studios' new indie divisions filled a void at their corporate parent companies, but also put the squeeze on the small, genuinely independent film distributors who didn't have the marketing budgets to compete. As a result, many went out of business.

By 1998, multiplex cinemas all over America were booming and celebrity salaries and contractual demands were starting to go through the roof. The average studio movie budget was well over $50 million, with many reaching over $100 million. Megastars like Tom Cruise, Sylvester Stallone, Harrison Ford, Demi Moore, and Julia Roberts were demanding script control and director approval. Their contracts included restrictions on their filming schedule, specifications for their trailer size, dietary demands, control over merchandising rights, and private jets for themselves and their entourage, including bodyguards, masseuses, personal chefs, assistants, and assistants to the assistants.

With production and marketing costs soaring, executives at the big studios needed to hedge their bets by making formulaic high-concept movies—sequels and spin-offs to existing hits—in an attempt to produce movies that would appeal to the widest possible audience and make the most amount of money. The kind of middle-budget, character-driven films I'd made in the eighties no longer fit Hollywood's new financial model, so the big studios stopped making them. A 1983 Oscar winner like *Terms of Endearment* would probably now only be made as a TV movie.

Meanwhile, the TV industry was also going through seismic changes. By the end of the nineties about 80 percent of American households had access to cable TV through cable hookup or satellite. Audiences were becoming more sophisticated and looking for bolder programming (the kind of edgy stuff that was taboo on advertiser-sponsored network TV) and were willing to pay premium fees for it.

HBO led the way. Its viewership took a big leap at the end of the '90s when HBO started to produce its own adult-oriented series, like *Oz, The Sopranos,* and *Sex and the City*—risky shows that were popular with both TV audiences and critics. Showtime was a little slower off the mark. It was creating new series, like *Queer as Folk*, but also producing feature-length cable movies to fill the void left by the studios: character-oriented stories with adult themes.

I would direct three movies for Showtime over the next few years. The first, *A Cooler Climate,* starred Sally Field and Judy Davis, based on a book by Zena Collier with a screenplay by Pulitzer Prize winner Marsha Norman. The only problem was that Showtime was filming all its movies up in Canada, and I now had a nine-year-old in school in New York City.

By the end of the 1990s, the Canadian dollar was cheap compared to the US dollar, so a movie could be produced in Canada for three-fourths of its American budget. Canada was referred to as Hollywood North. The Canadian film crews were experienced, genuinely friendly, and there was no language barrier (except for the interjection of "eh" at the end of every sentence, as in: "How do you like it up here, eh?").

Like *Desperately Seeking Susan* and *She-Devil, A Cooler Climate* was about two very different women and the impact they had on each other's lives. Unlike those other films, this one was a drama.

Sally Field was cast in the lead role, playing a middle-aged woman named

Iris who suddenly finds herself broke after a recent divorce. Having no specific skill other than being a homemaker, she finds work as a live-in housekeeper for a wealthy, bitter woman named Paula (Judy Davis).

Paula's life looks perfect on the surface, and Iris puts up with her daily abuse because she needs the money, but when Paula and her husband separate, an unlikely friendship develops between the two women as their situations reverse.

* * *

In the movie industry there's a lot of gossip that floats around about people, particularly actresses, who get a reputation for being "trouble" or "difficult." The Hollywood rumor mill is not unlike the one in high school. Sometimes the rumors are false. Sometimes they're started for malicious reasons—like an actress who dares to question the artistic intentions of her male director.

Seeing this through a female lens, I now view these rumors differently. I've known actresses who were considered trouble for refusing to undress when a scene didn't call for nudity. Or for not wanting to give a back massage or fellate a producer with a perverted sense of power. Some actresses (like the outspoken Ashley Judd, Rose McGowan, Annabella Sciorra, and Mira Sorvino) have gone public with their stories, having had years stolen from their careers after being (unofficially) blacklisted—victims of spiteful rumors that Harvey Weinstein floated around town.

I heard that Judy Davis had a reputation for being "enormously talented, but difficult." It was a rumor that started as a result of creative differences with legendary director David Lean over her starring role in *A Passage to India*. A role she would earn an Oscar nomination for.

Judy wasn't afraid to question authority. Some directors might take offense, but I just thought she was super smart. She had a tough exterior and could sometimes come across as brusque, but she was the type of person who didn't suffer fools. Our working relationship was straightforward. No games, no hidden agendas. If she had a question, I tried to answer it as best I could. Sometimes I'd say, "I don't know. What do *you* think?"

Sally Field kept to herself, but was a consummate professional. She'd been in the business for a long time, starting out at eighteen as the star of the popular 1965 TV series *Gidget,* followed by *The Flying Nun* (talk about a wacky '60s show premise!). She now had two Best Actress Oscars under her belt. But like many veteran actresses, at the ripe old age of fifty-two, she was too old to play Hollywood leading ladies and looked too young to play feisty old matriarchs. She was in that in-between place and was getting offered juicier roles on cable TV than on the big screen.

In the end, *A Cooler Climate* would be nominated for several acting awards. Both Sally and Judy got Screen Actors Guild and Primetime Emmy nominations, competing against each other in the Lead Actress category. Neither would win, which was probably a good thing—like having to choose the favorite of your two children.

Framing a shot in Vancouver, aka "Hollywood North."

Showtime was happy with the film and asked me to direct two more. But first, I would go to Barcelona to make a quirky detective mystery called *Gaudi*

Afternoon. My life was suddenly busy, and I was moving around a lot. I felt bad about uprooting Oskie, but I couldn't leave him home, and he seemed to enjoy the adventure. He would spend part of third grade in Vancouver, part of fourth in Barcelona, and part of fifth in Toronto. Like an army brat, he was learning to adjust to new places, new cultures, and make friends quickly. I just hoped that when he was grown up, he wouldn't resent me for not having had a more conventional childhood—one with a suburban backyard, a basketball hoop over the garage, Little League, and birthday parties at Chuck E. Cheese.

But let me rewind.

* * *

A year earlier, I had gotten an unsolicited script in the mail. It arrived in a plain manila envelope from a stranger named James Myhre in San Francisco. The screenplay's unusual premise and exotic Barcelona setting immediately grabbed my attention. That's the way things work. Something comes out of left field and catches you by surprise.

The script was based on the Lambda Literary Award–winning novel *Gaudi Afternoon* by Barbara Wilson. I wasn't familiar with Wilson's book, but learned it was part of a trilogy of mystery stories about a globe-trotting translator.

It followed the adventures of an American named Cassandra Reilly, a middle-aged book translator currently eking out a living in Barcelona. Her world is suddenly thrown into turmoil when she's approached by a mysterious American actress named Frankie Stevens to help track down Frankie's missing husband, believed to be in hiding in Barcelona. At first Cassandra has no interest in getting involved with this flamboyant stranger—then Frankie makes an offer the cash-strapped translator can't refuse. Soon Cassandra finds herself embroiled in a web of lies, mistaken identities, and double crosses—eventually coming to realize that no one is who they appeared to be.

After reading the script, I called James to say I was interested in helping him get the film made. And that's why we were now on a plane headed to Spain in search of a Spanish producer. The never-ending hustle for money to make movies!

Okay, that's the downside to independent filmmaking. A lot of time is spent searching for production money, and it can be exhausting. But once

you've found the financing, you usually have more creative freedom, so that's the trade-off.

In Barcelona and Madrid, James and I met with various production companies before finding Andrés Vicente Gómez, a producer with a hazy reputation, but a prolific track record. Andres liked the idea of shooting an English-language film in Spain and had the ability to pull together the money, if I could pull together a good cast. And I could. It would be an all-female ensemble starring Marcia Gay Harden, Juliette Lewis, Judy Davis, Lili Taylor, and six-year-old Courtney Jines.

Barcelona is one of the sexiest cities on earth. Dreamy, mysterious, and slightly surreal, especially at night when the old barrios dress up for show. It was also home to the early-twentieth-century *modernista* architect and designer Antoni Gaudí. Gaudí's work is fanciful and inspired by nature. His unfinished cathedral, La Sagrada Familia, looks like a dripping sandcastle. His sensuously curved benches at Park Güell (embedded with pieces of broken, brightly colored mosaic tile) look like wriggling serpents. His rooftop chimneys at La Pedrera resemble gigantic creatures from outer space. Gaudí's creations, like the characters in the movie, are not what they first appear to be.[23]

---

23. Antoni Gaudí was also not who he appeared to be. At seventy-three, Gaudí (a devout Catholic) was hit by a tram while taking his daily walk to confession. Because of his unkempt appearance, he looked like a beggar and was brought to a hospital, but given only rudimentary care. A day later, doctors realized his true identity, but it was too late. Gaudí died two days later.

Bingo Was His Name-O
(Traditional English children's song)

O scar and I arrived in Barcelona exhausted from our long flight from JFK to Madrid, then to Barcelona. Jonathan would join us a week later. He preferred to fly alone and I liked it that way too, giving me time to organize our accommodations in advance. Besides, Oscar was a great travel buddy. (Jonathan's aerophobia had gotten worse after he wrote *Turbulence,* which made it stressful to fly together.)

Oskie and I settled temporarily into a suite in the Hotel Calderon, then took a stroll along Las Ramblas, past the flower and bird vendors, past the wonderful Boqueria food market. No one eats dinner in Spain until 10:00 p.m., and at that hour you'll find restaurants filled with entire extended families, from babies to grannies. Of course, the Spanish take a siesta between 1:00 p.m. and 4:00 p.m., which seemed like a very civilized, but totally impractical, way to do business. Oskie and I ate tapas, bought a large bucket of Chupa Chups lollipops (better than their American equivalent, according to Oscar), then returned to the hotel and immediately passed out.

The next morning, I was scheduled for early meetings with the Spanish production team. The producer had arranged for an English-speaking assistant to look after Oskie while I went down to the lobby café to meet with various crew members. My new creative team. Most of them spoke English. A few didn't.

The director of photography, Josep Civit, suggested we shoot the film in CinemaScope because Barcelona, with its Gaudí architecture and gothic alleyways, was so visually striking. (I'd always said size doesn't matter, but maybe *screen size* does, if it enhances the story.) Josep was Catalan and spoke fluent English. The production designer, Antxón Gómez, who had designed several Pedro Almodóvar films, was Basque and spoke none. We communicated with a sprinkling of French, a lot of smiles, and big hand gestures.

The film crew was warm and professional. Spanish movie crews have a long history of working with American actors and directors, going back to the spaghetti Westerns of the mid-1960s. That's when Sergio Leone decided that a sleepy part of southern Spain would make a perfect (and cheaper) stand-in for the American Wild West and directed a trilogy of movies starring Clint Eastwood: *The Good, the Bad and the Ugly, A Fistful of Dollars,* and *For a Few Dollars More.* Other Westerns and Biblical epics would follow.

That afternoon, Oskie showed up in the hotel lobby looking upset. Bingo was missing! Bingo was the floppy brown stuffed dog that Oscar had had since infancy. Ten years later, he looked a bit mangled since Bingo traveled with us everywhere. He was our lucky charm.

Apparently, Bingo had gotten wrapped up in the sheets when house-keeping changed the bedding. The sheets, rolled into a ball with Bingo inside, were sent to a large commercial laundry somewhere in Barcelona, where they were tossed in with hundreds of other soiled hotel sheets. Now, I know this might sound silly, but this was probably more upsetting to me than to Oscar. I was sentimental, superstitious, and also feeling guilty about uprooting Oscar from his NYC school and dragging him off to Spain to be enrolled mid-term in an international school, where he would be the new kid and a non–Spanish speaker.

I'm usually good at compartmentalizing, but my mom brain took over and I could barely concentrate on my meetings until I got Bingo back.

After several emotionally charged phone calls with the hotel manage-ment, Bingo was finally tracked down, returned to our hotel room, and now resting comfortably on Oscar's bed, which meant that I could get on with my other job. Directing a movie.

* * *

I was excited to be working on a feature film again after nearly a decade of TV. There's a difference knowing you're filming a story that will be pro-jected on a big screen and viewed by a collective audience. And location scouting in Barcelona was a treat. I felt like a VIP with special access to all of the city's hidden treasures. We visited the private residential apartments designed by Gaudí. We went to secret underground rooms in churches that looked like caves. We scouted an old absinthe bar that had once been a hangout for Picasso, where the bartender insisted we each drink a glass of absinthe—the wormwood kind you drank through a sugar cube set on fire. I was slightly buzzed for the rest of the afternoon.

One evening we went on a location scout to check out a nightclub where we might film a scene. It was an old church that had been turned into a dance club. We arrived late at night to see the place in action. Bodies jostling, laser lights flashing, the sound system blasting, video projections flickering on giant screens.

When we arrived, I realized it was a *rave*. I'd never been to a rave before and never taken MDMA. (The drugs were different in the early '80s.) One of the young production assistants asked if I would like to try some. Although I admit my curiosity was piqued, it had been years since I'd taken anything stronger than a sleeping pill. I hesitated, looking around at the crowd of euphoric, sweaty twenty-somethings entranced by the techno music. I looked up at the bare-chested DJ perched like a god on the stage above the crowd, lasers flashing around him. I felt the throbbing bass pulsating through my body . . .

. . . and I suddenly saw myself through a camera lens.

That's what happens sometimes. It's like I'm seeing myself as a character in a movie, and what I saw was this: a middle-aged woman, clearly on the other side of a generational divide, who hadn't cut loose on a dance floor in nearly a decade (except for that time at her niece's bat mitzvah in Boca, but dancing like a fool in front of family doesn't count).

I declined the Ecstasy, but stuck around to watch the scene. After all, I was still a voyeur.

* * *

When you work on a film production, it's strange how quickly you bond with your cast and crew, especially when you're shooting on location. Then one day the filming ends and everyone goes their separate ways, promising to keep in touch, but moving on to another production where they will form another instant family. It's a nomadic lifestyle.

I had no idea how the film would be received by moviegoers or critics. I was aware of the movie's idiosyncratic tone and knew the gender confusion plotline was ahead of its time. It would be another decade before the words "transgender" and "nonbinary" entered the public conversation, and the acronym LGBTQIA+ didn't yet exist. But I was happy I'd had the chance to make a film with little interference and so few artistic compromises.

* * *

That winter, while I waited for *Gaudi Afternoon* to be released, Oscar changed his name from Oskie to Ozzy because it sounded cooler. He'd turned eleven, and Ozzy Osbourne was making headlines with his new reality TV show. I had turned forty-eight, and despite the cold winter weather, I started to get *hot flashes.*

In the spring, I traveled to Spain to do publicity for the film's opening in Europe, Japan, and Australia. In the summer, I crisscrossed the country for opening night galas and closing night screenings when *Gaudi* became a success on the international gay and lesbian film festival circuit. In September I was still waiting to hear news about the film's American distribution when something happened that I never could have imagined.

The world blew up.

Every Picture Tells a Story

(Rod Stewart)

At 8:45 a.m. on the beautiful blue-sky morning of September 11, 2001, a low-flying jet roared over our apartment building while Jonathan and I were drinking coffee. Jonathan had just returned from walking Ozzy to school a few blocks away. Suddenly we heard a *BAM!* I assumed it was a truck backfiring, but Jonathan said it sounded like a corporate jet and ran down to the street to see what was going on. I stayed upstairs for a few minutes, thinking he was just being overly dramatic. Looking out the window, I saw a crowd gathering below and pointing in the direction of the World Trade Center—a straight view down Thompson Street. I threw on a bathrobe and ran outside to see what was going on.

A plane had just crashed into one of the Twin Towers at around the sixtieth or seventieth floor. There was a gaping wound and smoke and flames were shooting out of the sides of the building. As everyone stood watching in shock, another fireball exploded from the second tower. We hadn't seen the second plane approaching since it came from behind.

Now smoke and flames were shooting out of both towers. It looked like a CGI special effect, or a scene from *The Towering Inferno.* I glanced around to see my neighbor, Daniel Day-Lewis, standing nearby, looking like an action hero who had come too late to the rescue. We all just stood in stunned disbelief, watching as the gigantic towers burned and the air filled with smoke. Then the sky around the buildings started to shimmer, as if glitter had been sprinkled in the air, and I realized it was all the broken shards of glass from the explosion, from thousands of windows shattering. The glass fragments were catching the bright morning sunlight like pieces of a broken mirror, twinkling as they fell to the ground.

Neighbors from nearby apartment buildings were watching from open windows above, listening to the news on TV and shouting down information as it became available. There was a report that another plane had crashed into the Pentagon. That was the first time I heard the words "terrorist attack," but the news was still sketchy. The street was getting crowded, so Jonathan and I headed up to our roof to get a clearer view. As if on autopilot, I grabbed our video camera, unaware that in five minutes the first tower would collapse. Thirty minutes later, the second.

9:40 a.m. On the roof in my bathrobe, unaware that the towers behind me were about to collapse and the world would change forever.

After the shock came the panic. No one knew if there would be more explosions to follow. I tried to call Ozzy at school, but cell service was sporadic. It was a breezy day and soot and fragments of burned paper were floating uptown in the wind, covering the sidewalk. You could smell burning plastic, fried computer systems, electrical wires, cables, all mixed with something else. Something noxious.

Jonathan and I hurried to our car parked in a garage nearby, passing by men and women in business suits covered in ash. They looked like the living dead. We drove to Grace Church School on Fourth Avenue, where all the students were gathered in the cafeteria and teachers were trying to keep everyone calm. Other parents were arriving now, too. We got Ozzy into the car and began to drive uptown. We feared staying in our apartment—it was too close to the burning towers, and there were rumors of a downtown gas explosion. Driving up Park Avenue, the streets were empty. Midtown looked like a ghost town. We drove straight through red lights, heading toward the Lincoln Tunnel, but the bridges and tunnels were closed. We made our way over to New Rochelle, where my sister lived. We spent the night there, listening to news of another plane that had crashed in a field in Pennsylvania.

The following day, we went to our house in New Jersey. Everything seemed artificially peaceful there, like nothing out of the ordinary had happened. But a sense of guilt washed over us. We felt like we'd abandoned NYC and couldn't just watch on TV as events unfolded. So we drove back into the city the next morning. There was a police barricade on Houston Street, and you needed to show ID to cross into Soho.

Inside our apartment, the windowsills were covered with thick black soot. The fires at the site of the collapsed towers were still raging. The newspaper photos and TV footage only told part of the story. They didn't convey the smell. The sickly scent of death and devastation that permeated downtown for months.

For one hundred days, a haze of smoke covered Lower Manhattan, and the streets of Soho were deserted as the towers continued to burn. I'd never seen West Broadway so quiet on a Friday night. The storefront windows displayed American flags, and on every available wall were handmade xeroxed fliers with photos of missing persons: *Have you seen my husband? Have you seen my father? My daughter? My son?*

But if there was anything positive in all this horror, it was proof that New Yorkers are resilient. NYC suddenly felt like a small village where everyone was pulling together, despite political, economic, racial, and religious differences—bonded by sadness and patriotism. There were impromptu candlelight vigils in front of churches, in parks. Three thousand people had been killed or were still missing. One was the father of Oscar's friend. He had dropped his daughter off at school that morning before heading to his office in Tower 1 and was never seen again. How do you explain that to a child?

* * *

The next few years were filled with chaos and fear as the events of 9/11 played out on a global scale. There was the invasion of Afghanistan, followed two years later by a war in Iraq. The world had dramatically changed, overshadowing whatever immediate plans I'd had for *Gaudi Afternoon*.

My concerns, along with the rest of the world's, were elsewhere, and *Gaudi* got lost in the shuffle. It would get a small art house release in mid-2002, then disappear.

Mamma Mia

(ABBA)

Although I haven't mentioned my mother in a while, she's been hanging out in the background of this story for the last few years, leading her own busy life.

It was now 2004 and my mother was about to go from a background player to a leading lady. My dad was seventy-four and had recently retired; my mother was seventy-two. They were living full-time in a retirement community in South Florida.

For those unfamiliar with the retirement scene in South Florida, Boynton Beach is a rapidly growing city in Palm Beach County. In what was once swampland and orange groves, there are now hundreds of instant communities popping up like sawgrass all over the Everglades, geared for people age fifty-five and above.

Older people move to Florida for three reasons: a) the warm weather, b) the nonexistent state income tax, and c) the all-you-can-eat early-bird buffets.

There's a similarity to many of these communities, although some are clearly more upscale than others. Their names evoke a glamorous vacation lifestyle: Valencia Glades, Palm Isles, Lotus Palm, Venetian Estates. The houses are painted in the colors of sherbert: peach, lemon yellow, and watermelon pink. The lawns are manicured and the streets lined with palm trees. Several communities are surrounded by manmade lakes. Although no one actually swims in these lakes because of occasional alligator sightings. Instead, people ride around in golf carts and play pickleball.

I understood why my parents liked it there. It was like summer camp for seniors. And in many ways, it had the same familiar, bubble-protected atmosphere of the suburb development where I grew up. Now imagine that suburb on steroids: brighter colors, bluer skies, more flamboyant tropical vegetation, where everyone is over sixty.

* * *

For the past twenty years, my mom has clipped newspaper articles about stories she found interesting and mailed them to me with little sticky Post-it notes: *Wouldn't this make a fantastic movie!* Then one day I got a phone call from my mother saying she urgently needed to talk to me. What motivated the call was the recent death of my mother's childhood friend, Marilyn, leaving behind a lonely widower, Dave.

Dave was an unassuming guy in his midseventies who had joined a local bereavement club for emotional support after Marilyn's death. Unexpectedly, he found himself back in the dating game again. Widows in the support group were suddenly hitting on him.

It started with casual invitations to go out for coffee ("just as friends"), then offers to go to the movies or out for a nosh (Dutch treat). One thing led to another, which eventually led to sex. Dave started to tell my father anecdotes about what it was like to be dating after forty years of married life and how different women were today. Bolder, more opinionated, uninhibited.

His stories included embarrassing dinner dates, awkward first kisses, and the strangeness of being intimate with someone new at this stage in his life. There was also the guilt and confusion of feeling disloyal to his deceased wife. Some of the stories were funny, some were sad. All were touching and about the desire for companionship and intimacy.

My father told Dave's stories to my mother and ended the conversation with: "Call Susan."

And that's what she did.

As my mother told me about Dave's experiences, I could see the film playing

304 | SUSAN SEIDELMAN

out in my head. But the timing was off. It wasn't a story I could focus on right now since I was about to start a new Showtime movie in Canada. So I stalled.

ME: Mom, if you like this idea so much, why don't you try writing the screenplay yourself?
MOM: I don't know how to write a screenplay.
ME: Go to Barnes & Noble and buy a scriptwriting book.

A few weeks later, I left for Vancouver to direct *The Ranch,* a movie about a group of women working in a legal brothel in Reno, Nevada.

* * *

When I returned to New York two months later, a thick envelope was waiting for me in the mail. Inside was a one-hundred-page screenplay called *The Boynton Beach Bereavement Club.* My mom had taken my advice. She had bought a *Screenwriting for Dummies* book. I should have known she would.

I didn't know what to expect when I sat down to read the script and didn't want to hurt my mother's feelings if I hated it.

Structurally, the story was messy, but it had many charming and honest scenes. Situations I could not have invented myself. The characters felt real, and included personal details that were sad, poignant, and very funny. It also felt like a movie I hadn't seen before: a bittersweet romantic comedy about the issues facing older people looking for love, companionship, and yes . . . sex.

I asked my mother if I could revise the script with a writer friend in Miami named Shelly Gitlow. She agreed. But sensing this was not the kind of movie that would typically be financed by a Hollywood studio, I half-jokingly said:

ME: So, do you want to produce it?
MOM: Uh . . . okay. (followed by a long pause) What does a producer do?
ME: They go out and find the money.
MOM: (another pause) Okay . . . I'll try.

I knew she would try. And suspected she would succeed.

* * *

Someone once gave me a dish towel that said: *Sometimes I open my mouth and my mother comes out.* But I wasn't becoming my mother. My mother was becoming me. She had always been strong-willed and ambitious for her children, but now, she was determined to push her own boundaries.

My mother met a young woman named Blair, the daughter-in-law of a friend, who had worked on Wall Street but given it up in search of something more creative to do. Blair had a friend, Deborah, also a former Wall Streeter, interested in getting involved in film production. Long story short, Blair and Deb joined us as producers. With their Wall Street connections, we then set about raising money to make the film. In the end, we found several investors who believed in the film's commercial potential and felt the story filled a void in the marketplace.

Our co-producer, Jamin O'Brien, came from South Florida and was able to pull in favors from local vendors, caterers, equipment rental companies—as well as a healthy investment from a real estate developer in Boynton Beach who saw the movie as good advertising for the retirement communities he was building in the area. It was a mutually beneficial relationship. He wanted the promotion. We needed the money.

The casting process went smoothly. There were many terrific actors in their sixties and early seventies—former movie stars, now relegated to small cameo roles—who were eager to star again in a romantic comedy. They appreciated the script's charm, but also its honesty about aging.

Actresses don't age well in Hollywood. With few exceptions, after forty, women are no longer considered desirable *leading ladies*. They have reached their "fuckable" expiration date. That's when they get cast as the mother of the leading lady. After fifty they play grannies. There is no denying the sexism and ageism that permeates the industry.

It's not the same for men. Men are allowed to gray and crinkle. It makes them sexy and "mature," and much has been written about the age disparity between male actors and their female co-stars. One classic example is the 1963 movie *Charade.* Cary Grant, at fifty-eight, is the star. His co-star and romantic partner is Audrey Hepburn, then age thirty-three. There was a twenty-five-year age gap and that was considered normal.

I cast Dyan Cannon to play the female lead role. She had been married to Cary Grant in 1965, thirty-three years her senior. (They would divorce by 1968.) Dyan would play a vivacious widow who was still an incurable romantic. Michael Nouri, of *Flashdance* fame, would play her younger lover. Ironically, Nouri and Dyan had been linked romantically in real life many years before, and had remained friends.[24]

Filming Dyan, at sixty-eight, rollerblading in Ft. Lauderdale *(Courtesy of Snowbird Films LLC)*

Brenda Vaccaro played a traditional housewife dealing with the sudden loss of her husband, learning how to overcome her pain and become independent.

Sally Kellerman played a divorcee who joined the bereavement club under false pretenses. Sally even had a nude scene, showing off her seventy-year-old kick-ass body, which was just as sexy now as it had been in the movie *M*A*S*H* in 1970.

---

24. Dyan was the first woman in the history of the Academy of Motion Picture Arts and Sciences to be nominated for an Oscar both in front of and behind the camera, receiving Best Supporting Actress nominations for *Bob & Carol & Ted & Alice* and *Heaven Can Wait* and a Best Live Action Short nomination for a film she wrote and directed, called *Number One*.

Joseph Bologna was a man dealing with the generational confusion of online dating.

Len Cariou played a shy widower who got to explore his newly awakened romantic nature as he bumbled through an awkward sexual encounter after many years of married life.

* * *

Making the film was a delight. The young crew was eager and hardworking. The veteran actors were good sports and happy to be a part of the process.

Since we were working with a limited budget, we had not allocated money to pay for background actors, but there were several big party scenes that needed to be filled with people. My mother was put in charge of recruiting extras.

I knew my mother's power of persuasion would come in handy. She posted flyers and drove around town to different senior centers, churches, and synagogues to drop off casting sign-up sheets. Being in a movie and rubbing shoulders with movie stars was a novelty in Boynton Beach, so she was able to recruit many more volunteers than we needed.

But, here's the thing about being a movie extra. Once the novelty wears off and you've taken a selfie with the stars, waiting around a film set can be pretty boring. Hours are spent sitting in a holding area while lights are set and rehearsals are blocked.

So how do you keep unpaid extras happy? My mother came up with an ingenious solution. She set up tables and ran card games—bridge, canasta, and poker. (She considered bingo, but that would have been too noisy.) This kept everyone occupied for hours. The only problem was, some of the elderly extras forgot they were there to make a movie and got irritated when the assistant director interrupted their card game to ask everyone to return to the set.

In the end, my mother and I made a good team. I'd been nervous that I would subconsciously revert to obnoxious teenage behavior, or she might do something embarrassingly mom-like in front of the entire crew. But that wasn't the case. The only awkwardness was what to call her at work. At home, she was Ma. On set I called her Florence and she called me "Sue" (my teenage name), but occasionally she'd slip and call me Suzie-Poo.

The LA actors were put up in hotel suites in nearby Boca Raton. To save production money, I moved into the guest bedroom at my parents' house in Boynton. I hadn't lived with my folks in over thirty years and forgot how high they turned up their air-conditioning and the amount of artificial flavorings they kept in their refrigerator. But it was nice spending time with them, and their home was roomy enough, so I didn't tread on their toes. But at one point, my mother suggested that I should start spending weekends at the hotel. When I asked why, she blushed and said, "Daddy thinks you're cramping our sex life."

From then on, I spent weekends at the Marriott.

Go Your Own Way
(Fleetwood Mac)

The film had its East Coast premiere at the Hamptons International Film Festival and got a great review in *Variety*. But finding a distributor would be tough.

Various distributors came to the screening and enjoyed the movie, but were skeptical about the film's commercial potential. They said older audiences (translation: audiences over fifty) were not a significant moviegoing demographic. Their key demographic was the eighteen- to thirty-four-year-olds. Yet I couldn't help thinking that my mother (now seventy-four) had more leisure time to see movies than I did, and I (now over fifty) went to the movies more than my fifteen-year-old son, who would rather play video games.

I thought the distributors were wrong and set out to prove it. The aging baby boomers were still the largest generation by population. Why weren't there more movies targeted for them?

Blair, Deb, my mom, and I were determined to figure out a way to self-distribute the film in places with a high concentration of residents over fifty—retirement areas like South Florida, Arizona, Palm Springs, and Southern California. This would be an intense DIY effort.

Being an independent filmmaker involved doing whatever the hell it took to get your movie out to the public. So I met with the owner of a privately owned South Florida movie chain, Frank Theatres, who agreed to play *Boynton Beach Club* in ten of his theaters as a tryout. The theater owner would take 10 percent of the ticket sales as a distribution fee and make money from the concession stand. This was an amazing deal, since there would be no middlemen to take a cut of the profits. But we, the producers, would have to do all the marketing and advertising ourselves, which turned out to be a lot of work and a great learning experience.

Our gamble paid off. Our little film was a box office success on its opening weekend in Florida, selling out almost every screening, with lines around the block. It even outperformed several of the big Hollywood movies playing in those very same multiplexes. We knew who our audience was and had figured out a way to reach them. Over the next few months, we got hundreds of calls from exhibitors across the country who wanted to book *Boynton Beach Club* into their theaters, and I suddenly recalled that famous line from the movie *Field of Dreams*: "If you build it, they will come." And they did.[25]

Unlike people whose lives shrink as they get older, my mother's world was expanding. She was doing press interviews, traveling to film festivals, and enjoying all the attention. Unafraid of change, at seventy-four my mother had reinvented herself, and it was wonderful to see her blossom. Little did she know that six years after the release of *Boynton Beach Club*, she, too, would be a single senior.

In 2011, my father, who always loved a good poop joke, died unexpectedly from an abdominal aneurysm that occurred while he was sitting on the toilet. Always fastidious, he tidied himself and made his way over to the nearby bedroom, where he passed away a few minutes later, sitting in his favorite armchair. It came as a shock to all of us, especially my mom, who had not expected him to depart that morning after a leisurely breakfast that included cupcakes from Magnolia Bakery I had sent for Valentine's Day. (I hope it wasn't the cupcakes!)

---

25. By 2010, Hollywood would finally recognize the box office potential of films targeted for older audiences when Fox Searchlight's film *The Best Exotic Marigold Hotel* (made for $10 million) grossed an incredible $139 million at the box office. This was followed by the success of TV series starring actors well over sixty, like *Grace and Frankie* (Jane Fonda and Lily Tomlin). In September 2023, ABC's *The Golden Bachelor,* a reality show about senior dating, would attract 11 million viewers and become the season's hit show.

Despite my parents' happy sixty-one-year marriage, the last few years had become increasingly difficult. My father was never officially diagnosed with dementia, but had been suffering from gradual memory loss and mild confusion. He began to repeat himself and frequently made up childlike rhyming jingles. His toughness had mellowed, and he became very, very sweet.

My dad had a memorial service in Florida that was attended by family and his many friends, one of whom sang his favorite song, "My Way." And it was true. He was an old-school guy, fiercely loyal to friends and family, who liked doing things his way. There were eulogies filled with funny anecdotes about his flashy taste, his obsession with cars, his generosity, and love of burned meat. (He wasn't happy until his steak looked like a lump of coal on a plate.) My father would have enjoyed his own very lively funeral, so I hoped he was watching.

Although in many ways my mother was independent, she was a romantic at heart. Having spent her entire life since age fifteen as a "couple," she didn't know how to be single, and I think she was lonely. After two years of widowhood, like the characters in *Boynton Beach Club*, my mother drifted into the world of senior dating. After a few casual, but lackluster, dinners with old codgers, she was introduced to a man named Bill. Bill had been a widower for many years and played the field. He was a sharp dresser and a people-pleaser with a successful salesman's gift of gab.

He and my mom would not have clicked had they met when they were younger. She would have found him a smooth operator. He would have found her too strong-willed. But my mother was now eighty-one and Bill was eighty-six and both had mellowed. They were in good health, looked twenty years younger, and still had a zest for life. They cuddled, danced, drank vodka martinis, and dined at steak houses. It was fascinating to watch my mom turn into a giddy teenager.

A decade later, my mother and Bill moved in together during the first outbreak of COVID. She was now ninety. He, ninety-five. The pandemic slowed them down, but only a little. In 2022, they drove to Disney World to go on all the rides, just the two of them—without grandchildren—simply to prove they could do it.

Push It

(Salt-N-Pepa)

S hortly after *Boynton Beach Club* was released, I was approached by a composer named Ned Ginsburg and a lyricist, Michael Colby, who were interested in turning the movie into a stage musical. Always up for a new creative
challenge, I offered to write the show's libretto (the "Book")—something I'd
never done before. I soon realized that musical theater was very different
from film, and trying to figure out when a character should stop talking and
suddenly burst into song wasn't so easy.

It took a lot of trial and error to get the right songs in the right spots
and weave them organically into the story. Along the way, a co-lyricist with
the melodious name Cornelia Ravenal joined the team. Then, in 2019, after
nearly a decade of stage readings and developmental productions, the musical had a successful three-week run at the Surflight Theatre in New Jersey. It
starred Andrea McArdle, Broadway's original Little Orphan Annie, now old
enough to play a character living in a Florida retirement community. Unfortunately, in early 2020, as we were preparing to move the show to a venue
in West Palm Beach, news of a mysterious virus lurking in the shadows put
an abrupt halt to our plans.

Damn! I've done it again! Let my story run away. Once more I'll press
PAUSE and rewind back to 2011—a time when the idea of a virus that
could devastate the entire planet would exist only in Steven Soderbergh's
sci-fi fantasy film, *Contagion*.

* * *

The next few years were spent developing scripts and directing episodic TV (some fun experiences, some less so), when I suddenly found myself with two movies going into production back to back. That's the crazy way this business works. Long periods of drought, then it pours.

One was a dance film called *Musical Chairs*. The other, a sports comedy called *The Hot Flashes*. Both were stories about underdogs staking claim to their value.

Musical Chairs was the passion project of Janet Carrus, one of the film's producers. It was a glimpse into a world I'd never seen before on film—wheelchair ballroom dance competitions—and set in a part of the city I'd never filmed—the Puerto Rican and Dominican neighborhoods of Washington Heights and Brooklyn.

Janet was the widow of Gerald Carrus, the founder of Infinity Broadcasting Corporation, the company that made Howard Stern and Don Imus household names. Sometime after her husband's death, Janet took up ballroom dancing and eventually became a semipro, participating in competitions around the world. While traveling in Europe, she heard about wheelchair ballroom competitions, which existed abroad but were not yet known in the United States. They were similar to traditional ballroom competitions—couples competing in various dance categories: salsa, tango, samba, waltz—but one of the dancers is disabled and uses a wheelchair. Janet showed me YouTube videos, and my mind was blown.

The screenplay by Marty Madden was sweetly romantic, teetering on the edge of sentimentality, but the characters were warm and quirky. Plus, I liked looking at traditional movie genres from a different angle. Having directed a New Wave screwball comedy, an AI rom-com, a father-daughter mafia movie, a feminist revenge comedy, a gender-bending detective story, and a date movie about single seniors, I was excited to make a wheelchair dance film.

Recognizing the importance of authenticity, the casting directors, Sig De Miguel and Stephen Vincent, knew we needed to put together a cast of able-bodied and disabled performers. In the film, the characters meet at a rehab center for spinal cord injuries, where they are cajoled into entering a ballroom dance competition. One is a former dance instructor, paralyzed in a Manhattan taxi accident. Another, a disabled Iraq War veteran with anger management issues. There is a punk rocker with a chip on her shoulder and a transgender African American woman refusing to let another of life's challenges bring her down.

This was Laverne Cox's first movie role, and I could not have envisioned that three years later, after a stint in the TV series *Orange Is the New Black,* she would be on the cover of *Time Magazine* with the headline: THE TRANSGENDER TIPPING POINT: AMERICA'S NEXT CIVIL RIGHTS FRONTIER. Besides being a talented actor, she was a savvy activist and an inspiring public speaker. In 2022 the Mattel Company would model a doll on her: the Barbie Tribute Collection Laverne Cox Doll!

Hard to imagine when I got my first white, blond Barbie in 1959 that there would one day be a Black transgender model.[26]

Laverne Cox and Morgan Spector get ready for the dance competition. *(Photo by John Clifford)*

We scheduled three weeks of rigorous wheelchair dance rehearsals to whip everyone into shape. Teaching the nondisabled actors how to maneuver

---

26. Fun fact: In the summer of 2023, a Barbie movie directed by Greta Gerwig, would gross over a billion dollars in worldwide box office. Gerwig's *Barbie* was even pinker than *She-Devil,* but with enough wit, diversity, and clever messaging about gender roles and empowerment to make it appealing to both lovers and haters of the original plastic doll.

smoothly in a wheelchair was harder than it looked. There were lots of chair topples during week one. By week two, the actors were getting the hang of it. By week three, they were doing wheelies.

During the making of the film, every preconceived notion I had about otherness and disability was shattered. It was inspiring to be around people who were not overcome by adversity, or defined by their disabilities, but had turned their abilities into something poetic. I fell in love with the cast and they fell in love with each other. I remember a few times while filming the ballroom dance sequences, I'd shout, "Cut!" and be genuinely surprised by who got up out of their wheelchair and who remained seated. The dancers had become so unified, I'd forgotten who was able to do what.

* * *

Over the thirty years I'd worked on film productions, I'd never had a personal injury despite all the heavy equipment being lugged around, the time pressure, and the number of bodies crowding a set. But there's a first time for everything.

On the fifth day of filming, we were shooting a scene in a dance studio off Fifth Avenue. It was St. Patrick's Day, and you could hear the sounds of shouting and drunken laughter coming from the street below. While waiting for the lights to be set, I happened to be standing in an archway where the set dressers had hung a heavy velvet curtain from a metal pole on the ceiling. I didn't notice the pole until it came crashing down on my head. I must have momentarily glanced up, because the metal pole smacked me right in the eye, almost knocking me down. I was dazed for a few moments, unsure of what had happened, then my eye began to swell into an enormous purple egg. A doctor was called to the set to check for a concussion. Thankfully, I didn't have one, but I was sent home to recuperate. I would direct the rest of the film with a big black eye that lasted well over two months. I looked like a battered woman and couldn't help notice the curious sideways glances of people I passed on the street. A look that said, "I wonder what she did to get that?"

After the shoot ended, I spent the next few months in the editing room with Keiko Deguchi, watching the movie come to life. I'd worked with

Keiko on my last three films, and she was a trusted collaborator, with the patience of a saint. I watched as she put in the beautiful, haunting score composed by Mario Grigorov. The music made me choke up, and when I glanced over at the usually unflappable Keiko, she, too, looked like she was about to cry.

Musical Chairs had its premiere at the Miami International Film Festival, where it got a standing (and seated) ovation and went on to receive a 2012 GLAAD nomination for Best Film in a Limited Release. But I wasn't there to celebrate. I was now in preproduction in New Orleans on *The Hot Flashes,* a project I'd been involved with, off and on, for several years.

Pulling together the financing had been difficult, but through sheer resolve, its first-time screenwriter/producer, Brad, and his partner, Nina, had managed to find investment money to kick-start the production. New Orleans (post–Hurricane Katrina) was offering lucrative tax incentives to film there and, suddenly, there was a rapidly approaching start date. I had little time to unwind from one film before moving on to the next. But in the unpredictable world of moviemaking, you embrace an opportunity when it comes your way because you never know when another will come along.

The Hot Flashes plot went like this:

Following the death of a former teammate, a group of middle-aged women (the 1982 Texas state girls' basketball champions) decide to reunite after thirty years and challenge the current teenage girls' champs to a series of basketball games to raise money for breast cancer awareness. But first they have to get over their old high school grievances, get back in shape, and prove they still have what it takes to be winners.

In many ways I was the perfect director for the film.

1. It had five roles for actresses around age fifty.
2. It was about women going through a midlife crisis who wanted to feel valued. (I could relate.)
3. It was a comedy with a positive social message.
4. It had an atmospheric setting—a small town in Texas: big sky, cowboy hats, and pickup trucks.
5. It was about basketball . . .

. . . STOP! FREEZE! That's where things got a little tricky.

Okay, I admit it. I've never been sporty and knew little about basketball. (Remember when I said this would come back to haunt me? Well, now it did.)

Growing up in the 1960s, girls weren't encouraged to be athletic, and there were few female team sports offered at my high school. The only sport my girlfriends and I engaged in was smoking pot behind the Del Ennis Bowling Lanes.

Of course, girls could be cheerleaders, but that wasn't considered a sport.

Starting in tenth grade, we were forced to take gym class twice a week. And please don't get me started on those hideous royal blue gym bloomers that sat in our lockers for months, unwashed. The class consisted mostly of calisthenics—jumping jacks, sit-ups, and running in circles around the perimeter of the gymnasium. Plus a weekly swim in the school's over-chlorinated pool. (No one wanted to dunk their head underwater and have to redo their makeup.)

I faked my period twice a month. In the '60s, menstruation was still a legitimate excuse to get out of swim class since most girls used sanitary napkins and belts.[27] Tampons were thought to be bad for virgins, and most of us still were.

Of the few female team sports offered, the most popular was field hockey. But the ground surrounding our school was frequently soggy, so by the end of a game you were miserable and covered in mud. Girls' soccer didn't exist in the 1960s and girls' basketball wasn't popular in our predominantly white suburban high school. But even if it had been, at four feet, eleven and a half inches, I'd never have made the team.

The attitude toward female sports changed radically in the early '70s, thanks to Title IX. This new federal law required that women be given equal opportunities to participate in all school sporting activities. It was also intended to teach girls about team building, competition, and how to accept

---

27. The beltless maxi pad was not invented until 1972. The sanitary belt was patented in 1956 by an African American inventor named Mary Beatrice Davidson Kenner.

defeat or victory gracefully, leadership skills that would come in handy a decade later when more women entered the workforce.

Suddenly, it was cool for girls to be jocks! But by the time Title IX came into effect, I'd almost finished college and was on my way to New York to study filmmaking. Team sports, and the lessons they might have taught me, were no longer on my radar.

* * *

I'd been upfront with Brad about my lack of basketball experience, but I loved the script's characters and theme. So few movies dealt with menopause as a significant stage in a woman's life. In mainstream cinema, the subject was taboo, considered too unsexy to document on film, a joke on an old lady's T-shirt: *I'm still hot, it just comes in flashes now.*

For me, basketball would be the vehicle, not the main point.

I was working again with casting directors Kerry Barden and Paul Schnee. It would be our fourth movie together, and we were able to pull together a terrific cast of former Hollywood leading ladies who were now at an age when they were no longer getting lead roles in studio comedies.

The film starred Brooke Shields, still staggeringly beautiful at forty-eight. And for someone with such a famed and controversial childhood, she was extremely down-to-earth. But what stood out most was that like the character Brooke played in the movie, she was a hard worker. Someone determined to prove her self-worth. Coincidentally, Brooke had also once been a Susan, having starred in the popular '90s sitcom *Suddenly Susan.*

Brooke played Beth, the small-town Texas housewife who comes up with a plan to reunite her former teammates and challenge the current high school girls champs to a series of games to raise money for the town's defunct mammogram mobile. She names her team the Hot Flashes (for obvious reasons) and figures that between the profits from the game's concession stand and proceeds from the town's betting pool (knowing that all the men in town will bet *against* the middle-aged ladies), they could raise enough money to get the mammo-mobile back in operation. All they needed to do was win.

One of Beth's former teammates, a shy lesbian car dealership owner named Ginger, was played by a redheaded Daryl Hannah. Another was

Clementine, the trampy, chain-smoking cashier at the local Piggly Wiggly. Melanie Griffith was cast in the role.

Melanie had auditioned for *Desperately Seeking Susan* thirty years earlier. I'd wanted to work with her ever since watching her wonderful performances in *Something Wild* and *Working Girl*. She had on-screen warmth and vulnerability. And a great voice. But when she showed up in New Orleans, she seemed distracted. During the team's first basketball training session, she was often on her phone, and I wondered if there was something stressful going on in her private life that I was unaware of. (A year later, she and husband Antonio Banderas would separate.) After three days, Melanie left the production. In a press release, it was called "creative differences"—a catchall phrase that often has little to do with creativity. In retrospect, I think it was one of those right person/wrong time situations. At the last minute, Virginia Madsen stepped in and did a fantastic job on and off the court.

Then there was Roxie, played by Camryn Manheim, an out-of-shape hippie who specialized in baking pot-laced desserts. The fifth team member was Flo, played by Wanda Sykes, the town's mayor, who was seeking reelection and didn't want to jeopardize her chances of winning in this predominantly white small town by doing anything that seemed too Black.

None of the players had set foot on a basketball court in decades. But after a few rusty practice sessions and some heated attempts to reconcile old, festering high school grudges, they band together to prove they can still strut their stuff.

We had hired a basketball consultant to train the actresses and teach them some plays. What they lacked in athletic prowess, they made up for with determination. The cast bonded during basketball camp and ran their asses off on court for ten hours a day, nine days straight. Pretty impressive for a group of fifty-year-olds.

* * *

It was while filming *The Hot Flashes* that I realized I was getting old(er).

The first time one of the crew members, a local makeup artist, called me Mrs. Seidelman, I glanced around expecting to see my mother. But he was talking to me. "Please, call me Susan," I said. The next time he saw me, he hesitated, then called me ma'am, and I understood he was a southern gentleman of thirty and I was a woman of fifty-eight. He was simply too polite to call a woman his mother's age by her first name. Then I looked around at all the other crew members and noticed, for the first time, that I was the oldest person on set. I flashed back to *Desperately Seeking Susan,* when I had been one of the youngest, and was surprised to realize that three decades had gone by without me noticing.

In the summer of 2013, we had our premiere in Los Angeles. All the actresses showed up to lend their support. When the reviews came out, they were kind, but mixed. The movie was called "enjoyable" and praised for having "its heart in the right place," but the screenplay was criticized as "predictable" and the basketball games "messy." Both things were true, so this came as no surprise.

Despite *The Hot Flashes'* sympathetic message, the script needed more bite, and the games needed more excitement. I remember one reviewer called the film "well-intentioned." In 1982, when I'd made my first film, *Smithereens,* being well-intentioned had never been my goal. I wanted to be bold.

I still did.

Thankfully, the actresses' performances were applauded, and they were nominated for a Best Ensemble Cast Award by the Women Film Critics Circle. Working with the cast had been the highlight of the job.

It's a wrap!

In the end, both *Musical Chairs* and *The Hot Flashes* were films about outsiders wanting to break out of the boxes they were stuck in, a thread woven through many of the movies I'd made over the past thirty-five years. And their message was this: "I'll show you." The words I whispered when Bobby C broke my heart in eighth grade.

I'll show you all!

The Times They Are A-Changin'
(Bob Dylan)

I could tell you about other films I've made and the ones that came close but slipped away. Suffice it to say, getting any movie produced is a battle, no matter what the budget level. And at some point, I had to ask myself this: *Did I still have the fight? The hustle? Was there something else I'd rather be doing?* (Nothing I could think of.) Secretly I worried I had nothing new to say. Isn't that the fear of all creative people? Maybe it was time to pass on the lessons I'd learned from my successes and failures to the next generation of storytellers.

* * *

In the fall of 2013, I returned to teaching. I'd been an adjunct professor in NYU's film department off and on for a few years and taught an intensive six-hour advanced directing workshop once a week. This was a class where seniors get to make the thesis film that will hopefully open doors for them after graduation.

University film programs had changed dramatically since I was a student, becoming more competitive and much more expensive. Suddenly everyone wanted to be a director, and many universities now had serious film departments. NYU's graduate film school was no longer located in a funky building in the East Village at East 7th Street and Second Avenue. It had moved into an impressive high-rise called Tisch School of the Arts, on Broadway.

The atmosphere was different, too. More pragmatic. The students read industry trade papers, studied the latest box office results, followed film biz websites, and were plugged into social media. They were up to date on the hottest agents and how to submit their films to the top festivals. (They emailed a link.) They also had access to a vast array of new digital tools—although all the latest technology is no substitute for a good story well told.

I remembered how hard it had been to find a mentor when I was starting out. It was my time to pay it forward. But it wasn't a selfless desire on my part to be a teacher or role model. I had a selfish motivation as well. I enjoyed being around young people. I liked hearing about what movies they watched, what music they listened to, what podcasts they thought were cool. I loved their enthusiasm. They were a reminder of who I'd been, and I hoped they could hold on to that passion for as long as possible, knowing the film business can turn even the most confident optimist into a self-doubting cynic.

In his play *Speed-the-Plow,* David Mamet wrote: "Life in the movie business is like the beginning of a new love affair: it's full of surprises, and you're constantly getting fucked."

Everyone knows the movie industry is mean-spirited and shark-infested, but it's also dazzling, exhilarating, and euphoric, which is why everyone puts up with all the nasty shit.

And there was another change I noticed. My students talked about TV series with as much enthusiasm as feature films. At the time, the multihyphenate Lena Dunham was an inspiration to them. It was a combination of Dunham's youth (she was still in her twenties and already writing/producing/directing and starring in the successful HBO TV series *Girls*), mixed with her unorthodox creativity and fearlessness. I liked Dunham's work, too, recognizing that different generations share universal experiences, only dressed (or in Lena's case, sometimes undressed) in different clothing.

By 2015, nearly half of my Advanced Directing Workshop were women. It had become more commonplace for young women to see themselves as directors, producers, and cinematographers.

And it was true, there were many more indie films and TV series being directed by women, who were no longer referred to as "women directors." Simply "directors." (No qualifying adjective needed.) But even so, this was not reflected in the industry at large. Still, very few women were given the opportunity to direct the big-budget studio movies. That was almost exclusively the domain of men. And there was still a large sexist pay gap. Of the one hundred top-grossing movies in 2015, only 7.5 percent were directed by (white) women. Yet, each year the gap between the number of men and women in my NYU class was closing, until in my final year, 2019, there would be more women than men. And my advice to students:

Claim what you can do and do it with confidence.

Stay curious.

Make stuff.

Goodbye Yellow Brick Road
(Elton John)

O nce I'd made it to Manhattan, I thought I would never leave. I'd become the person I'd always wanted to be—an authentic New Yorker. I effortlessly rode the crowded subway during rush hour. I liked the hum of all-night traffic coming from Houston Street, the laughter of drunk party people stumbling along Thompson Street at 4:00 a.m. I'd learned to navigate around the piles of dog shit on the sidewalk. I even liked the taste of NYC tap water and grown accustomed to the scent of garbage in the air when the weather turned warm.

Then one day I woke up and knew it was time to go.

I'd lived in the same Soho loft building for thirty-four years. I'd watched my neighborhood go through changes: the dark deserted streets of the seventies, the unfinished artists' lofts of the early eighties, the yuppie real estate boom of the nineties, the devastation of 9/11, the subprime mortgage bust of 2008, when the shops on West Broadway were shuttered. But what I was feeling now was different. It was like the slow fade of a once-intense love affair. Many of the things I'd loved about life downtown—the colorful residents, the funky bookshops, the mom-and-pop food stores, pop-up art galleries, performance spaces, and dive bars—no longer existed. Or, if they did, I was no longer frequenting them. A pastrami sandwich at Katz's Deli now cost thirty bucks.

But, maybe that's the magic of New York City. Like the people who gravitate there, the town is constantly reinventing itself. In that way, it's like no other place on the planet, and there will always be an influx of new people, dreamers, scammers and rogues, arriving to make the city their own. And after living there for forty-three years, New York was in my blood, a part of who I was no matter where I lived.

* * *

In 2017, Jonathan and I sold our loft and moved full-time to our house in the country. Built before the Revolutionary War, in 1768, with thick plaster walls, insulated with a mixture of mud and horsehair, the house drips purple wisteria flowers in the spring. It stays naturally warm in the winter and cool in the summer. There is no need for air-conditioning. It had been restored and renovated by its various owners over the last three centuries, but you can still feel the ghosts of the past. Fortunately, they were not scary. It's a house with a history that's carved into the huge stone fireplaces, wooden beams, and wide pumpkin pine floorboards. It's surrounded by hay fields used as a thoroughfare by herds of deer. Hawks fly in circles overhead. Directly across the road is a woodpecker preserve. I listen to them pecking away all day, and they really do sound like their cartoon cousin, Woody.

I was nervous about leaving the hustle and bustle of Manhattan. Worried that our new country life would be too secluded, too provincial. What I didn't know was that a few years later the entire world would go into a pandemic lockdown.

Life is full of unpredictable twists and turns. And the universe must have a sense of humor because in one of life's little ironies, I was now a Jersey Girl. This was the state that had been the butt of several jokes in my earlier films. The last place I thought I'd ever end up.[28]

Here's a Jersey joke from *Desperately Seeking Susan:*

---

28. Okay, a lot of cool people came from New Jersey: Sinatra, Springsteen, Jack Nicholson, Queen Latifah, Bon Jovi. (Is Bon Jovi cool?)

INTERIOR. MAGIC CLUB—NIGHT

SUSAN enters the nightclub, carrying her suitcase, and is greeted by her friend, the CIGARETTE GIRL.

CIGARETTE GIRL: My God, Susan! Where have you been? Everyone thought you were dead!

SUSAN: (deadpan) No. Just in New Jersey.

* * *

The name of our town is Stockton. It's on the Jersey side of the Delaware River, across an iron bridge from Bucks County, Pennsylvania. The largest nearby town, New Hope, had been a popular getaway for the New York theater crowd in the 1940s and '50s. An artsy and liberal place where gays, lesbians, and thespians all felt comfortable at a time when few places were as welcoming. Some of Bucks County's famous residents included Oscar Hammerstein, James Michener, Patricia Highsmith, S. J. Perelman (author of the Marx Brothers movies), Dorothy Parker,[29] the singer Pink, and members of the alt-rock band Ween.

In the 1960s, New Hope became popular with tourists and lost some of its charm. Its Main Street filled with ice cream parlors and hippie tchotchke shops selling tie-dyed T-shirts, crystals, and bongs. But despite the tourism, New Hope retains its eclectic and liberal attitude. Visit a local diner and you'll find a pig farmer and a carpenter sitting at the counter alongside an aging drag queen.

Our country friends are a creative and diverse group: antique dealers, painters, writers, musicians, cooks, and scientists. There's a forager who picks the wisteria hanging from our house to sell to fancy restaurants in Manhattan to decorate exorbitantly priced salads. Another who finds chanterelles hidden in the woods. Few have any connection to the film business, and I sometimes

---

29. Dorothy Parker once said: "London is satisfied, Paris is resigned, but New York is always hopeful," which instantly made me want to move back to the city!

miss conversations about New Icelandic Cinema or gossip about what A-lister was caught in the latest Hollywood scandal. On the other hand, I'm reminded that there are four distinct seasons. Something I'd lost track of living in Soho.

* * *

I turned sixty-five and was now technically a senior citizen. I could buy senior-priced movie tickets and get 5 percent off at the local supermarket on Senior Tuesdays.

But here's the truth—I didn't like getting old. I didn't like the wrinkles, the saggy neckline. I hated the occasional moments of memory fog. Despite the *60 is the new 40* slogan on T-shirts and dish towels (and I plead guilty to using that catchphrase in *Boynton Beach Club*), *Sixty is not forty!* Sixty is sixty, only now dressed in Lululemon.

The Bette Davis quote, "Old age ain't no place for sissies," was more accurate.

Definitely older, hopefully a little wiser (*Photo by Oscar Brett*)

Meanwhile, pop culture was becoming unrecognizable. I first noticed this over a decade earlier when I went to the supermarket and saw there were no longer movie stars on the covers of the magazines at the checkout counter. We had entered the era of reality TV with celebrities like Paris Hilton, the Osbournes, the Bachelor, the Real Housewives, and, to everyone's surprise, the future president Donald Trump. A few years later, attention would shift to another generation of *influencers* including the entire Jenner-Kardashian clan. And then there were all the new Instagram and TikTok celebs who were simply famous for being famous.

Wren's wishful thinking in *Smithereens* had become reality.

I thought of my grandmothers at my age. Nana H, with her false teeth suspended in a glass of water, and Nanny S, with her blond wig resting on a stand on her dresser. Thankfully, I still had a full head of thick hair and all my own teeth! Although my vision wasn't as sharp as it used to be. When I looked at myself in the mirror, I was in soft focus. On the positive side, it was like having my own built-in diffusion filter. In that way, nature has been kind.

I stretched the skin above my eyelids and under my chin. I watched the ads online for Botox and miracle creams and considered all the things I could do to look younger. In a culture that worshipped youth and desirability, being attractive was not just about vanity. It had financial, political, and transactional ramifications, especially if your livelihood was in the public eye. (Worse for women, but older men now felt it, too.) Then I remembered the week I'd spent in India with the French actress Jeanne Moreau. We were both on the jury of the New Delhi Film Festival, so we spent six or seven hours a day watching movies and having lunch together. I was in awe of her. She'd been my idol since I first saw her in François Truffaut's film *Jules and Jim*. At the time of the festival, 1996, I was in my midforties and she was in her late sixties and very beautiful. Elegant. European actresses wore their age differently than American women. The folds under her eyes and the faint lines around her mouth made her look sexy. She had a slightly crooked smile that said "I dare you to fuck with me." She looked like a woman who lived a fascinating life. And she clearly had. It was written on her face.

How wonderful to have a face that told an interesting story.

It's the End of the World as We Know It
(R.E.M.)

In February 2020, I was invited by the University of Texas at Austin and the Alamo Drafthouse Cinema to give a talk and screen a movie. There was news on TV about a mysterious virus from China that had spread to Italy, but there was still no cause for alarm. Jonathan told me to wear a mask on the plane. I did, but was the only person on the plane wearing one, and after a while my glasses fogged up, so I took it off.

Three weeks later, on March 11, the world went on lockdown. One of the early casualties was Mark Blum, the talented actor in *Desperately Seeking Susan*. He died in a New York hospital emergency room on March 25, just two weeks after COVID-19 was officially declared a global pandemic. It hit the news big-time and made this surreal situation all too real.

Mark Blum and Madonna *(Courtesy of MGM Media Licensing, photograph by Andrew Schwartz)*

For the next two years, I spent much of my time puttering around at home dressed in a T-shirt and pajama bottoms. I stopped wearing a bra. I no longer went to the hair salon after everyone there came down with COVID. I Zoomed with old friends and noticed that several had let their hair go gray. Who knew the pandemic would start a fashion trend?

In May 2021, our home was suddenly infested by a swarm of Brood X cicadas. They had emerged from inside the earth after spending seventeen years dormant underground, now coming out to mate. They covered the sides of our house, came down the chimneys, and dropped from the old stone fireplaces. They filled the air with their deafening mating hum, like something out of a sci-fi movie, or a biblical plague. There was nothing we could do but wait the five weeks it took for them to run their life cycle, then die.

In August, Oscar married a beautiful and intelligent woman named Eva. They stood in front of a municipal clerk in New York City wearing face masks. Sadly, Jonathan and I were unable to attend the ceremony since the city clerk's office only allowed one witness, and we were two. Instead, they decided on a photographer friend who took their wedding photo against a painted backdrop of City Hall.

Ozzy and Eva get married (*Photo by Julian Kapadia*)

* * *

During the height of the pandemic, Jonathan and I drank too much. Our cocktail hour (I won't call it a Happy Hour, because we weren't always happy) moved from 5:30 p.m. to 3:30 p.m., followed by dinner at 4:30 p.m. (our Early Bird Special). When the food in our local supermarket began to disappear, we stockpiled canned goods: SpaghettiOs, Beefaroni, baked beans, Campbell's soup. It brought back childhood memories of my mother's home cooking. Surprisingly, we weren't depressed, although there was much to be depressed about: new strains of virus, climate change, nightly stories of sexual abuse and racial violence. But we were lonely. We were social creatures, alone in a big house in the middle of nowhere. We missed family dinners. We missed hanging with friends. Time became elastic. Days felt like weeks, months like years.

Strangely, now that I had all this free time, I wasn't sure what to do with it. It was hard to focus on the future with so much uncertainty, so I found myself turning to the past as if visiting a foreign country. Once again, I began taking notes. Some were just random thoughts and memories that occurred to me in the shower as I was shampooing my hair. Some were middle of the night musings that popped into my head when I found myself awake at 3:00 a.m. And I suddenly had the urge to email, phone, Zoom with people I hadn't spoken to in decades. To check my recollections against theirs. In some cases, to say things I'd neglected to say, like "I'm sorry" for some slight, some wrongdoing, some bad judgment call I'd made in the past. Or simply to say "I love you."

After much hesitation, I decided to contact my old boyfriend, Yan, the man who broke off our engagement in 1979, giving me the kick in the ass I needed to jump-start my career.

I'd heard from a friend that he was now retired, having enjoyed a successful career as an economist and consultant to the White House. He had gotten rich, but his personal life had been complicated. He was currently living in Santa Monica with his fourth wife. We hadn't been in touch for a long time, but I knew he'd followed my career over the years. I wondered if he was surprised by the path my life had taken. But that wasn't the reason I wanted to contact him.

There's an event I've avoided talking about because I worried it might color this story in an unwanted way. Plus, I could never find the right words. Yan was the only person who might help me fill in some of the gaps. Although this happened forty years ago, it influenced several of the films I'd go on to make. It was a story about the powerful taking advantage of the powerless.

I had an old email address for Yan, but wasn't sure it was still valid. I emailed and a few hours later, he emailed back. I wanted to ask him about what happened during the spring of 1978, when we had gone on vacation to the island of Guadeloupe.

I was twenty-six. We were staying at a French hotel on the beach where they offered scuba lessons to guests. I'd never gone scuba diving before—neither had Yan—and the fish in that part of the Caribbean were spectacular because of a coral reef nearby. We decided to give it a shot.

The scuba operation was run by a group of young Frenchmen with the laid-back style of hippie beach bums. They had long hair, streaked blond by the sun, and permanent tans. They looked like guys who spent their entire life in flip-flops and cut-off jeans. We joined a group of about eight hotel guests, all diving novices. We were given some basic scuba instructions, then taken out on a boat with three guides. We reached a spot near the reef, and two of the instructors helped the group put on their masks and tanks (no wet suits necessary) and climb into the water. The third guide stayed behind with the boat.

Underwater there was a spectacular world I'd only seen in Jacques Cousteau documentaries: a huge coral reef, home to glowing angelfish, sea anemones, sponges, gigantic sea turtles, and eels. The only sound I could hear was my own breathing echoing inside my mask.

I was looking around, mesmerized by schools of fluorescent fish, when the next thing I knew, Yan and the other tourists were nowhere in sight. Without realizing it, I had been separated from the group. All I could see in front of me were vibrant fish and the dark sea beyond. Then I saw the scuba instructor come up alongside me. He started swimming in a circle around me, like he was performing some sort of mating ritual. He then took hold of my hips, pulled me in front of him and began rubbing his body against mine.

I started to panic, but there was no one around. Just the two of us and fish. I was too shocked to push him away with any force. Terrified he would leave me stranded underwater to run out of oxygen and die on the ocean floor. I had no idea where I was, or how to resurface.

I felt helpless . . . and yet, and yet . . . here's the strange thing that happened. Some self-preservation instinct kicked in, my mind disconnected from my body, and I watched this underwater scene play out as if I were watching a film. Part of me was thinking: "Take mental notes. One day you'll put this in a movie."

How crazy was that?! But it helped me not to panic. I was being raped by a stranger whose face was covered by a snorkel mask, and I'd turned this into a movie scene. Pause! Eject! EJECT!!!

Instead, I peered out of my slightly fogged goggles, as if through a camera lens, and focused on the fish swimming by, silent witnesses to this abuse. I watched as globules of semen floated by in slow motion, suspended in the sea water. On the soundtrack, all that played was the echoey sound of my own breathing amplified by my mask—inhale, exhale, in and out, in and out.

My mind and body reconnected when I reached the surface and climbed back on the boat. The other two scuba guides and the tourist group were already onboard, waiting. Yan was there, too. I wondered if the other scuba guides knew what had happened. I suspected they did and that this was some sick underwater game they played. A competition. I was sure I wasn't the first tourist this had happened to, nor would I be the last.

Did they privately exchange high-fives?

Thinking back on it now, what upsets me most was my silence. That I never spoke out. Not to Yan, not to the authorities, not to anyone. Maybe I was in shock. Or felt ashamed. Maybe I thought Yan would think that I'd been complicit in what happened. This was a time when women were still held accountable for men's bad behavior (even today, some still are).

So, I said nothing during the boat ride back to the hotel, sitting next to Yan, shivering with a wet towel around my shoulders. When the boat docked, I got off and we walked back to the hotel. I didn't turn around to see if the scuba guide was watching or drinking beers with his buddies.

Afterward, I blocked out this memory for many, many years. I locked it away in a filing cabinet in my brain, where it stayed until the #MeToo movement started to speak out in 2017. And the more vocal they became (not just women—men, too) the more this memory refused to stay hidden. That was when I decided to email Yan, to see if he remembered anything about that day on the scuba boat over forty years ago. I told him what had happened, and he seemed genuinely surprised. He had no idea that anything out of the ordinary had occurred and said I should have told him. I was glad we had this exchange. Just mentioning it to him provided some closure. I didn't know that would be our last communication. A year later, Yan died of cancer. Since the pandemic was still raging, his funeral was held virtually. I asked his wife, the woman he had finally found happiness with, if I could attend. She was gracious and sent me a Zoom link.

*   *   *

These days, I don't wear my feminism casually, as a woman's right to control her own body is being challenged across the country. But thankfully, abuse of power and bad behavior are no longer considered "business as usual."

And I never did put an underwater rape scene in any of my films. Instead, I'm telling that story now—without cover—so that others in similar situations (one in six women, one in thirty-three men in the US, one in three women worldwide) will know that it happened to me, too.

Both Sides Now

(Joni Mitchell)

It's life's illusions I recall
I really don't know life at all

Last year I turned seventy. When I was a kid, I used to think fifty sounded old. Then I pushed it back to sixty. But seventy is seventy. The number speaks for itself. Yet, inside there's still the ghost of that fifteen-year-old girl who boogalooed on *Super Lou's TV Dance Party*.

But even at this age, I'm desperately seeking something. Isn't that what this journey is all about? Desperately seeking love, sex, success, health, wisdom, peace, kindness, hope.

Maybe what I'm seeking now is a way to age gracefully while still retaining a little bit of *bad*.

* * *

Copies of *The Hollywood Reporter* pile up in our mailbox, then are moved to stacks on the kitchen table, where they sit unread for weeks. They report news about a movie industry I no longer recognize. Too many comic book heroes. Too much CGI. Too many unfamiliar stars, in unfamiliar TV series, airing on unsubscribed-to streaming channels.

Sometimes I'll catch a movie or show starring an actor I've known. My contemporaries. They are now cast as grandparents. John Malkovich looks like a distinguished elderly gentleman. Meryl Streep still exudes style and class as her hair has turned from blond to silver. Madonna is still fearless, but no longer looks like the Madonna I knew. (But I no longer look like the young filmmaker who directed her.)

Movies used to be a cultural touchpoint. Not anymore.

Movie theater attendance has dramatically dropped, and several of the large theater chains have gone out of business. The decline started even before the pandemic. COVID only sped things up. Most people now watch movies at home, but no matter how big your TV screen, it's not the same experience. Watching TV at home, I find myself putting the show on pause to make a cup of coffee, transfer my clothes from the washer to the dryer, send a quick text. Maybe I'm not paying full attention, knowing I can always rewind. Nothing can replace the pleasure I once felt from disappearing into another world, in a dark movie theater, munching buttery popcorn. Even the sticky floor was part of the experience.

* * *

Jonathan and I have trouble sleeping some nights. We lie in bed at 2:00 a.m. and have the kind of conversations we used to have when we smoked harsh pot, the kind with seeds and stems that always made you cough. Only we're not stoned. We're wide awake and staring out at the moon shining through our bedroom window, overlooking the hay field. We're having a semiphilosophical, quasi-religious, cosmic conversation about life and death, space and time, past and future—the kind of trippy talk that only makes sense in the middle of the night if you've taken shrooms, or just fallen in love. Then we look at each other and Jonathan says it seems like we've been on an extended thirty-seven-year-long first date. We both smile because at that moment what he says feels true.

And on those strange, wakeful nights as I lie in bed thinking about my past, I realize there's something else that's true. I've stuck to the mission I set for myself when I first decided to make movies forty years ago. To tell unusual stories about uncommon women. The proof is right there in the films.

*   *   *

Recently, several nice things happened:

In October 2022, I was invited to the Mystic Film Festival in Connecticut to receive a Lifetime Achievement Award. I was honored, but my emotions were mixed, aware that these awards are given at the end of someone's career. (Although, who knows, maybe I'll have a reboot?!)

In December 2023, *Desperately Seeking Susan* was added to the National Film Registry as part of a small selection of films preserved by the Library of Congress for their historic, cultural or aesthetic contribution to American Cinema.

Making Mr. Right, long forgotten, was rediscovered by Kino Lorber and put out on DVD with a director's commentary.

Smithereens aired on Turner Classic Movies, something I never would have imagined back in 1982 when I made this rebellious punk movie. (Was that a sign that I, too, had become a classic?)

I still keep in touch with my former film students and am always excited to hear when one has gone on to make a movie of their own.

Oh, and here's another bit of news. I went to the doctor and found out I'd shrunk half an inch. But if anyone asks, I'll still round up to five feet.

*   *   *

Oscar and his wife, Eva, now live in Brooklyn near Prospect Park. Ozzy, a video producer, has inherited his father's ability to move around the kitchen effortlessly. Unlike the Seidelman women, he's a creative and excellent cook. He's also affectionate and kind; what my mother would call a real mensch. For now, Oscar and Eva say they don't want kids, that the world is too messed up, filled with moral confusion; but maybe the world will get better and they will change their minds.

Meanwhile, I'm granny to an adorable half terrier, half dachshund named Anchovy. She's proof that size doesn't matter. She stands ten inches high and is the girl boss of the entire family.

Anchovy *(Photo by Oscar Brett)*

* * *

The virus is hanging around, but life has slowly returned to normal. A different normal. And I find myself itching to get back out into the world and have an adventure. I'm not sure what that will be, but there are several things on my bucket list I need to tick off.

Although, I'm still being cautious, still superstitious. Still on the lookout for signs and signals from the universe. For example, a few months ago I dropped a magnifying mirror that rested on my bathroom countertop. It hit the floor and cracked—a harbinger of bad luck. I hadn't broken a mirror in decades, so it came as no surprise when two days later, Jonathan and I both came down with COVID after having avoided it for the past three years. And as I type these words, I glance up at the time on my computer screen and it's 11:11, and I can feel my old friend Turk smiling down at me.

* * *

Few parents name their daughters Susan anymore. It's a name that has gone out of style.

But names go in cycles, so maybe there will be a future generation of Susans and Barbaras and Debbies to carry on the moniker of their grand-mothers and great-grandmothers.

I can't wait to see what those new Susans get up to. I'm not the first, and won't be the last, in a long line of restless young women who come out of nowhere to say: "I'll show you."

These days I spend my time in front of a laptop. Typing, editing, re-vising. Jonathan has also written a book, a dystopian novel that a famous French director has optioned for a TV series, so maybe one day you'll get to see it. We work in two separate parts of the house and meet up in the late afternoon for a gin and tonic on the porch. I haven't read his book. He hasn't read mine. We both agree it's better that way. Our lives are already so entwined, it's important we each have a world of our own to retreat to.

In the early evening, when the sun is low, I sometimes dance around our back lawn (where only the deer can see me) while Jonathan smokes a cigar, swinging in a hammock nearby. We turn the volume up loud—Donna Summer, Tina Turner, Dusty Springfield, and my favorite, Amy Winehouse singing "Valerie."

Our young neighbors walk their dogs down our country lane, past our house, and every once in a while, they catch me by surprise. Here's what they see:

A five-foot-tall 😊 seventy-one-year-old woman in a Yankees cap, bop-ping around her garden like the Energizer Bunny. But what they cannot see is that I once wore white go-go boots and danced in the window of a psyche-delic clothing boutique, wrapped towels around naked models at the Conti-nental Baths, was a former homecoming queen who hung out with punks, watched helplessly as friends died of the gay cancer, walked the red carpet at Cannes, watched the Twin Towers fall, and got to play Let's Pretend with some pretty extraordinary people.

They wave and I momentarily stop dancing and wave back.

Everyone has a story to tell. This is mine.

Acknowledgments

With thanks to the special Susans in my life.

My agent (Susan #1), Susan Golomb, whose response to an unsolicited email (which I thought would go directly to junk mail) gave me the encouragement and support I needed to keep writing.

My pal, playwright Susan Cinoman. Thanks for your great instincts and always interesting conversations.

Thank you, Susan Kerns, the editor of the *ReFocus* book about my work, who unknowingly planted the seed in my brain to tell this story.

And special thanks to my original partner in crime, Susan Berman, who was there at the start.

* * *

This book would not exist without the great advice and guidance of Elizabeth Beier, my very smart, savvy, and stylish editor at St. Martin's Press. Thank you for the opportunity to put these memories and musings out into the world.

Thank you, Jonathan Brett, for your many creative talents and strongly felt opinions. You have made the past thirty-seven years a wonderful adventure.

With love and admiration for my clever, affectionate, and kindhearted son, Ozzy Brett, who also had the intelligence to marry Eva Shapiro, the first person I trusted to read this manuscript while still a work in progress.

Thank you, Samantha and Hannah Brett, for letting me into your lives. I am fortunate to have you all as family and don't ever take that for granted.

With immense indebtedness to my mother, Florence, who passed on her fearlessness as well as her curiosity about all things offbeat and quirky. I lucked out.

Thank you to my sister, Denise (Zeesie); my brother, Richie (the Bird Baby); and my father, Michael, who handed down his earthy sense of humor, his rock-solid reliability, and bad eating habits.

And with sincere appreciation for friends who were generous enough to read early drafts of this manuscript (the ones filled with typos, bad grammar, and unedited ramblings), and took the time to share their thoughts and ask all the right questions: Brenda Robin Citron, Marion Frank, Danielle Winston, and Mona Astra Liss. And thanks to Steven Seighman for his delightful book design, Laurie Henderson for her meticulous care throughout the production process, and Brigitte Dale for her help and patience.

Thank you, Julie and Bill Levinson, for providing shelter from the storm when our house flooded and you graciously lent us yours so I could continue writing in a beautiful place.

And finally—with genuine gratitude to all the actors, producers, screenwriters, cinematographers, designers, editors, musicians, and crew members I've had the honor to collaborate with over the past four decades. Thank you for accompanying me on this journey, and sometimes leading the way.

People

Aaron Spelling
Abe Beame
Abel Ferrara
Adele Bertei
Adelle Lutz
Aidan Quinn
Al Goldstein
Alain Resnais
Alan Arkin
Albert Camus
Albert Finney
Alberto Moravia
Alex Comfort
Alfred Hitchcock
Alfred Newman
Alice Guy
Alison Bechdel
Alison Maclean
Allen Ginsberg
Alvin Schwartz
Alvin Toffler
Amanda Plummer
Amos Poe

Amy Heckerling
Amy Winehouse
Anaïs Nin
Andrés Vicente
   Gómez
Andrew Lloyd Webber
Andy Mondshein
Anita Sarko
Ann Magnuson
Anna Karina
Anna Levine
   Thompson
Anne Sexton
Annette Bening
Annette Funicello
Annie Golden
Anthony Bourdain
Antón Gómez
Antoni Gaudí
Antonio Banderas
Antonioni
Sir Arthur Conan
   Doyle

Arto Lindsay
Audrey Hepburn
Barbara Boyle
Barbara Ehrenreich
Barbara Ling
Barbara Stanwyck
Barbara Streisand
Barbara Walters
Barbara Wilson
Barbra Streisand
Barry Diller
Barry Gordy
Barry Manilow
Barry Sonnenfeld
Barry Strugatz
Ben Weber
Bernd Eichinger
Bernie Brillstein
Bert Parks
Bess Myerson
Bette Davis
Bette Gordon
Bette Midler

Betty Friedan

Billy Hopkins

Billy Wilder

Blair Rosenfeld

Bob Marley

Bob Rafelson

Bob Weinstein

Bon Jovi

Brad Rijn

Brenda Lee

Brenda Vaccaro

Bret Easton Ellis

Brian DePalma

Brooke Shields

Bruce Springsteen

Bruce Willis

Bruno Ganz

Burl Ives

Burt Bacharach

Camryn Manheim

Candace Bushnell

Carole King

Carole Lombard

Carrie Fisher

Cary Grant

Cecil B. DeMille

Charles Grodin

Charles Manson

Charlton Heston

Cheryl Browne

Chris Elliott

Chris Noth

Chris von Wangen-
heim

Christine Vachon

Christo

Christopher Durang

Christopher Lee

Chubby Checker

Claude Chabrol

Cliff Arquette

Clint Eastwood

Coen brothers

Corey Haim

Courteney Cox

Courtney Jines

Craig McKay

Crispin Glover

Cruella de Vil

Cyndi Lauper

Cynthia Nixon

Daniel Day-Lewis

Darren Star

Daryl Hannah

David Arquette

David Berkowitz

David Bowie

David Denby

David Lean

David Leland

David Mamet

David Newman

Dean Martin

Deborah Kerr

Deborah van Eck

Demi Moore

Dennis Quaid

Diana Ross

Diane Keaton

Diane Sawyer

Dianne Wiest

Dick Clark

Dion

Divine

Don Imus

Donald Trump

Donna Summer

Doris Dörrie

Dorothy Arzner

Dorothy Hamill

Dorothy Parker

Drew Barrymore

Dustin Hoffman

Dusty Springfield

Dyan Cannon

Dylan Thomas

Ed Begley Jr.

Ed Lachman

Eddie Albert

Eille Norwood

Elaine May

Ellen Chenoweth

Ellie Greenwich

Emily Lloyd

Enrique Iglesias

Eric Clapton

Eric Mitchell

Eric Roberts

Eva Gabor

Eva Shapiro

Eve Arden

Eve Babitz

Farrah Fawcett

Federico Fellini

Floyd Byars

Fran Leibowitz

Frances Ford Coppola

François Truffaut

Frankie Valli and the
   Four Seasons

Fred MacMurray

Gary Coleman

Gary Oldman

Gene Siskel

President George Bush

George Clooney

George Lucas

George Peppard

Gerald Carrus

Germaine Greer

Gerry Goffin

Giancarlo Esposito

Giancarlo Giannini

Gilles Jacob

Giorgio DeLuca

Giulietta Masina

Glenn O'Brien

Glenne Headly

Gloria Estefan

Goldie Hawn

Grace Kelly

Grandmaster Flash

Gregory Corso

Greta Gerwig

Griffin Dunne

Groucho Marx

Hal Ashby

Hal David

Hans Christian An-
   dersen

Harrison Ford

Harvey Keitel

Harvey Weinstein

Hayley Mills

Heather Whitestone

Henry Sheehan

Herb Ritts

Hermann Hesse

Holly Golightly

Howard Chandler
   Christy

Howard Hawks

Howard Shore

Howard Stern

Hugh Grant

I. M. Pei

Ida Lupino

Ingmar Bergman

Ira Hurvitz

Italo Calvino

Jack Lemmon

Jack Nicholson

Jacques Cousteau

Jacques Rivette

James Cameron

James Dean

James Michener

James Myhre

James Russo

James Taylor

Jamie Lee Curtis

Jamin O'Brien

Jane Campion

Jane Fonda

Janet Carrus

Janet Maslin

Janis Joplin

Jason London

Jay Leno

Jay McInerney

Jean-Luc Godard

Jean-Michel Basquiat

Jeanne Moreau

Jean Paul Gaultier

Jean-Paul Sartre

Jeff Barry

Jeff Koons

Jennifer Jason Leigh

Jerry Blavat

Jerry Leiber

Jerry Lewis

Jim Carrey

Jim Jarmusch

Jim Jones

Jim Morrison

Joan Didion

Joan Micklin Silver

Joan Tewkesbury

Jodie Foster

Joel Dean

Joel Tuber

John Cale

President John F.
   Kennedy

John Ford

John Gotti

John Huston

John Lurie

John Malkovich

John Milius

John Sayles
John Turturro
Johnny Mathis
Jonathan Brett
Jonathan Demme
Joni Mitchell
Josep Civit
Joseph Bologna
Joseph Heller
Joseph Papp
Judith Crist
Judy Davis
Judy Holliday
Julia Roberts
Julia Sweeney
Julian Schnabel
Julie Christie
Juliette Lewis
Kate Millett
Katharine Hepburn
Katherine Riley
Kathleen Turner
Keiko Deguchi
Keith Haring
Kelly McGillis
Kenny Scharf
Kerry Barden
Kevin Costner
Kim Cattrall
Kristin Davis
Kurt Russell
Kurt Vonnegut
Larry Gagosian
Larry Levan
Larry Mark

Laura Branigan
Laurel and Hardy
Lauren Bacall
Sir Laurence Olivier
Laurie Frank
Laurie Metcalf
Laverne Cox
Lawrence Ferlinghetti
Lawrence Kasdan
Lee Quinones
Len Cariou
Lena Dunham
Lenny Bruce
Leonard Goldberg
Leonardo DiCaprio
Leora Barish
Leroi Jones
Liberace
Lili Taylor
Lillian Hellman
Lily Tomlin
Linda Fiorentino
Lionel Newman
Little Eva
Little Richard
Lizzie Borden
Lois Weber
Lou Reed
Louis Malle
Lucille Ball
Lypsinka
Madonna
Malcolm McLaren
Malcolm X
Marcia Gay Harden

Margaret Dumont
Mario Grigorov
Mark Blum
Mark Friedberg
Mark Kamins
Mark R. Burns
Marlo Thomas
Marlon Brando
Marsha Norman
Martha Coolidge
Martin Ransohoff
Martin Scorsese
Marty Madden
Mary Quant
Mary Tyler Moore
Maryse Alberti
Mel Gibson
Melanie Griffith
Melissa Manchester
Mervyn LeRoy
Meryl Streep
Mia Farrow
Michael B. Jordan
Michael Douglas
Michael Gazzo
Michael Nouri
Michael Patrick
  King
Michael Peyser
Mickey Rourke
Midge Sanford
Mike Medavoy
Mike Newell
Mike Nichols
Milan Kundera

Miloš Forman
Mira Sorvino
Miranda Richardson
Molly Haskell
Molly Ringwald
Mona Davis
Nancy Spungen
Natasha Trethewey
Neil Jordan
Neil Sedaka
Nicholas Pileggi
Nicole Holofcener
Nora Ephron
Oliver Stapleton
Oliver Stone
Orson Welles
The Osbournes
Oscar (Ozzy) Brett
Oscar Hammerstein
Oscar Wilde
Ovid
Ozzy Osbourne
Pamela Koffler
Paris Hilton
Patricia Arquette
Patricia Field
Patricia Highsmith
Patrick Demarchelier
Patti Smith
Patty Duke
Paul Castellano
Paul Lynde
Paul Newman
Paul Schnee
Pauline Kael

Pedro Almodóvar
Penelope Tree
Penny Marshall
Peter Falk
Peter Gabriel
Peter Jennings
Phil Spector
Pierre-Henri Deleau
Pieter de Hooch
Preston Sturges
Prince
Princess Diana
Queen Latifah
Quentin Tarantino
Randa Haines
Randy Newman
Ray Charles
Ray Liotta
Rebecca Miller
Regina Ziegler
Renata Adler
Richard Branson
Richard Edson
Richard Gere
Richard Lester Myers/
    Richard Hell
President Richard
    Nixon
Ricky Martin
Ricky Ricardo
Risa Bramon
Robert Downey Jr.
Robert Joy
Robert Shaye
Robin Byrd

Robin Williams
Rock Hudson
Rockets Redglare
Roger Corman
Roger Ebert
Roman Polanski
Ron Nyswaner
Rona Gail
Ronnie Spector
Rosalind Russell
Rosanna Arquette
Roseanne Barr
Rosie O'Donnell
Roy Helland
Roy Lichtenstein
Rudy Dillon
RuPaul
Rutger Hauer
S.J. Perelman
Sally Field
Sally Kellerman
Sam Cohn
Sammy Davis Jr.
Santo Loquasto
Sara Driver
Sarah Jessica
    Parker
Sarah Pillsbury
Scott B
Scott Rudin
Sean Penn
Sergio Leone
Seymour Stein
Shadow Morton
Sheila Benson

Shelly Gitlow

Sheri Lewis

Shirley MacLaine

Sid Vicious

Sidney Lumet

Sig De Miguel

Sissy Spacek

Skinny D'Amato

Spike Lee

Stanley Kubrick

Stéphane Audran

Stephen Bray

Stephen Vincent

Steve Buscemi

Steven Soderbergh

Steven Spielberg

Steven Wright

Stoller

Stuart Dryburgh

Susan B. Anthony

Susan Berman

Susan Boyle

Susan Hayward

Susan Sarandon

Suzanne Vega

Sylvester Stallone

Sylvia Plath

Tama Janowitz

Terry Gilliam

Thomas Newman

Tim Monich

Tina Turner

Tippi Hedren

Todd Haynes

Todd Phillips

Todd Solondz

Tom Arnold

Tom Cruise

Tom De Haven

Tom Hanks

Tom Verlaine

Tony Bennett

Truffaut

Twiggy

Uma Thurman

Valerie Jarrett

Versace

Veruschka

Victor Hugo

Vidal Sassoon

Vincent "The Chin"
  Gigante

Vincent Canby

Vincente Minnelli

Vincent Price

Virginia Madsen

Virginia Woolf

Vivien Leigh

Walter Mirisch

Wanda Sykes

Warren Beatty

Werner Herzog

Werner Sherer

Wes Anderson

Wes Craven

Whoopi Goldberg

Will Patton

Will Smith

William Goldman

Willie Garson

Wim Wenders

Woody Allen

Yvonne De Carlo

Zena Collier

Zsa Zsa Gabor

Recommended Viewing

Some of my favorite movies were directed by women. This list is totally subjective, based on my taste. It includes independent, mainstream, documentary, experimental, and animated films, and leans heavily on English language movies simply because I've seen more of them.

Apologies to those filmmakers I've forgotten to mention. I'm sure I'll periodically wake up in the middle of the night kicking myself for leaving someone out.

In alphabetical order:

Maren Ade: (Germany) *Toni Erdmann* (2016)

Chantal Akerman: (Belgium) *Jeanne Dielman, 23 quai du Commerce, 1080 Bruxelles* (1975)

Allison Anders: *Gas Food Lodging* (1992), *Mi Vida Loca* (1993)

Gillian Armstrong: (Australia) *My Brilliant Career* (1979), *Starstruck* (1982)

Andrea Arnold: (UK) *Fish Tank* (2009), *American Honey* (2016)

Dorothy Arzner: *Dance, Girl, Dance* (1940)

Shari Springer Berman (with Robert Pulcini): *American Splendor* (2003)

Kathryn Bigelow: *The Hurt Locker* (2009), *Zero Dark Thirty* (2012)

Lizzie Borden: *Working Girls* (1986)

Jane Campion: (New Zealand) *An Angel at My Table* (1990), *The Piano* (1993)

Niki Caro: (New Zealand) *Whale Rider* (2002)

Liliana Cavani: (Italy) *The Night Porter* (1974)

Gurinder Chadha: (UK) *Bend It Like Beckham* (2002)

Joyce Chopra: *Smooth Talk* (1985)

Vera Chytilová: (Czechoslovakia) *Daisies* (1966)

Martha Coolidge: *Rambling Rose* (1991)

Sofia Coppola: *The Virgin Suicides* (1999), *Lost in Translation* (2003)

Julie Dash: *Daughters of the Dust* (1991)

Donna Deitch: *Desert Hearts* (1985)

Julie Delpy: (France) *2 Days in Paris* (2007)

Claire Denis: (France) *Beau Travail* (1999)

Maya Deren: *Meshes of the Afternoon* (1943)

Doris Dörrie: (Germany) *Men . . .* (1985)

Lena Dunham: *Tiny Furniture* (2010)

Ava DuVernay: *Selma* (2014), *13th* (2016)

Nora Ephron: *Sleepless in Seattle* (1993), *Julie & Julia* (2009)

Emerald Fennell: (UK) *Promising Young Woman* (2020), *Saltburn* (2023)

Valerie Faris (and Jonathan Dayton): *Little Miss Sunshine* (2006)

Greta Gerwig: *Lady Bird* (2017), *Barbie* (2023)

Bette Gordon: *Variety* (1983)

Debra Granik: *Winter's Bone* (2010)

Lee Grant: *Tell Me a Riddle* (1980)

Catherine Hardwicke: *Thirteen* (2003), *Twilight* (2008)

Leslie Harris: *Just Another Girl on the I.R.T.* (1992)

Mary Harron: *I Shot Andy Warhol* (1996), *American Psycho* (2000)

Amy Heckerling: *Fast Times at Ridgemont High* (1982), *Clueless* (1995)

Marielle Heller: *Can You Ever Forgive Me?* (2018)

Nicole Holofcener: *Walking and Talking* (1996), *Friends with Money* (2006)

Patty Jenkins: *Monster* (2003), *Wonder Woman* (2017)

Tamara Jenkins: *Slums of Beverly Hills* (1998), *The Savages* (2007)

Jennifer Kent: (Australia) *The Babadook* (2014)

Barbara Kopple: *Harlan County U.S.A.* (1976), *American Dream* (1990)

Diane Kurys: (France) *Peppermint Soda* (1977), *Entre Nous* (1983)

Jennie Livingston: *Paris Is Burning* (1990)

Phyllida Lloyd: (UK) *Mamma Mia!* (2009)

Barbara Loden: *Wanda* (1970)

Ida Lupino: *The Hitch-Hiker* (1953), *The Bigamist* (1953)

Alison Maclean: *Jesus' Son* (1999)

Maria Maggenti: *The Incredibly True Adventure of Two Girls in Love* (1995)

Sharon Maguire: (UK) *Bridget Jones's Diary* (2001)

Penny Marshall: *Big* (1988), *A League of Their Own* (1992)

Elaine May: *The Heartbreak Kid* (1972), *A New Leaf* (1971)

Daisy von Scherler Mayer: *Party Girl* (1995)

Nancy Meyers: *Somethigang's Gotta Give* (2003), *It's Complicated* (2009)

Rebecca Miller: *Personal Velocity: Three Portraits* (2002)

Mira Nair: (India) *Salaam Bombay!* (1988), *Monsoon Wedding* (2001)

Jan Oxenberg: *Thank You and Goodnight* (1991)

Euzhan Palcy: (France) *Sugar Cane Alley* (1983)

Kimberly Peirce: *Boys Don't Cry* (1999)

Sarah Polley: (Canada) *Away from Her* (2006), *Stories We Tell* (2012)

Sally Potter: (UK) *Orlando* (1992)

Gina Prince-Bythewood: *Love and Basketball* (2000)

Lynne Ramsay: *We Need to Talk About Kevin* (2011)

Dee Rees: *Pariah* (2007), *Mudbound* (2017)

Kelly Reichardt: *Wendy and Lucy* (2008), *Certain Women* (2016)

Marjane Satrapi: (France) *Persepolis* (2007)

Nancy Savoca: *True Love* (1989), *Household Saints* (1994)

Céline Sciamma: (France) *Tomboy* (2011), *Portrait of a Lady on Fire* (2019)

Emma Seligman: *Shiva Baby* (2020)

Coline Serreau: (France) *Three Men and a Cradle* (1985)

Joan Micklin Silver: *Hester Street* (1975)

Celine Song: *Past Lives* (2023)

Penelope Spheeris: *The Decline of Western Civilization* (1981)

Barbra Streisand: *Yentl* (1983), *The Prince of Tides* (1991)

Betty Thomas: *The Brady Bunch Movie* (1995)

Justine Triet: (France) *Anatomy of a Fall* (2023)

Agnès Varda: (France) *Cléo from 5 to 7* (1961), *Vagabond* (1985)

Margarethe von Trotta: (Germany) *Marianne & Juliane* (1981)

Claudia Weill: *Girlfriends* (1978)

Lina Wertmüller: (Italy) *Swept Away* (1974), *Seven Beauties* (1975)

Olivia Wilde: *Booksmart* (2019)

Chloé Zhao: *The Rider* (2017), *Nomadland* (2020)

About the Author

Joan Vidal

Susan Seidelman, a graduate of NYU film school, was born in Philadelphia, lived for many years in Manhattan, and currently resides in New Jersey.